MURDER, MYSTERY & MY FAMILY

MURDER, MYSTERY & MY FAMILY

A TRUE-CRIME CASEBOOK FROM THE HIT BBC SERIES

KAREN FARRINGTON

FOREWORDS BY JEREMY DEIN QC AND SASHA WASS QC

BBC
BOOKS

1 3 5 7 9 10 8 6 4 2

BBC Books, an imprint of Ebury Publishing
20 Vauxhall Bridge Road,
London SW1V 2SA

BBC Books is part of the Penguin Random House group of companies
whose addresses can be found at global.penguinrandomhouse.com

Penguin
Random House
UK

Copyright © Chalkboard TV 2019

Main text by Karen Farrington

This book is published to accompany the television series entitled *Murder, Mystery and My Family*, first broadcast on BBC One in 2018.

Murder, Mystery and My Family is a Chalkboard TV production.

Commissioning Editor: Lindsay Bradbury
Executive Producer: Mike Benson

First published by BBC Books in 2019

www.penguin.co.uk

A CIP catalogue record for this book is available from the British Library

ISBN 9781785944772

Typeset in 11.75/19 pt Baskerville MT Std
by Integra Software Services Pvt. Ltd, Pondicherry

Printed and bound in Great Britain by Clays Ltd, Elcograf S.p.A.

Penguin Random House is committed to a sustainable future for
our business, our readers and our planet. This book is made
from Forest Stewardship Council® certified paper.

CONTENTS

FOREWORD
by Jeremy Dein QC

I was called to the Bar in 1982. My dream was to defend in the criminal courts, to become a jury advocate, to be a voice for those ill-equipped to speak for themselves. With support from many others, my ambition was realised. Thirty-seven years later, I have lived and breathed the criminal justice process daily. I have experienced the highs and lows, not just for myself, but, much more importantly, for those thrown into the system nationwide. I have witnessed emotions of all types, at all levels, in every shape and size. Horror, devastation, anger, sympathy, remorse, regret: the full range. But nothing could have prepared me for *Murder, Mystery and My Family*, and the cruelty of the death penalty.

Glad though I am to have gained profound insight into this concept, its effects will remain with me forever. Miscarriage of justice is bad enough, but when the story ends with questionable, even wrongful, state killing, there is no going back. At least, not in any meaningful way. That, above anything, is the all-embracing mischief behind the death penalty. But there are plenty more, as I believe our programme starkly reveals.

Guilty or not, in the cases Sasha and I reviewed, the defendant was generally hanged, then buried within the precincts of prison grounds. True, the individual concerned had been found guilty of murder. But the routine way in which the punishment was handed down, then swiftly administered, was astonishing. Sarah Chesham, Emily Swann, Charlotte Bryant and Louis Calvert – and other women like them – were executed following trial by 12 landowning, upper-class males. Those hanged – fast tracked, largely after rushed appeals – could not be brought back. Justice was final; worse still, so was injustice.

On a more positive theme, throughout my involvement in *Murder, Mystery and My Family*, I was overwhelmed by the quantity, and quality, of research done by the Chalkboard TV production team. The footprints of criminal justice are never an easy thing to retrace but, in preparation for filming, no stone was left unturned to investigate the truth behind these women's journeys to the gallows. Sasha and I owe a massive debt of gratitude to the Chalkboard squad, whose tireless endeavours enabled us to analyse each case fully informed and confident of our ground. Thanks to everyone concerned, and I mean everyone.

In the process of reviewing these cases from the perspective of defence counsel, however, I encountered many truly disturbing features of historic criminal justice. There is scope to highlight a mere handful here. A prime example: how the justice process, indeed society, historically viewed women. Derogatory attitudes that were adopted towards females emerged starkly, and the unfair prejudice they faced when striving to secure just verdicts cried out.

As far back as 1839 – the year of the earliest case we reviewed – and for a long time thereafter, there was an all-embracing perception that just being charged with a crime meant a woman was untrustworthy, discreditable, simply a low-life. Though it was not this debasing of women alone that caused me discomfort as the reality of our historic criminal justice system dawned.

Another notable concern that consistently stood out amidst the piles of papers and quagmire of information confronting us was naked judicial effort to promote the integrity and credibility of police officers, sometimes to the point of no return. Glowing judicial references for the investigating police, even in trials where the defendant hotly disputed the confessional testimony, were undoubtedly a recipe for injustice. While the accused was frequently referred to as 'The Man' or 'The Woman', the judge would commonly commend to the jury the police officer's years of experience and seek to emphasise their professional reputation. Once, in an attempt to persuade the jury to believe police evidence, the trial judge compared lies on oath to conspiracy to murder. Astounding. It inevitably follows that all of this was infinitely damaging to a defendant, rendering a fair trial nigh on impossible. No doubt class, gender and narrow-mindedness, rather than malice, were the primary cause. This was, of course, no consolation to the soon-to-be-executed accused.

As our programme unfolded, a further troubling area related to the field of expert evidence came to light. The prosecution's favouritism towards select experts was perhaps unsurprising, but the way in which these witnesses were sometimes made to seem infallible before the jury left a dreadful taste. From a defence perspective, this inevitably created overwhelming difficulties. Particular prosecution experts were viewed as 'untouchable', which meant an intimidating atmosphere crept into the trial. So powerful were the reputations of certain prosecution experts – for example, Sir Bernard Spilsbury, the pathologist who gave evidence in Edith Thompson's case – that on occasions the defence would not dare to be seen to challenge their testimony. This approach was flawed, indeed dangerous, as it meant that often the defendant was deprived of a fair trial, the very cornerstone of our criminal justice system today. A truly worrying state of affairs.

The spotlight shone on the criminal justice process by *Murder, Mystery and My Family* raised many other historical questions. Crucially, how could a defendant have been deprived of entitlement to give evidence for so long? It is now impossible to believe that the accused was effectively gagged until the year 1898. And what, overall, was the true quality of defence – indeed how many hanged defendants were poorly, even terribly, represented?

In the midst of all this, and much more, the families involved in the various series cases showed huge dignity and patience throughout. The pitfalls in the process that shone through as the root cause of prospective injustice were treated with respect and understanding – testament to the families, if fortunate from the point of view of the system itself.

Overall, I feel immensely privileged to have imported my years of defending to this unique project. I was reminded throughout of the paramount importance of fair trial, and the indispensability of strong and fearless defence of the accused. Gladly, the death penalty is now a distant memory in the United Kingdom – but criminal justice is not. The many condemned who feature in the programme *Murder, Mystery and My Family* vehemently protested their innocence. The vast majority, including the five women in this book, were executed. Innocent or guilty, there is a single lesson to be learnt from this unique programme – never again.

FOREWORD
by Sasha Wass QC

When I was invited to participate in a series looking at historic capital cases, that is to say those resulting in the death penalty, I had little idea how challenging the project would be. The researchers working for Chalkboard TV not only found cases where there were justifiable reasons for concern, they also unearthed a surprising amount of contemporaneous material. This included trial transcripts and judges' notes. These legal documents revealed expert analysis by pathologists, toxicologists and ballistic experts. There were also trial exhibits that had been retained, which had been put before the jury, such as photographs of the key participants in the various cases and crime scene drawings. This wealth of material not only revealed a fully rounded picture of each case but also painted the social and historic environment in which these trials took place.

The other source of information we were wary of but found useful came from contemporary local and national newspaper reports. Photographs of victims, the accused, witnesses, their homes, the local areas and sometimes scene of the crime illustrations all provided helpful backdrops to the cases and brought the stories alive. Professional court reporters, who would have attended more than just the prosecution's opening speech and not simply returned to court days or weeks later to hear the verdict, also proved invaluable.

However, as in today's news environment, the hunt for readership often resulted in overly simplistic summaries of complex evidential and trial issues. Secondly, it was not unknown then, nor is it unknown today, for grandstanding lawyers to make unsupported allegations and inflammatory attacks in court to provide bait for lazy journalists to repeat in the press where they hoped to be protected from libel charges by court privilege. For these two reasons we were cautious about over-reliance on press reports and were careful to verify them with other sources wherever possible.

One of the most interesting results of our various reviews was the difference between police investigations then and now. For example, the police's methods of taking and recording statements was far less rigorous and accountable than it is today. In three of the thirty cases reviewed throughout the programme, we were of the opinion that the defendants' confessions, unsupported by any other evidence, were wholly unreliable and the convictions were consequently unsustainable. Judge Radford, who oversaw each case, shared our concern.

In the area of scientific evidence, there have been substantial developments enabling more accurate analysis of material, using techniques that were not available to investigators in the cases we reviewed. Modern trials routinely include evidence of DNA profiling, CCTV, automatic number plate recognition technology, internet communications and telephone evidence, enabling the whereabouts of individuals to be tracked at certain times. These new techniques provide far greater certainty in identifying perpetrators and assisting jurors in their task. None of these forensic tools were available to investigators, scientists and lawyers at the time of these trials. So even if we could have used them to confirm the guilt or innocence of the accused, they cannot be used to test conclusions determined in the past – it would be arrogant and unfair to judge historic cases through the prism of modern-day technology. However, we did review the available contemporary material and scientific analyses produced in the trials to determine whether evidential interpretation, analytical mistakes or documented evidence had been missed at the time. Where valuable new evidence had come to light, we considered it in our deliberations.

Had modern-day scientific evidence been unearthed we would have made determinations to that effect. Today, where such fresh evidence is uncovered, the Court of Appeal considers it and convictions may be quashed. In legal systems applying capital punishment, the verdict may be technically reversible, but the outcome is not. As it transpired, our main criticisms and dissatisfaction giving rise to disagreements with the historic cases reviewed arose from what we perceived to be failures in investigations, mistaken or partial analysis of the available material at the time or flaws in the judicial process.

The oldest case we reviewed was tried in 1839, and there have been numerous changes in the law since then. We reviewed each case according to the laws that applied at the time. However, some injustices, viewed with the benefit of hindsight, were so palpably unfair as to cause us to challenge the verdicts. We felt that despite the then accepted legal practices, judicial intervention ought to have been applied.

Prior to 1898, a defendant was not allowed to give evidence in their own defence. For example, Sarah Chesham, who was tried in the 1850s, was not only prevented from testifying in her case, but the state did not even provide her with a lawyer to speak on her behalf. She had no chance to participate in the trial that resulted in her execution. Unsurprisingly, we had little difficulty concluding that she had suffered a miscarriage of justice. (The Chesham case is addressed in Chapter One.) Today, matters have turned full circle in that a defendant who elects not to give evidence will be warned by the judge that the jury may be directed to hold their silence against them.

The Homicide Act 1957, the Suicide Act 1961 and the Coroners and Justices Act 2009 have all introduced new criteria that enable charges of murder to be reduced to manslaughter in certain circumstances: for example, in cases of diminished responsibility and loss of control. Case law is constantly developing in response to evolving standards. For example, case law now recognises the mental impairment suffered by battered women and allows juries to return verdicts of manslaughter where abusive relationships provide the backdrop to a killing. Had this syndrome been understood at the time of the trial of Emily Swann, whose case is dealt with in Chapter Two, she may well have availed herself of a partial defence to murder (reducing her conviction to manslaughter) and her life would have been spared.

Other changes in the law since the cases we reviewed have included the abolition of the double jeopardy rule. This rule prevented defendants who had been previously acquitted standing trial for a second time on exactly the same charge. Today, if significant new evidence arises in a previously determined case, a retrial may be ordered by the Court of Appeal so that justice is finally and correctly served with the benefit of the new evidence.

There has also been a radical revision of the approach taken to a defendant's previous criminal history. The Criminal Evidence Act 1898 provided a shield to a defendant who had been in trouble on a previous occasion, preventing the defendant's past crimes and misdemeanours from being revealed to the jury to avoid prejudicing their opinions, and was only lost in exceptional circumstances. The Criminal Justice Act 2003 now enables prosecutors to routinely present evidence to a jury of a defendant's 'bad character', which may include their criminal history.

Since 1839, the date of the first case we were asked to reconsider, sentencing has also changed quite radically. The most significant statute being the Murder [Abolition of the Death Penalty] Act 1965. Murder thereafter was and continues to be met with a mandatory sentence of life imprisonment. Lost to history is the symbolic placing of a black handkerchief on the trial judge's head to indicate the convicted defendant was to face the hangman's noose.

Between 1965 and 2003, the court would pass sentence of life imprisonment following a conviction for murder without specifying the length of time for which a defendant would actually remain in prison. This 'minimum term' or 'tariff' was determined at a later date by the Home Secretary of the day. For example, when I defended Rosemary West in 1995, the trial judge, the late Mr Justice Mantel, was not empowered to fix the minimum term that Mrs West would actually spend in prison, merely to make a recommendation. He stated in court: 'If attention is paid to what I think, you will never be released.' At the time of writing, it is still not known publicly what Mrs West's minimum term will be.

Following the passing of the 2003 Criminal Justice Act, sentencing for murder has become much more transparent, with a minimum term set down in open court. Schedule 15 to the Act sets out various starting points according to the type of murder in question. For the avoidance of doubt, the 'minimum term', which is often misunderstood by the public, refers to the time a convicted person must actually spend in prison (without any discount for good behaviour) before they can apply for parole. A life sentence with a minimum term of, say, 30 years means that the convicted defendant will remain in prison for 30 years before they are eligible to apply for parole. There is no guarantee that the prisoner will be released on licence.

During the course of *Murder, Mystery and My Family*, Jeremy Dein and I were fortunate to be able to meet and engage with the descendants of those whose cases we were reviewing. Reactions to the case reviews by later generations were often emotional. In one case, a family member came specially from Australia in order to participate in the review process. For some, the revelation that they had 'a murderer in the family' came as a complete surprise. Others regarded the fact as a matter of intellectual curiosity. In the case of Charlotte Bryant in Chapter Five, the conviction radically altered the course of the lives of the family. As a consequence of the execution of one parent for murdering the other, the Bryants' five children found themselves orphaned. They were unceremoniously separated from each other and placed into different care home facilities.

Many of the family members who contributed to the television series heard evidence about their forebears' murder trials and convictions for the first time. They acknowledged and respected the scrutiny of the review process that challenged the evidence, applying the rigour of modern judicial standards and attitudes. Constraints of air time prevented the wealth of evidence available being broadcast, but the salient points were aired in front of Judge Radford, who was privy to all of the material still held on file and in the press, which was reassessed by both counsel.

Family members sat nervously on the edges of seats awaiting Judge Radford's determinations and hoping for exoneration of their ancestors. In some cases, the decision reached was not the positive outcome the living descendants had hoped for. The majority of those disappointed by the review outcomes took comfort in the fact that justice had been done in the past and that their forebears had been fairly and properly convicted of murder.

During the course of each programme, the investigative review process involved a gruelling journey by family members to the site where one of their relations had lived or where they had met their death at the direction of the state and to their final resting place. It was often a traumatic experience for the living descendants to witness their deceased relative's grave. A common practice in the past was for the body of the person executed to be buried inside the confines of the prison, rather than on consecrated ground. The life taken by the judicial process was often only marked by a small numbered token the size of a coin fixed to a prison wall. Their last resting place was stripped of individuality and humanity, seemingly as a further punishment and recognition that they had taken another person's life. Such criminals were seen as unworthy of respectful burials, no matter what positive contributions they may have made to society during the course of their lives.

Between the year 1900 and 1964 approximately 800 people in Britain were hanged, many of them desperately protesting their innocence. It is not unusual for those justly and properly convicted of a crime to protest their innocence, blame others, live in denial, attack the police or blame their lawyers rather than accept their guilt. But in rare cases, new evidence has and still does come to light. Mistakes in the adjudication of justice have been made and will no doubt continue to be made, no matter how many safeguards are put in place to avoid this occurrence. Addressing real and perceived miscarriages of justice is a function of a civilised judicial system. If mistakes are discovered, prison sentences can be quashed, compensation ordered, apologies made and compensation offered. This is plainly impossible where capital punishment has been carried out. It is primarily for this reason why, despite the natural, emotional and reflexive human desires for revenge and retribution in kind, many civilised societies now opt for life imprisonment as the punishment for homicide. Nothing can make amends for a wrongful hanging: death is irreversible.

INTRODUCTION

P rior to 1964, trials that ended in a hanging were not necessarily rarities. When a defendant's guilt was beyond any scintilla of doubt, juries returned the appropriate verdict and sombre judges donned a black cap to deliver the dreadful sentence.

But what if mistakes had been made by police as they gathered evidence or by barristers as they set out cases in court? Could the juries have been influenced more by coarse manners and unorthodox habits than by the facts laid before them? Were contraventions of social mores the rationale for deadly verdicts rather than evidence? Were mistakes made that cost defendants their lives?

In the series *Murder, Mystery and My Family*, living relatives put forward cases for reinvestigation in the hope of finding misinterpreted – or missed – evidence that might have influenced the outcome of those trials. Two barristers guide troubled descendants through knotty legal aspects, alongside an array of experts who help to shed new light on old casework. At the very least, the reputation of those in notorious prosecutions can be reconfigured, given what's uncovered.

This book takes a forensic look at the cases of five women whose journeys to the gallows were marked by a series of daunting pitfalls and hurdles that they could not overcome. Placing them under modern scrutiny has revealed considerable doubt about the wisdom of the verdicts at their trials.

Murder remains inexcusable, no matter who the perpetrator. However, unsafe convictions that fulfil a dubious public appetite are equally indefensible, especially when the penalty is death. It is this tormenting thread that links them. All the women featured in this book lived in what was overwhelmingly a man's world. There were some female journalists at work by the turn of the twentieth century, but pioneer policewomen weren't employed until the First World War. Women jurors, solicitors and barristers weren't seen until the 1920s – and then only in insignificant numbers. The first woman MP to take her seat in Parliament was Nancy Astor, following a by-election in 1919. Although women won the vote in 1918 it wasn't offered on equal terms with men until a decade later. Even then, equality under law did not add up to equal treatment. Men had greater currency than women and for these women the consequences of society's bias were extreme.

Each of the five had dramatically different circumstances, although some facets of their lives were similar. Charlotte Bryant, Sarah Chesham and Emily Swann were unable to read or write – although Charlotte and Emily's mothers were literate. This trio, along with Louie Calvert, had children who were left motherless or orphaned – and in abject misery – when the death sentence was carried out. Charlotte and Louie sometimes worked as prostitutes, a common response to poverty among women at the time, but the others didn't. Some 170 years ago, Sarah worked for a pittance on the land while 90 years have elapsed since Edith Thompson had a busy metropolitan job. Louie Calvert alone was accused of killing someone other than a husband. In each of their stories there is absorbing detail alongside some broader themes.

Sarah Chesham was a scapegoat rather than a murderer, in an era when people perceived the peril of poisoning to be widespread. In fact, the all-consuming poison panic was a symptom of other issues that preoccupied society at the time, not the cause of the country's dire misery. Thousands of people perished after contracting cholera and no one knew how to stop the disease. In 1848, when the country was gripped by the fear of arsenic poisoning, there was a rash of revolutions around Europe and the British government apparatus itself began to creak. While there were some victims of poisoning, who'd had arsenic unobtrusively slipped into their food and died in agony, public anxiety escalated out of hand and was misdirected onto the shoulders of women like Sarah.

Sarah's husband Richard died from tuberculosis. Although an iota of arsenic was found in his body, everyone was agreed there was far too little to affect his health. Yet this was judged to be a sign that she administered minute amounts of the drug in order to weaken him so he couldn't survive his final illness. She was targeted because her reputation was already in tatters. Although she had been cleared of murdering two sons and a baby by poisoning some years before, no one believed she wasn't guilty. Now an alliance of vicious neighbours and sanctimonious bigwigs wanted to make sure she was convicted of attempted murder, mostly to satisfy a primitive desire for vengeance. Sarah lived at a time when ignorance and superstition ran riot. Alone out of the five, she died after a conviction for attempted murder and was the only one to endure a public execution.

Emily Swann was without doubt implicated, along with her lover, in the killing of her husband William. She admitted to being present when he was attacked and he almost certainly died in her arms. Like many others at the turn of the century, she was a big drinker, with causes possibly rooted in childhood tragedy and marital discord, and was drunk when the attack happened. Women like Emily who imbibed too freely and then got into trouble with the law were considered such a problem for society that, where possible, they were institutionalised. It's a sign of how seriously this 'sin' was taken. So any sympathy for her among the jury evaporated when the circumstances of her husband's death became apparent. Jurors ignored the fact that there was scant evidence of any injury caused by a wielded poker on William's dead body, while Emily was too small to inflict physical damage on her husband. Moreover, they were apparently unconcerned that she had been previously attacked by her husband and unaware of the emotional consequences that might have brought.

When her husband was killed, Edith Thompson was also in an adulterous relationship. Lover Freddy Bywaters was their lodger and he eventually stabbed Percy Thompson. After he was arrested,

Freddy insisted Edith had nothing to do with the murder. But to investigators she seemed an older woman bending a younger man to her will. Her letters betrayed her, they thought, with talk of poisoning to end her marriage. In fact, the love notes were flowery flights of fancy written by someone infected by high drama who dreamt of an alternative life to her own. Evidence about her gaining access to poison or being part of the stabbing plan was absent. As an independent woman pursuing a career in a country still teetering after a catastrophic war there was little sympathy and no small amount of resentment inspired by her hopes and dreams. Many men affected by the conflict wanted to see women – who'd so recently been drawn into the workplace to replace absent fighters – return to the kitchen, fast.

National newspapers of the era would have us believe Charlotte Bryant was a foul-mouthed, money-motivated, self-centred woman who killed her husband in order to re-ignite the interest of a lover who'd deserted her, without a care for the ensuing fate of a brood of children. Following the death of Frederick Bryant, her life was raked over by journalists, policemen, solicitors, barristers, judges, civil servants and government ministers. At the end of it, she was found wanting in every department of her life.

Charlotte was not a gracious, glowing woman and was neither passive nor submissive; in other words, she did not fall in line with the feminine stereotype that prevailed in the 1930s. In fact, she turned out to be the polar opposite of everything expected of a woman, according to the establishment norm. In the absence of evidence against her, was she tried on her reputation?

Charlotte, like the other women in this book, became a sensation at a time when the term 'broadsheets' meant the same as tabloids today. She was convicted as a female killer, an impulse thought to run counter to nature, and her trial created a maelstrom of persuasive publicity – not all of it rooted in fact. Hers was not an isolated example.

Charlotte was not only considered vulgar, but she was an outsider in her community. Her Northern Irish accent marked her out when she arrived in a sleepy Dorset town at a time when there was no love lost between the English and the Irish. Even at the best of times she was a challenging character who had severely limited emotional intelligence. When charismatic Leonard Parsons crossed her path she launched into a relationship that seemed like it might take precedence over her existing family. Yet she kept returning home, to a husband observers said she hated and to children she was accused of neglecting. Her domestic arrangements were far more nuanced than many realised.

She was found guilty of poisoning her husband even when there was no proof she had either bought or administered arsenic. The evidence against her came from a key witness who herself had the opportunity to poison the victim. This witness insisted a tin of weed killer kept in the kitchen had been burnt on a domestic fire as Charlotte tried to cover her tracks. Yet the expert whose testimony appeared to confirm this got his sums wrong. The ash in the grate wasn't supercharged with arsenic residue after all, as another specialist pointed out after the trial had finished. It may not have been the remains of a tin of weed killer. But still, Charlotte did not get a second hearing to review the evidence of the burnt tin, a pivotal part of the case against her.

Louie Calvert was by all accounts an unprepossessing figure who schemed her way into family life and executed an audacious plan to bring home a baby that wasn't hers, having promised her husband she was pregnant. Still, that didn't make her a murderer. Although she was found guilty of killing her landlady there were two stout pieces of evidence that backed up her story of a man being present and cast an element of doubt on the prosecution case. And though there was circumstantial evidence against her, there was a troubling lack of motive. Louie was a hard-bitten ex-convict who was not concerned by a spell behind bars. She had stolen many times before, without killing in the process. Once again, she was a woman who had contravened her era's accepted standards of female behaviour, and quality of evidence was sacrificed in order to obtain a conviction.

Courts could not shine the spotlight of DNA findings from crime scenes until recently, to help establish guilt or imply innocence. Instead, juries got their bearings from the way defendants looked and acted. There was a willingness to take people at face value, that is, judging them by their demeanour, rather than scrutinising the facts. Jury members might have been looking for traces of remorse to enhance the image of an accused woman, but why would there be any if she was innocent? The jury might have decided someone was behaving as if they were guilty. In reality it is impossible to deduce someone's innocence or guilt by the way they seem.

The headlines at the times of these women's respective convictions screamed their guilt. Today, investigations by two experienced, clear-eyed barristers have pulled up perplexing new slants on their stories. But what would a modern judge decide about the safety of these verdicts?

THE CASE OF
THE POISON PANIC

SARAH CHESHAM

In the middle of the nineteenth century, a tuberculosis diagnosis was like a death sentence. As many as one in four people living in cities were carried off by what was often known as 'galloping consumption', with its spread accelerated by cramped and unsanitary living conditions. Tuberculosis was an insidious, stealthy disease that thrust its unwelcome tentacles everywhere. Although it is closely associated with the lungs, it sometimes affects other parts of the body, and it certainly didn't stay contained within metropolitan areas or the rigid social boundaries that existed at the time, claiming numerous luminaries like composer Frédéric Chopin and poet John Keats alongside rafts of the industrial poor. Back then, no one knew that bacteria were to blame for this dreaded disease, also called phthisis, scrofula or the white plague, nor how to stop its rampant progress. It wasn't until 1882 that Robert Koch – later dubbed 'the father of bacteriology' – began unpacking its mysteries.

Farm worker Richard Chesham didn't live in a city but nonetheless succumbed to the ravages of the disease, possibly through drinking infected milk, the hazards of which were not fully addressed for another 100 years. When he fell ill in 1850, his persistent, hacking cough echoed around the house where he and his family lived in Clavering, Essex. Gasping for breath and with the foul taste of blood-veined phlegm in his mouth, he was weary and wincing with chest pain. As the crackle of his lungs was audible not only to doctors but to his family as well, there was no doubt about the nature of his affliction and everyone knew that his chances of survival were abysmally low.

By turns perspiring and shivering, he became increasingly skeletal, although his wife Sarah tried feeding him a soft concoction of rice and milk in the vain hope he would find new strength. He died on 16 May 1850 and was buried in the graveyard of St Mary and St Clement that same month, though his family were too poor to put up a permanent headstone.

His death was followed by a post-mortem that revealed, as expected, tubercles in his lungs – growths that indicated the presence of tuberculosis. Yet before long, his widow was standing in the dock, accused of attempting to murder him as part of a sustained poisoning campaign. Further investigation had also uncovered a tiny amount of arsenic in his body, though far too small to kill him. Science was once again behind the game. No one realised it was natural to harbour some of the poison inside the body, and that almost everybody did. And arsenic was a widely used substance at the time, so ingesting a small amount was probably fairly common. But it was the scintilla of evidence that those following the trial craved, so that Sarah Chesham would at last feel the full weight of justice.

It wasn't the first time she had faced the ordeal of a court case and the ensuing public scrutiny; Sarah had already been tried in three poisoning cases. The fact that she was found to be innocent in each did nothing to sway public opinion about her culpability. Once again she was demonised. At her fourth and final trial she was publicly acknowledged as 'Sally Arsenic', a nickname that found favour inside the courtroom and with the public at large.

In court, Sarah – who was illiterate and ill-educated – struggled to keep up with proceedings. Crucially, she had no lawyer, no one at all to represent her, to fend off scurrilous charges by vengeful neighbours or tainted testimony by a nationally regarded scientist. Her guilt was presupposed and she was duly sentenced to death. As it turned out, a case of tuberculosis was every bit as fatal for Sarah Chesham as it was for her husband.

*

The Cheshams were among some 1,150 residents in Clavering village, tucked inside the Essex county boundary where it butts up against Hertfordshire and lying eight miles from the market town of Saffron Waldon. Clavering was mentioned in the Domesday Book, with a number of smallholders listed. Although in 1850 farming was still its biggest business by far, there were now grocery shops, a drapery, millers, beer houses, bootmakers, tailors, a wheelwright, a saddler and a blacksmith at work there.

The village's timber-framed thatched houses are still in evidence today. By modern standards it's a rural idyll, but when the Cheshams were there life was far from satisfactory for the majority of its inhabitants. Housing was notoriously poor, with a grass thatch making homes damp while small windows left them dark. Rats, mice and insects of all varieties made their homes in the walls and floors.

Richard Chesham married Sarah on 29 June 1828 and, together with both of the witnesses, signed the marital certificate with an 'X' – the equivalent of a signature for those who are illiterate. Although churches had made strides into education provision, the Cheshams had grown up in an era when education for children of working families was barely known.

Since 1839 two schools had opened. In 1833 there had been new legislation to restrict child labour in factories and, in the same year, the House of Commons approved a £20,000 grant to promote education. Still, schooling was not mandatory at the time, and no one in rural areas was expected to stay beyond the age of ten. Both schools were a long-awaited beacon of hope for farm children, although the youngsters might not have seen it that way at the time.

Ignorance and poverty were just two of the reasons for Sarah's persecution. Fear of disease and political uncertainty at home and abroad helped to stoke the flames that left Britain a simmering pressure cooker at the time.

While Richard was in his early twenties when they wed, Sarah, aged just 17, was below the legal age for marriage and needed her parents' consent, which was duly forthcoming, perhaps because Sarah was pregnant. Richard and Sarah's daughter Harriet was born in February the following year. There followed five sons:

Philip born in 1830, John in 1832, Joseph in 1834, James in 1837 and finally George in 1839.

Richard was one of some 200 farm hands in Clavering registered on the 1841 census, all aged between 10 and 85. Life on the farm was hard and Richard would have been expected to turn his hand to a variety of tasks, including threshing, ditching, hedging, mowing, carting, cutting wood and making faggots. Although agricultural wages had risen during the Napoleonic Wars at the beginning of the nineteenth century, they had flattened out by the time of Richard's death. Best estimates have his earnings at about £20 a year when he died – worth just £2,670 today.

Women and children also undertook farm work, as Sarah and her children surely did, but they were paid even less than adult men. Nor was there much food to be had. The era is best remembered for the Irish Potato Famine, which caused devastation and diaspora in virtually equal measure in Ireland, still part of the British Empire at the time. England also suffered from bad harvests during the decade before Richard's death, which is often referred to as 'the Hungry Forties' due to the scarcity of food during that period.

Richard's low wages were barely sufficient to support himself, his wife and their six children, and men like him were pinioned to the very lowest rungs of the ladder, with few opportunities to improve their living standards. Democracy wasn't a lever for change, with only one man in seven entitled to vote. Just 16 men in Clavering were able to vote in the Parliamentary election of 1847 – and some of those were not resident.

Symptoms of the overwhelming poverty were clear with the so-called Swing Riots that began in 1830 in southern England, a protest against high rents, church taxes and agricultural mechanisation. In Dorset, the first trade unionists, the Tolpuddle Martyrs, began organising in 1833 in response to reduced wages. Then in 1836 the Chartist movement got underway, with people like Richard in its sights. It campaigned for a vote for every man aged 21 and above, as well as a secret ballot and improvements in electoral practice. Midway through the century, the Chartist movement was at its most active, with its greatest petition – said to be six million strong – delivered to Parliament in 1848.

Yet it's unlikely that farm labourers like Richard would have paid much attention to the political landscape and its turbulence. Although he stood to gain from the success of the Chartists and similar movements, he had plenty of other distractions to keep him occupied.

In January 1845, the youngest four boys were taken ill, producing such copious amounts of vomit in their upstairs bedrooms that it poured through the ceiling of a downstairs room, on to the table and floor belonging to their neighbours, the Deards. Two – Joseph and James – died within days of one another. Dr Stephen Hawkes, who arrived to find James in his final throes and Joseph already dead, was convinced that English cholera was the cause of their demise.

At the time, Asiatic cholera and English cholera were viewed as two distinct diseases, with both casting long shadows over British society. The former made its mark in Britain after sweeping through the population like several tidal waves during the nineteenth century when soldiers and sailors returned from far-flung colonies, bringing the infection back with them.

Those who were struck down had virulent diarrhoea, so much so that their bodies might even turn blue for want of water. Other symptoms were lethargy, confusion, seizures, sickness and a racing heart. Given the way that cholera killed indiscriminately and at speed, it seemed like a modern plague and was the subject of much conversation and speculation. At the time, no one knew cholera was carried by contaminated water. The fear of the next epidemic felt tangible.

Meanwhile, English cholera was considered to be a separate intestinal disease, closely associated with dysentery in the minds of doctors, as it usually occurred in the late summer as a consequence of seasonal heat and poor hygiene. However, its source was probably the same as the foreign illness that was causing so much terror at the time. A toxic combination of raw sewage and household rubbish was deposited onto domestic midden heaps – open air town dumps – and noxious liquid from these often leaked into ditches that led to streams from where drinking water was drawn. Thus it seems likely there was little distinction between the two diseases.

Although Joseph and James died in the depths of winter, Dr Hawkes still seemed satisfied that English cholera was probably to blame. That's what he wrote on James's death certificate anyway, while he marked the cause of death for Joseph as 'unknown' on the basis that the lad had died before he arrived, so he hadn't witnessed the effects of the illness for himself. With the symptoms of arsenic poisoning – diarrhoea, nausea, vomiting, racing heart and muscle cramps – so similar to cholera, it's perhaps not surprising that it could pass under the radar. Initially, it seemed like no one would ever know the real cause of their deaths.

The boys were buried together in a single coffin in the graveyard attached to Clavering's church. A grieving Sarah seemed reluctant to have their bodies subjected to post-mortems, claiming she couldn't bear to see them cut open.

On the face of it, the family tragedy seemed nothing short of grotesque bad luck. But people in the village soon began wondering aloud if the deaths were a family misfortune – or the result of doctored food or drink. This reflected a national obsession with poisoning that was at this time reaching its peak, stoked by the popular press and fuelled by fears that ran deep through Victorian society. Even the scientific journal the *London Medical Gazette* had published a series of editorials about this 'great moral evil' under the title 'On the Increase of Secret Poisonings in This Country'. It blamed the perceived epidemic of poisonings on popular fiction, while others argued that press reports based on court cases in which poisoners were dealt with were tantamount to 'how to' guides. Certainly, heightened awareness of poisoning would have increased the number of suspected cases.

Still, the talk surrounding Sarah Chesham may not have grown beyond gossip had it not been for another unexpected death 18 months later, this time that of a baby.

*

After his birth in December 1845, Solomon Taylor lived with his mother Lydia in the village of Manuden, which was about half the size of nearby Clavering. She claimed that her infant son was healthy until he was unexpectedly visited by Sarah Chesham on a number of occasions, a view that was backed up by at least one doctor.

Solomon's father was wealthy tenant farmer Thomas Newport, who lived at Curles Farm, which was where Lydia once worked. She was just 17 when he, nearly a decade her senior, first propositioned her. Unsurprisingly, when she became pregnant she was released from her job and returned to her mother's home, apparently resisting Newport's enthusiastically made case for having an abortion, for which he offered to procure the necessary medicine. Later, after giving birth to his son, Lydia took him to a magistrates' court to sue for maintenance, while her mother also pestered him for payments.

Two rival theories emerged at the time concerning Solomon, Sarah and farmer Newport. The first was that Newport was enraged and embarrassed by Lydia's public pursuit of cash and paid Sarah to exact revenge on his behalf, by killing the child. Others believed that Sarah herself was having an affair with Newport, and poisoned Solomon in a fit of jealousy.

In a further dimension to this toxic triangle, young Joseph Chesham had been accused of theft by Newport who, on another occasion, had beaten him with a stick, causing him to fall and injure himself. This happened just before Joseph's death, and on more than one occasion Sarah blamed Newport squarely for it. None of the above was ever definitively proved, but Sarah's rat-infested family home was owned by Newport, which would have given him some leverage over her.

Bizarrely, Sarah was believed to have poisoned baby Solomon long before his death, and his illness was conflated with the deaths of Joseph and James. Society was looking for a scapegoat and Sarah fitted the bill. Coupled with this there was a keenness among a police force still finding its feet to prove its worth to the public purse. Hence the observations of one James Player seem to have become pivotal. He said that the previous summer, when passing the Chesham household, he heard Sarah say to one of her remaining sons: 'You little dog, hold your tongue, you ought to be where the others are.' Player shared this information with Lydia Taylor and her mother, who duly passed it on to a police constable. This ambiguous outburst by Sarah, overheard by Player, assumed extraordinary weight, tantamount to an admission, during the subsequent investigation.

Prior to the Rural Constabulary Act in 1839, Britain's cities and counties had different approaches to maintaining law and order, including night watchmen and parish constables. This new law permitted the establishment of police forces much like the one that had already been in existence in London for a decade. Authorities in Essex had wasted no time in appointing a chief constable, Captain McHardy, at the start of 1840. But the new force came at a high cost, and ratepayers often complained that it was too expensive, with the result that policemen were particularly keen to investigate alleged crimes of the sort that would justify their value to the local population. Lydia told them a persuasive tale. She said that, although she was barely acquainted with her, Sarah Chesham had visited several times and on each occasion surreptitiously fed baby Solomon something. On the first occasion, in January 1846, a year after James and Joseph's deaths, Sarah was holding Solomon when he became ill.

'Lord! Lydia, he has turned as callow as a rat,' Sarah announced, but insisted she had only fed him sugar.

In May that year Lydia and Solomon visited Sarah, who at one stage took the child and rushed across a field with him to confront Newport. By the time Lydia caught up she said Solomon bore pink marks around his mouth. The following month, Sarah visited Solomon again, this time when Lydia was at work. On this occasion Lydia's mother believed that the baby – now six months old – had once more been fed something that had a catastrophic effect on his health.

Of course, there was little by way of concrete evidence to back up Lydia's words. The police didn't seem to question why Lydia and Solomon visited Sarah if it was thought she was a killer. For Sarah's part, she said she was there to commiserate with Lydia about her fate at Newport's hands, to find common ground in a shared enmity.

Still, Sarah was arrested on 11 August 1846 and taken to Newport police station, where she was held in custody. Police officers searched her house and showed enormous interest in a collection of ointments she possessed, but there seemed little that would befit a poisoner's arsenal. Perhaps she was perceived as 'a wise woman', one who practised folk medicine in an age where science was beginning to prevail. In any case, the cloud above her head wasn't about to lift.

Six days later, magistrates ordered that her sons' bodies should be exhumed. Their blackened corpses were identified by the local vicar, and the remaining contents of their stomachs were packaged up and labelled before being sent to London for analysis. Once examined, it seemed as if the rumour-mongers had got it right. Joseph and James died from arsenic poisoning. Newspapers operating without the legal constraints that govern reporting today all but accused Sarah of murder.

On Friday 21 August 1846 the *Essex Standard* implied that Sarah was thought guilty by her own family: 'Since her apprehension much has been said on the subject of the deaths, and subsequent speedy disposal, of two of her own children, who died about 18 months ago; and it was remarked that neither during the examination, nor since she has been in custody, has her husband been to see her, or sent anyone to inquire about her.'

The consensus in newspapers at the time was that she rubbed a salve on the baby's lips that was impregnated with poison, most likely arsenic.

On 22 August, the *Ipswich Journal* related how Sarah was seen sneaking an unknown substance into Solomon's mouth: 'The child was almost instantly convulsed, and manifested the usual symptoms of being poisoned. The mouth was besmeared with something similar to yellow salve, and the prisoner was accused of having attempted to destroy it. She however decamped, and escaped detection until Tuesday week, when she was apprehended.'

Of course, many medical applications of the era contained arsenic. Those in Sarah's possession had already been taken and tested, and found to be benign. Nor was she close by when Solomon finally died. The ill-fated child passed away on 27 September, the cause of death unclear, by which time Sarah had been in custody for six weeks. Yet everyone was united in the view that Sarah had questions to answer.

In the autumn there were two inquests. The first looked more closely at the circumstances of the untimely deaths of Joseph and James Chesham. The venue was the Fox and Hounds public house in Clavering and the coroner was Charles Carne Lewis, who held the post for 50 years before his death in 1882, aged 74. He was a man of influence, as he was also clerk to the magistrates in his corner of Essex and registrar at the county court. Carne Lewis heard evidence about the circumstances of Joseph and James's deaths from their elder brother Philip Chesham, by now 16 years old. Joseph had died on a Sunday night, and James the following Tuesday. On the Saturday night before Joseph's demise, Philip told how he had come home to a supper of 'a few potatoes and a morsel of meat' before going off to share a bedroom with them. Although he didn't see it himself, he thought his brothers were fed gruel that night by their mother.

On the Sunday, both boys 'appeared very sadly', he said. Joseph emerged from the bedroom to be sick while James was complaining of a headache. Although they couldn't face food, they were chronically thirsty – a typical symptom of poisoning. They returned to share a bed upstairs, both groaning in pain. Sarah was with them, calling out at one point to Philip, 'Get up and see Joe go off,' meaning that he should be at his brother's bedside as he died.

Spending all of Monday at work, Philip did not see James alive again. He and another brother, John, were taken ill at around the same time and had medicine from Dr Hawkes, which appeared to help, as both returned to full health.

Downstairs neighbour Elizabeth Deards told the coroner that, before Joseph and James died, Sarah was concerned enough about appearances to say to Elizabeth: 'I shall soon hang on Chelmsford gallows and be buried underneath it.' Afterwards she was seen grieving for her lost sons, looking 'wild and bad about the eyes', and seen standing against the door frame and crying for them.

The inquest into the death of her sons found that Sarah was guilty of murder. While she was behind bars awaiting a hearing on those joint charges, the second inquest into Solomon Taylor's death was held at the Cock Inn in Manuden. In addition to Lydia and her mother, there were other witnesses. A Mr D. Wodehouse reported that he was passing Mrs Taylor's house when he saw her rush out crying. When he entered, he saw Solomon Taylor foaming at the mouth, with his eyes rolled back in his head. According to Wodehouse he instantly accused Sarah of being responsible. But Sarah insisted to him that she had only put a piece of bread in his mouth and picked a stick for him to suck on.

John Cowell said he had seen the accused in the company of Mr Newport in 'improper situations'.

However, the hard scientific facts made any result far from straightforward. Doctors agreed that the child had died from intestinal issues but they couldn't say whether his death was from natural causes or the work of a poisoner. The jury reflected this in its verdict, saying that Solomon Taylor had died from mesenteric disease of the glands, but whether from natural causes or otherwise there was insufficient evidence to show. Despite this, the coroner added the charge of murder of Solomon Taylor to her charge sheet and she now faced trial over the three deaths.

As officials deliberated, Sarah was herself struggling for survival. The jail, near Chelmsford, was scheduled for improvements but for now had 210 single cells measuring 2.5 by 2 metres, with a height of 2.75 metres. In addition there were 14 larger cells, measuring 4 metres by 2.5 metres, that each contained four beds. Awaiting trial, Sarah would not have been expected to do hard labour like convicted prisoners, but she was subject to a fearful diet that amounted to little more than a daily ration of poor quality bread and gruel or rice on alternate days. At the time, prisoners awaiting trial could receive help from people outside, especially in terms of supplies. With this in mind, Sarah wrote to Newport, with the aid of a prison matron, asking for his help. In some ways the letter throws up more questions than it answers, although its heartfelt and urgent tone is indisputable:

> *You know you ruined me and have brought me to all this trouble and you know 'tis true, and my friends know the same ... You deserve to be here more than I do for you did it, not me, and you know that I have told*

you that I would speak of it times and times and you told me not to be a damned fool … 'Tis your money that keeps you out of prison – you deserve to be here more than me. Mr Newport, you shall support me for I am suffering for the crime that you did. You caused the death of my poor children. I am wretched and always shall be for you know what I have upon my mind and I cannot never be happy any more, and if you do not suffer in this world you will in the next.

The letter was never delivered to Newport but sent instead to the Home Office, where it was kept as a piece of incriminating evidence for use against Sarah during her forthcoming trial, although it lacked the hoped-for confession. She waited in vain for a response from Newport in terms of food and warm clothing, remaining unaided in her bleak existence behind bars.

At the time, Newport had problems of his own. In January 1847 he was himself arrested, although he won bail the following month. But he was now enmeshed in the poisoning scandal and would stand trial accused of inciting Sarah Chesham to kill Solomon Taylor.

*

On 11 March 1847, Sarah appeared at the Essex Lent Assizes, charged with the murder of her son Joseph. Lord Chief Justice Thomas Denman was presiding at the trial, which was held in the Shire Hall at Chelmsford. With the notion of prosecuting and defence counsel still in its infancy, Sarah was to enjoy a stroke of good fortune. To fight her case, she was allocated Charles Chadwick Jones, an immensely experienced barrister who had been appointed a serjeant-at-law, a highly respected ancient but now defunct legal title. Still, his task would not be easy. Up against him there were three able prosecuting counsel: Montague Chambers, Thomas Chambers and Charles Wordsworth, a first cousin of the poet William.

The ace in the hand of the prosecution was the evidence of Professor Alfred Swaine Taylor – something of a pioneer in forensic science, although, it was later proved, not beyond making errors that would fundamentally affect a trial. Taylor was among the first to shape medical jurisprudence, proving that anatomical investigation could assist in the prosecution of the law. For him, there was no doubt that Joseph's stomach contained several grains of arsenic that were responsible for his death. However, Serjeant Jones brought in witnesses, such as the Reverend George Brookes, to testify that Sarah was a good mother who appeared stricken with grief at the death of her sons.

Two witnesses admitted that Sarah had asked them for arsenic to counter a rat invasion. There seemed little doubt that the issue with vermin was real but, more to the point, neither had actually supplied her with it, so there was no evidence she had any poison at hand with which to end her sons' lives.

One witness, Mary Pudding, told the court that Sarah was reluctant to have a post-mortem carried out on the pair after they died. However, the desire to keep dead bodies whole was not unusual at the time, borne out of religious and superstitious reasoning.

A copy of Sarah's intercepted letter to Newport was read out in court, although not before Serjeant Jones made it clear that she was duped into writing it by authorities hoping for an outright admission that wasn't forthcoming.

In his final address, Jones reminded the jury that no motive for the terrible killing had been outlined in court, and he appealed to them to ignore the malicious gossip and sensational newspaper reports that had been circulating. After just ten minutes deliberating the verdict came back: not guilty. The jury's foreman explained why. 'We have no doubt of the child having been poisoned, but we do not see any proof who administered it.'

The second trial, dealing with the death of James, followed quickly on from the first. Philip Chesham was called as an unwilling candidate for the prosecution case. He was understandably hesitant to testify against his mother and came out with one affecting line that ably contributed to her defence: 'My mother has been a good mother to we.'

Professor Taylor believed that James's body contained as much as 30 grams of arsenic, enough to kill three or four adults. But he knew how difficult it was to show that poison had been administered and by whom. This case would once again prove his point.

In the dimming light of the early evening, the judge did his second summing-up of the day and sent the jury out to consider a verdict. For the second time it came back as not guilty.

The third trial – Sarah's trial for the murder of Solomon Taylor – took place the following day, with Lydia Taylor's vivid testimony key to proceedings. Sarah's son John proved tongue-tied on the stand – and for good reason. He had been coached by his employer, a friend of Newport, to give damning evidence against Sarah to save Newport's skin. Fortunately, the judge realised what had happened before much damage was done. And this time, forensics worked in Sarah's favour. Professor Taylor analysed the contents of the medicaments at the Chesham household to find that most were only dangerous when administered in large quantities. Moreover, he was adamant that there was no poison in baby Solomon's stomach, so Sarah was duly acquitted for the third time. The case against Newport, charged with procuring Sarah to poison Solomon Taylor, also failed.

If Sarah and Newport were not responsible for Solomon's death, then who was? It's difficult to say with certainty at this distance, but at the time an unknown number of babies and toddlers were falling victim to a medicine called Godfrey's Cordial, also known as 'Mother's Friend', a bottle of which stood on the shelves of the Taylor household. Available without recourse to a doctor, it was administered for a wide range of symptoms including colic, dehydration and diarrhoea. Although it seemed benign, the cordial in fact contained a potentially harmful single grain of opium in every two-ounce dose. Sometimes it succeeded in putting children into a deep sleep, as the giver intended. However, the unlucky ones were fatally poisoned by the drug, usually given by the hand of a loving parent.

As far as Sarah was concerned, she had endured inquests, magistrates' hearings and three trials, and was found innocent every time. But, whatever the real cause of Solomon's death, most people in Clavering thought that Sarah had got away with murder.

*

So what made them so certain? What was it about the deaths of James and Joseph Chesham and Solomon Taylor that so caught the public's attention?

Poisoning cases put unbridled fear into the heart of Victorian society. The nuts and bolts of the poison panic were that people suspected foul play even when none had occurred because the threat of death from arsenic, the popular choice of poisoners', was at the forefront of their minds. When fear prevailed, truth was more easily concealed behind an elaborate fable ushered in by society at large.

Undoubtedly, there were women who broke with the convention of being homely nurturers and killed partners, parents, children or rivals, with arsenic being their weapon of choice. Equally, today we know much more about societal behaviour and how public thinking can be coaxed down a particular route when the real causes of a community's difficulties, the issues that are shaking foundations and causing deep concern, are hiding in plain sight.

Properly called arsenic trioxide, it came in the form of white powder that could easily be secreted in food or drink. It wasn't the only poison available, but it was seen as the toxin of choice at the time. Scots toxicologist Robert Christison, a pioneer in the study of poisons who made a name for himself at the trial of the infamous body-snatchers Burke and Hare, dared to put some on his tongue and testified that it was tasteless. It was said to bear a mild odour of garlic.

In its white-powder form, arsenic was relatively commonplace in Victorian homes and businesses. It was used to killed vermin including fleas, lice and bedbugs, as a fungicide, for health purposes, in cosmetics and, in a different form, as a food colouring and to create a popular shade of green in wallpaper. Farmers steeped seeds in it before they were planted – and hungry children who saw seeds or treated grains on the floor might well stoop to scoop them up.

It was an era when hand-washing for hygienic purposes was unheard of, even among operating doctors. Only in 1846 did Hungarian doctor Ignaz Semmelweis make the first recorded conclusions about how the lack of hand-washing contributed to patient deaths in hospitals. It wasn't until a decade later that Florence Nightingale introduced this fundamental hygienic measure as she cared for soldiers injured in the Crimean War.

Professor Taylor had himself warned of the hazards posed by reusing bottles that had once stored arsenic products. He investigated several deaths caused by residual poisoning from a bottle not properly cleaned before being used for either foodstuffs or drink. On one occasion, he said, 370 children became ill after arsenic was used alongside soda to remove the fur from the inside of a steam boiler, with the water being subsequently drawn off to mix with the children's milk. Fortunately, after treatment they all recovered. Years later he told a Parliamentary committee about being 'frequently consulted' about drugs being sold to people who didn't use them properly or deadly drugs being mistakenly dispensed in the place of less harmful ones, sometimes with dire consequences.

However, it was deliberate poisoning that was most feared by Victorian society. Inflexibly paternalistic, it was structured so that men occupied the upper echelons while women of all classes adopted a more lowly position. Nor was there any desire among men to give up their exalted status. With divorce the preserve of the very wealthy and opportunities for jobs and travel limited, there was no escape for wives trapped in an unhappy marriage or female servants wanting to flee an abusive master. Without doubt, a few women realised that poisoning presented them with the opportunity for a new life, but deaths by accidental consumption, from contaminated hands or food, surely outweighed the numbers of murders committed by vengeful spouses, greedy descendants, miserable staff or weary parents. Still, if it was used to kill, there was only a relatively slim chance of the would-be murderer being spotted in the act, particularly if they lived with their victim and could administer it in food or drink without being seen. As well as it being readily available and hard to detect, proving its purchase was all but impossible at the time. It was upon this foundation that suspicions evolved.

One weekly newspaper, *The Leader*, asked: 'If you feel a deadly sensation within and grow gradually weaker, how do you know you are not poisoned? If your hands tingle, do you not fancy it is arsenic?'

The sight of smiling friends or relations at the table or a tasty-looking meal on the plate in front of you was no guarantee that food had not been adulterated, the newspaper declared. And when that stark realisation became instilled in the distrustful hearts of men, the dark shadows of death by poisoning were spotted everywhere and an overarching narrative centred on domestic skulduggery quickly began to take shape.

The ground shifted in 1836 when science caught up with felony thanks to an experiment that proved arsenic's presence. James Marsh unveiled a new process – replacing other rudimentary tests that had previously existed – in which a solution drawn from a body that contained arsenic was found to produce the gas arsine when it came into contact with hydrogen, from which the metallic arsenic could be recovered in definitive quantities. Not only was there a tell-tale yellow smear that indicated the presence of arsenic but there was an opportunity to work out just how much of it was in the corpse. After he published these results in the *Edinburgh New Philosophical Journal*, Marsh's test was lauded as being 'elegant in its simplicity'. He won the admiration of other eminent scientists of the era and the Large Gold Medal from the eminent Society of Arts, its highest award.

Marsh's technique was further refined and, in 1841, a different test, pioneered by Hugo Reinsch, involving hydrochloric acid and copper foil, was unveiled. As it happened, both were good but not fool-proof. Nonetheless, these innovations were beckoned in by a grateful male population, convinced that this would skewer the plans of poisoners once and for all. According to the *Pharmaceutical Journal* in 1841, poisoning had been 'happily banished from the world'.

Yet that turned out not to be the case. Between 1839 and 1848 the Old Bailey, the country's foremost court, saw more than three times as many poisoning trials as in the previous decade – 23 compared with 7. The threat still loomed large, it seemed. Cases that arrived in court were viewed as 'the tip of the iceberg' by the popular press and there was little doubt in many people's minds that numerous women were toying with the idea of poisoning, if not actually carrying it out. It became common currency in domestic conversations at the time, with women threatening to use it or fearing they would be accused of it. Between 1840 and 1850, 167 people were charged with murder or attempted murder, of which 87 were women. That's a little more than half.

To protect themselves from a perceived assault via easy-to-execute villainy, men in pivotal positions in the police and the courts decided there would be no mercy shown to women found guilty of poisoning. Once found guilty, they would feel the full force of the law as a deterrent to others.

The poison panic largely ran in parallel to Britain's cholera epidemics. In the summer of 1849, when newspaper columns were alive with stories of poisonings, the deaths from cholera in London alone escalated from 22 in the first week of June to 339 a week by mid-July. Theories were rife but no one knew what was behind the disease that could kill within hours. It was an underlying terror that claimed far more lives than poisoners. Yet the sensational antics of domestic killers seemed far more digestible by comparison, because with them came a physical target for people's fear and fury.

*

Famously, the first poisoner in this episode of moral panic was Frenchwoman Madame Lafarge. Born Marie-Fortunée Capelle into a middle-class family, she wed husband Charles Pouch-Lafarge in 1839. She believed him to be a wealthy industrialist when in fact he was from peasant stock and stony broke. He married her believing her dowry to be a passport to future security. When she arrived at his run-down property after the marriage and realised she had been duped, Marie shut herself in a bedroom and begged her new husband to release her from the marriage, threatening suicide.

This he refused to do, as he needed her money, but he did agree not to approach her for sex until his estate was flourishing once more. In 1840, Charles was struck down by something his family branded 'la maladie Parisienne' – one of those metropolitan 'miasma' illnesses associated with crowds and poor hygiene. Despite meticulous care from his wife, his condition continued to worsen until he finally died. His family doctor was convinced he had suffered from cholera, with virulent epidemics the subject of popular public anxiety at the time. But some members of the household suspected Marie had smuggled arsenic into his food and drink in order to kill him.

She was ultimately arrested and put on trial, charged with his murder. More people were now able to read than ever before and the cost of newsprint had fallen, making newspapers more accessible. As a result the court case became an international sensation. It was not an open-and-shut case and public opinion was sharply divided about her guilt. The evidence against her was compelling but circumstantial. Marie insisted that the arsenic found in the house was to combat rats. At first Marsh's newly developed test for arsenic seemed to indicate there was no poison in the body of Charles Pouch-Lafarge. But then an expert performed the same test a second time on the contents of the victim's stomach and proved that they contained a residue of the poison. Madame Lafarge was given a life sentence with hard labour. She died of tuberculosis in 1852, aged 36.

She was, it seems, a murderer, and rational science proved her guilt. The compelling story lent some Continental glamour to this most hideous of crimes. In Britain, Charles Dickens coined the phrase 'Lafarged' for anyone who had been poisoned, as more suspected cases came to trial and public fears about the limitless capacity of poisoners for murder and mayhem continued to rise. No doubt the patriarchy was primed to succumb to hysteria, with the threat of revolution nipping at its heels and fuelling insecurity. This led to women like Sarah Chesham finding themselves accused of killing their children. And yet this was a period in which rampant childhood illnesses claimed young lives so often and indiscriminately; losing a third of children born into a family was considered normal. Drilling down into whether women were killing their children or if those deaths were accidental is tricky territory. However, a new insurance-style scheme was said to have thrown temptation into the path of some unscrupulous mothers.

This possible motive for infanticide identified at the time came from the burgeoning network of 'burial clubs'. This was a system in which members could contribute a small sum regularly to pay for a nominated person's funeral, with the promise of a payout when it was needed. It particularly appealed to working-class people with limited means as it meant they avoided the shame of having a pauper's burial or one paid for by the parish. People set great store by funerals in Victorian times and the prospect of themselves or their loved ones being buried in a pauper's grave, without ceremony or memorial, was abhorrent to many. Some families were so determined to sidestep this public shame that they kept dead bodies inside their homes until they could scrape together the money for a decent funeral. In 1843 social reformer Sir Edwin Chadwick reported to Parliament that a respectful burial for themselves and their families was perhaps 'the strongest and most widely diffused feeling amongst the labouring classes', who had far more inclination to invest money in it than, say, healthcare or education.

At first, burial clubs were universally welcomed. By the early 1840s, one estimate made in Preston, Lancashire, had 25,000 to 30,000 residents belonging to burial societies, paying a total of £4,000 in fees each year, mostly in individual amounts of halfpennies and pennies.

In their purest form, burial clubs did shield hard-pressed families from the cost of funerals, which were made more expensive still by the need for sets of mourning clothes for those attending. However, the principle didn't always translate into perfect practice. The rules allowed people to nominate partners, siblings or offspring for burial clubs without their knowledge. Thus working-class women fell under suspicion of belonging to burial clubs to cash in on their children's lives. One child allegedly belonged to 19 burial clubs – although as that would have entailed 19 separate, regular payments it seems a remarkable exception rather than the rule.

In May 1848, Mary May registered her brother William Constable with the New Mourner's Friend Society without his knowledge. A month later, the labourer became ill and swiftly deteriorated. May fell under suspicion after using her brother's given name with the burial club rather than the one he commonly used – Spratty Watts – as well as mistakenly attributing the wrong age to him. Having him buried quickly – a matter of good public hygiene in the summer weather – also bolstered the case against her. As the police and the local vicar investigated, newspapers grossly exaggerated the number of her children who had died prematurely (she's thought to have had six children, although only one survived, but gossips put the number at an almost impossibly high 16).

In an era of high child mortality it was statistically probable that a woman with a family would have lost children. However, in cases such as these, it was often quickly assumed that all those who had been previously lost to the multitude of childhood diseases must have in fact fallen victim to the poisoner's regime. Mary's first husband had also died, and the idea she had poisoned him also gained currency, although it had never been mentioned before.

An inquest was held into William Constable's death. When given the opportunity to speak, Mary May told the coroner: 'All I've got to say is I never done the crime, and I don't know who did. I never gave him anything in my life, only what I shouldn't mind taking myself.'

Still, the jury returned a verdict of wilful murder. At her trial, May was represented by Charles Chadwick Jones, who had done a fine job on behalf of Sarah Chesham at her three trials the previous year. The substance of his defence was similar, that May was a dutiful and affectionate sister and mother, that erroneous ages were often given out at the time and that the £10 sum paid to her was not a proper motive. Moreover, May could not profit from events. The parish paid for the funeral as Spratty Watts had no money. However, she was unable to claim the money from the burial club because she was a married woman and, at the time, was unable to receive money. According to the burial club administrator it had to go to her husband, or might have been used to reimburse the parish fund. Certainly she didn't receive any cash from the transaction. May had been introduced to the burial club by her friend Susannah Forster, the village schoolmistress. Chadwick Jones claimed a policeman who posed as a friend to May elicited statements from her that were confusing, contradictory and even incriminating.

It was to no avail. The jury came back with a guilty verdict and the judge, Sir Frederick Pollock, declined to follow their recommendation for mercy. Hers would be the first hanging in Chelmsford for nine years and the first of a woman since 1804. She saw her husband in the condemned cell shortly before the sentence was carried out. Later, he hanged himself just before he was to be re-married to May's schoolmistress friend Susannah Forster. One popular story said that May had pledged to haunt him if he wed again. In 1850, burial club payments were limited to £3.

That Mary May and Sarah Chesham lived in the same county – albeit miles apart in an age when transport was difficult – was seized upon by newspaper commentators. Having convinced their readership that poisoning was something of a norm, journalists flirted with the idea that there was a secret society of female poisoners in Essex. It was even said that Mary May had admitted that

Sarah Chesham was her teacher in the dark arts of poisoning – something Sarah would stoutly refute until her death.

Newspapers conflated the notion of burial clubs with the deaths of the Chesham boys, although that never formed part of the case against Sarah, whose crimes were now seen as systematic. The newspapers' message was even more effective for being speedy, after the invention of the electric telegraph in 1844, which added a heady immediacy to reports. To add fuel to this fire, Hannah Southgate – a neighbour of Mary May – stood trial for poisoning her first husband, Thomas Ham. His body had been exhumed in April 1847 and was found to contain arsenic. Chief witness against Hannah, who had quickly re-married to farmer John Southgate, was their servant Phoebe Reed. Reed's evidence was persuasive, but when she revealed in court she'd had five children, only two of which belonged to her husband, and was pregnant with an illegitimate sixth, the spotlight swung away from Hannah and on to her – guilty not of poisoning but of lax morality.

Hannah was found not guilty, but there followed a rash of denunciations against local women thought to have poisoned victims in the recent past. Similar waves of hysteria, with one woman implicating the next, had happened some two centuries before when witch-finding peaked in the area. Ultimately, most accusations were quietly forgotten. But the national horror stirred up by suspected domestic poisonings continued.

Eighteen-year-old Catherine Foster was found guilty of murdering husband John in Suffolk after putting arsenic in his dumplings. Chickens that pecked at the uneaten suet also died. Initially, the doctor thought his death had been caused by English cholera, but a post-mortem discovered evidence of the poison. At the trial, her lawyer pointed out it would be difficult for her to have a fair trial, given the distribution of handbills prior to its opening that proclaimed Foster a murderess. Her lack of emotion also played badly in newspaper reports. Strangely, she made a half-hearted confession before declaring she hoped to spend eternity with her dead husband. Once she was found guilty, an estimated 10,000 people watched her hang in Bury St Edmunds in March 1847.

On 21 August 1849, Mary Anne Geering was hanged in Sussex for a sustained campaign in which she poisoned her husband, Richard, and two sons, George and James. A third son in the household, Benjamin, was ill until being removed by the family doctor. Subsequently he made a recovery. At least two were in a burial club and Richard had a small inheritance that Geering had already accessed before being arrested. Professor Taylor found a mighty seven grains of arsenic inside Richard's decomposing corpse. At Lewes Assizes it was proved that Geering had purchased arsenic, and her claims of a rat infestation were denied by other members of the family.

Two days later Rebecca Smith was hanged in Devizes, Wiltshire, for poisoning her baby son, who died when he was just three weeks old. She also confessed to killing a further six of her newborns using poison rather than asphyxiation, perceived to be a milder method of murder at the time, for which she was more harshly penalised.

Two others died of natural causes while the eldest, a daughter, was never harmed.

Smith's trial on 9 August 1849 lasted an entire day, with local women freely sharing their suspicions about the conduct of a woman they hardly knew. She and her family had moved to Westbury in 1843, and struggled to make friends and allies there. After deliberating for just 30 minutes, the jury returned a guilty verdict, although with a recommendation for mercy. That husband Philip was a violent drunk was noted and earned her some sympathy. Nonetheless, she was sentenced to death, a reflection of the seriousness with which the law viewed the use of poison.

Her miserable domestic circumstances inspired two petitions: one from the citizens of Devizes, who didn't want a 'demoralising' public execution in the town, and the other, signed by nine people in her family – although not husband Philip. It claimed Rebecca was well brought up but pinned the troubling crimes on a hope-lessness and despair that arose from domestic misery. Still, Home Secretary Sir George Grey was unmoved – and bizarrely measured the penalty by the feelings of people in her local parish. Years later he wrote that she had poisoned her own children and that there was reason to believe she had poisoning several more before. That's why there was no sympathy for her in the neighbourhood, he said, and a general feeling that the punishment was just.

Despite other women being found guilty of poisoning – and all the above ultimately confessing to their crimes – it was Sarah who remained in the crosshairs as far as society was concerned.

Could Sarah – or any of the other women whose cases are outlined above – have been persuaded to use poison as a result of the flurry of poisoning cases that were the talk of the town? Did she yearn for fame and notoriety? While the court cases and hangings were doubtless the subject of local conversation, she could not read so she wasn't subject to the excitement caused by newspaper coverage in the same way others were.

Writer and politician Edward Bulwer-Lytton did little to help her cause. A prolific writer, he coined the phrases 'the great unwashed' and 'the pen is mightier than the sword'. His 1846 novel about poisoning cases featured a heroine called Lucretia Clavering, with the name rooted both in the Borgia family – famous for its arsenic murders during the Italian Renaissance – and Sarah's home village. Its plot lurched from one sensational killing to the next. It was, of course, published when Sarah was an innocent woman and four years before her conviction for murder.

Professor Taylor was among the vocal critics of Bulwer-Lytton and other authors who focused on poisonings. 'A large proportion of modern novels may be regarded as convenient handbooks of poisoning,' he said. He believed Bulwer-Lytton's novel might even account for the bulge in the number of cases. Every page had detailed descriptions of how murders could be successfully perpetrated, alongside tips about how to avoid detection.

Bulwer-Lytton, a friend to Benjamin Disraeli and Charles Dickens, was a poor writer who has since been lampooned on numerous occasions. But many commentators at the time feared his book gave some dignity or even welcome notoriety to assassins.

The Times branded it a disgrace to the writer and 'a shame to us all'. Nonetheless, it further inextricably linked Sarah to the crime of murder in the minds of a broad, book-reading public.

*

After Richard Chesham died on 16 May 1850, a post-mortem was duly held and tuberculosis was declared the cause. Still, an inquest into his death was held the following month, once again at the Fox and Hounds Inn in Clavering. This was not standard procedure at the time, but instigated because of the cloud now enveloping his widow Sarah. Her home was treated like a crime scene, when the facts said that nothing untoward had happened. Essex-based doctors found Richard's left lung in considerably worse condition than his right, as well as three pints of fluid in the chest. But Professor Taylor was once more called upon and again found evidence of arsenic. This time, though, it wasn't present in the quantities that the Chesham boys had had in their systems. It was, he admitted, too small a quantity to say that it was the cause of death. But other findings helped to muddy the waters.

Taylor also tested a bag of rice found in the Chesham household after Richard died and discovered that the white dust visible among the rice grains in the canvas bag was arsenic, enough to kill six adults. Although Richard was surely dying anyway, this was enough to persuade Professor Taylor that he had been gradually poisoned in small doses, to accelerate his death: '[The doses] would excite great pain and anguish and debilitate and exhaust the patient and where there were consumptive symptoms they would tend to weaken the bodily power.'

From here, the bag of rice began to assume great importance. The inquest heard from Sarah herself, who denied giving rice to her husband but admitted that, before his death, there were intermittent bouts of illness and her husband was 'like a raving madman with a pain in his stomach'. Referring back to the death of her sons, she implied that Thomas Newport was responsible for their deaths. Everyone agreed the rice belonged to Sarah's father.

There was other potentially damning evidence given by Richard Chesham's mother, also called Sarah, who flatly contradicted her daughter-in-law's claims concerning the rice. Richard had been fed rice by his wife, the older woman insisted, and was given thickened milk only seven hours before his death. This was accepted, even though more arsenic would presumably have been present in Richard's corpse had it been true.

George Willings, the relieving officer responsible for helping the poor in times of hardship, told the inquest that Sarah Chesham applied for an order to see the parish doctor on 4 February. Afterwards Richard's health yo-yoed and sometimes he complained of vomiting and of pain in his chest and body. Mr Hawkes, the doctor, said that he attended Richard from February, when he complained of pain in his bowels, purging and sickness. This continued periodically for six weeks until Richard was overtaken with consumption.

John Timewell Clarke, the superintendent of police who discovered the rice in a kneading trough, described how Sarah became agitated when he took it away for further investigation. Yet despite these snippets of suspicion, the jury at the inquest wasn't convinced that there was any more to Richard's death than met the eye. After deliberating for a short time, the jurymen decided Richard had indeed died from tuberculosis. The coroner, Mr Lewis, had no choice but to accept the finding. Nevertheless, he was keen to pin something on Sarah, apparently swayed by local opinion and newspaper reports. He suggested that it might now be a case for the magistrates, and Superintendent Clarke agreed to investigate further.

Behind the scenes, the proposed investigation went far beyond the remit of the local constabulary. The police work continued, in tandem with an appeal to the government for financial and practical assistance in what became something of a witch hunt. In London, barrister H. Hawkins was among those who became involved. He targeted Sarah after Richard's inquest, justifying his bizarre actions by saying, 'Morally speaking, there can be little doubt of arsenic being the cause of these intermittent attacks of illness.' He was entirely taken with the view of people in the village that, despite the outcome of the inquest, the dead man had been poisoned by his wife.

Hawkins asked for guidance as to whether the best legal minds at large in British society at the time – the Solicitor General and the Attorney General – felt that there was sufficient evidence to arrest Sarah Chesham and have her prosecuted and convicted for murder. In a letter to them he acknowledged there was a lack of strong medical proof that would be necessary to secure a conviction, but said that public feeling was so strong that some further investigation should take place.

These were chilling words indeed. Such was the infamy of this case, that a well-positioned barrister was urging two of the most powerful legal men in the country to take action against an uneducated woman without resources to draw on. Although these were all educated, worldly men, they refused to acknowledge the results of the post-mortem showing that Richard had indisputably died from tuberculosis. Hawkins subsequently fades from history, but his contribution to this corner of it, nudging a dubious call for prosecution over the line, is starkly apparent.

Professor Taylor was duly quizzed again about whether his evidence was robust enough to secure any kind of conviction. His written reply to the magistrates' clerk probing for breakthrough evidence was unequivocal: 'I am afraid there would not be any chance of a conviction, if the woman were committed for trial under the statute for administering poison with intent.'

It wasn't because he was convinced of her innocence, although at least his concern was for proper process. He pointed out that none of Richard's vomit in the period leading up to his death had been analysed. The case being too speculative, the professor said: 'Morally speaking there can be little doubt of arsenic having been the cause of these intermittent attacks of illness but there is a want to that strong medical proof which is necessary for conviction.'

Although forensic scientists were relatively few in number, Professor Taylor was perhaps the most eminent in the field. He was without doubt cautious and rigorous, and at this time no one doubted his expertise. So when he spoke against Sarah in this way, it really counted for something. However, his reputation would be damaged by two later trials – of William Palmer, a convicted poisoner from Staffordshire, and of Dr Thomas Smethurst, who poisoned his wife in 1859 – where his findings were disputed. Accomplished lawyers put the great claims made for toxicology on trial in these cases as they battled to defend their clients. Taylor's cause wasn't helped by a growing competitiveness among toxicologists and, for a while, he found himself vilified in the national press. Although Palmer continued to deny his guilt, he was eventually hanged.

One article, originally in the *Monthly Homeopathic Review*, raved: '… we would not extinguish the life of a flea on the ground of the science of Dr Alfred Swaine Taylor. It is a shame and a sin, that so blundering an experimentalist – blundering on his own showing – should be allowed to give an authoritative opinion that may take away, that has taken away, men's lives.'

Taylor would attempt to answer public criticism in the 1859 edition of his book *On Poisons, in Relation to Medical Jurisprudence and Medicine*, devoting pages to the justification of his actions.

But this was all in the future. For now, his word and his work went unquestioned. The clerk to the magistrates, Mr Collins, was forced to look elsewhere for evidence against Sarah Chesham that might 'stop the wretched woman in her horrid career'. Her neighbour Hannah Phillips seemed a likely candidate for its supply. She had spoken at the inquest as a friend of Sarah. Although she declared that Sarah had hidden poison under a slab and then warned her not to talk about it, the inquest seemed little moved by her words.

Now when she was questioned she found a lot more to say that would cast a shadow over Sarah. It seems likely that the pair – once firm friends – had fallen out. Hannah spilled the beans about how Sarah had recently advised her to go to a butcher's and get the ingredients for mince pies and that she should 'season it' – implying the addition of arsenic. If Hannah didn't know how to season it, the conversation continued, then Sarah would do it for her as there was 'no sin in killing husbands such as theirs'. This was because both men suffered with ill health and were considered a burden on their households. She insisted that Sarah Chesham lived unhappily with her husband and had another man ready to take his place. Hannah accounted for not telling everything she knew to the inquest by saying her husband was fearful of losing his job with John Newport, a brother of Thomas. However, on hearing that Sarah Chesham had urged his wife to poison him he had changed his mind.

The clerk wrote to the Home Office, wondering if her evidence would be worth great weight, given that it was so belatedly given. Clearly it ticked enough boxes, as ultimately the Home Office gave the go-ahead for further action. After the government gave the nod, the magistrates' hearing got underway in September, to test the evidence gathered against Sarah.

Once again, newspapers played to popular opinion from the outset, with one calling Sarah Chesham 'an already notorious woman' and another saying she was 'the alleged poisoner of her husband Richard Chesham and two children'. While she was indeed going through the relevant legal process after being suspected of playing a part in her husband's death, she had, of course, been cleared of killing her children and she was not being charged for a second time with those offences.

Among the three presiding magistrates at Newport in Essex were Captain Henry Byng of the Coldstream Guards, who had been a page of honour at Queen Victoria's wedding. One of the other magistrates was a colonel. Socially, the gulf between the bench and the prisoner was immense. This is important because working-class women like Sarah – compelled to undertake menial labour to feed their families – were compared in their minds with the norms of genteel society at the time and found wanting. The lionised female figure of the day was a homemaker, educator, carer, nurturer, a keeper of the moral compass, who was fragile and serene. She might possibly be a cook but was definitely a source of goodness – and the profile of Sarah Chesham and women like her was certainly at odds with that. Sarah was a long way from the idealised women of Victorian Britain.

Still, it wasn't the first time she found herself at the mercy of the establishment, and Sarah found the courage to put up a sparky, albeit rambling, defence for herself: 'I am innocent enough of my poor husband's death. Mr Hawkes told me it was decline and nothing else ... I never gave him any poison. I had no reason to do it. He was a good husband to me. I am sure nobody lived more comfortably together than we did although Hannah Phillips says we did not. I did everything for him as far as I could do in every respect.'

Richard had told Mr Brookes, the vicar, that she had done her wifely duty and, she added, he hardly ever ate rice. Sarah in turn pointed the finger of guilt at Hannah Phillips, saying it was she who had asked for poison to administer to her husband: 'There's plenty know what sort of a woman she is. She is not good. Three different times she asked me for poison. I told my poor husband and he told me not to say anything about it.'

But it was Hannah Phillips's words – now even further embellished – that seized the headlines the next day when, for the first time, her full account became public. Married to a labourer, she became friendly with Sarah Chesham after her return from Chelmsford jail. According to Hannah, Sarah had claimed Newport had murdered her sons, offering them a halfpenny each if they accepted the sweet he offered. The coins were placed with them in the coffin, she said.

Newport wanted Sarah to poison Lydia Taylor and their son, Solomon, Hannah told the magistrates, and she continued to weave a compelling tale. According to her testimony, Sarah gave some arsenic to the child, but Newport became angry because she refused to poison the mother when she had the opportunity. She also claimed that Sarah had hidden the poison outside her home, in a lane, and retrieved it on her return from the trials. When Hannah had no idea what arsenic looked like, it was Sarah who told her it had a similar appearance to flour.

When Sarah talked about her dead sons it was in grief, Phillips confirmed, focusing the thoughts of the magistrates not on the case in hand but on those that happened four years previously. She then related the latest episode, about how Sarah advised her to make a poisoned pie to rid herself of a difficult husband. Sarah, she insisted, had adulterated food that she gave to her husband and sons for their lunches in the fields.

Phillips made it sound like Sarah was perpetually turning out poisoned pies, and had a grudge against her husband. After her husband died, Sarah was said to have cried to Phillips: 'I have sent myself to hell all through he [meaning her husband].' After the inquest, Phillips revealed that Sarah had begged her not to reveal their conversations surrounding poisons. Yet it was only her testimony that related to supposed confessions by Sarah, or her use of poison.

John Pilley, a constable, confirmed that Sarah told him Newport was responsible for poisoning her children, using an adulterated peppermint drop. Sarah also produced for Constable Pilley a bottle said to contain arsenic. It was given to her by Newport, she insisted, because he wanted her to kill Lydia and Solomon Taylor. However, as sensational as this seems, the bottle wasn't sent to Professor Taylor for analysis. And Newport's examination by the magistrates was brief and relatively painless. He said he had never given Sarah any poison or arsenic – and nothing else was apparently asked of him.

Their minds made up, the magistrates said they would commit her for trial at the next assizes for administering poison with intent to kill and murder. When she heard this, Sarah made a strange but telling request. She asked if she might be taken before a witch who would be able to discover the identity of the real murderer, if indeed there was one at large. It reveals the depth of superstition that lay over Essex villages at the time and a lack of faith in established routes to justice that prevailed among the working classes. The magistrates declined the request.

Aged 42, Sarah stood trial at the Essex Lent Assizes in March 1851 before Mr Justice Campbell, who had succeeded Denman as Lord Chief Justice. There were two lawyers for the prosecution but, with Serjeant Jones now seriously ill, no one to act for the defence. She was charged with feloniously administering poison to her husband Richard with intent to kill, to which she pleaded not guilty.

Crowds flocked to the trial, keen to glimpse a woman whose reputation as a child and husband killer preceded her. It would be impossible to recruit a jury that did not know of Sarah's reputation. Still, at the outset of the trial the judge implored the jurymen to dismiss everything they had heard about her beforehand and focus solely on the evidence. Against this backdrop, Hannah Phillips took the witness stand, repeating everything she had told magistrates previously and also calling Sarah 'Sally Arsenic', a casual but caustic epithet, as she gave her version of events. Without a counsel in place to defend her, no challenge was made against the use of language like this, and it was duly repeated in the next day's newspapers.

Physician Dr Stephen Hawke had come in for some criticism after the death of the Chesham boys for not being rigorous enough in his pursuit of the real cause of death. He felt so vilified he had taken to writing letters to a national newspaper to defend himself. With their father Richard, he had already stated tuberculosis was to blame – which indeed it was. But at the assizes, Mr Hawke changed his version of events and said there was 'some irritant poison' inside Richard's body – something he had never stated before – and that Sarah had opposed a post-mortem. It all helped to stack the evidence against her, and Sarah had no one in court to dismantle the case as it was being constructed.

The relieving officer, George Willings, had recently passed away, but his deposition, including the fact that Sarah told him the dead man had taken nothing but milk and rice, was read out. For the first time, Charles Clayden, a farm labourer who worked with Richard, gave evidence that he had seen Richard eat a meat pasty and some dumplings during the harvest before his death. This was presumably introduced by the prosecution to prove that the victim had indeed eaten some of Sarah's homemade pies.

Yet there was evidence in her favour during the eight-hour trial. Her father James Parker confirmed he had bought the rice in question and had eaten two helpings with no ill effects. Also, although she testified that Sarah had fed Richard rice before his death, her mother-in-law confirmed that she was a good wife.

According to the account in the *Essex Standard* on 7 March 1851, Justice Campbell acknowledged she had acted with 'uniform kindness' to her husband and that consequently no motive could be assigned for the deed. But, he warned the jury, if the evidence convinced them, it was their duty to bring back a guilty verdict. A newspaper said that a guilty verdict was returned within a few minutes. Now the judge adopted a sombre tone as he told Sarah the evidence against her was overpowering: 'I have no doubt in saying that you have been most justly convicted and there would be no safety for the lives of mankind if, when guilt so flagrant and heinous were established, such a verdict as this were not recorded.'

He was apparently overcome with emotion when he passed the death sentence. It wasn't his only option, however, with imprisonment or transportation also applicable for the crime. Sarah was sentenced as if she were a serial killer, despite the fact that the charge was one of attempted murder. Like everyone else, the judge seemed convinced she had confessed to the killing of her sons, even though she was not facing trial for those offences nor had given any such confession. It seems he was relying on something Hannah Phillips had said rather than Sarah herself, who continued to maintain her innocence. However, there was no Court of Appeal in 1851 – that didn't come into existence until 1875 – and Sarah had no means of challenging the skewed views of the criminal justice system of the day.

If the prejudices of the court were not enough to deal with, Sarah became the target of a press campaign that was nothing short of extraordinary, implying that she had killed an unknown number of children, even beyond her own two sons. Everything that was reported was bedded in vivid but fanciful terms. The fact that she did not betray emotion when she was sentenced to death and walked unaided from the dock 'with a firm step' immediately went against her.

In *The Globe's* 7 March edition she was branded 'a masculine-looking woman', presumably to make her seem more capable of terrible crime. Referring back to her previous trials, the newspaper said: 'Although the evidence was most cogent and left very little doubt of her guilt she obtained a verdict of acquittal.'

On 13 March, the *Cheltenham Chronicle*, describing her in prison, spoke of her callousness and that she appeared to be 'altogether devoid of remorse'.

But these comments were tame compared to the *Falkirk Herald*, published on the same day: 'The woman has thus led a notorious and almost public career for upwards of four years … [and] the prisoner was regarded as a professed murderess in her own neighbourhood and that mothers lock their children up when she was seen about the premises …

'It is nothing less than wholesale indiscriminate and almost gratuitous assassination.

'There was no passion, no resentment, no prospect of plunder. There was not even the pretext of poverty.'

As the colourful report continued, the *Herald* accused her of recruiting other women as poisoners and taunting them if they couldn't find the courage to kill.

That week's *Dundee Courier* was more vivid still: 'For six slow months Sarah Chesham watched her husband gradually sinking in a long death beneath the food which she cunningly prepared with minute doses of a tormenting poison. But this horrible crime, for which she is justly doomed to suffer the last penalty of the law, is by no means the only one laid to her charge. She seems to have poisoned habitually and for the mere love of slaying.'

Sarah was such a committed poisoner, it was said, that she carried poisoned sweets with her to lure local children and satisfy 'a vampire appetite'. She was also accused in the press of being the head of a gang, with the already executed Mary May one of many pupils recruited by her: 'So successful was she in this endeavour that the name of poisoner became as potent a word of terror among the inhabitants of the villages and hamlets in the neighbourhood of Clavering as that of a witch was wont to be some two centuries ago.'

The Courier went on to accuse the juries who had freed Sarah previously of being guilty of dereliction of duty. Meanwhile, the *Limerick Reporter*, which had Sarah eclipsing Madame Lafarge in notoriety, declared: 'The narrative of the dark and sinister career of this hell kite is such, in truth, as almost to exceed the limits of credibility. Reason shrinks from believing in full the horrors attributed to her ... In this woman, or rather we should say in this fiend, we find not only a poisoner but a school mistress of poisoners ...'

Perhaps the worst and most perpetual offender was *The Times*. From its distant London base it had always had plenty to say about Sarah Chesham and, like the rest of the printed media, not necessarily anything that was rooted in fact. In its reports about Sarah, *The Times* framed her as a 'reputed poisoner, a woman whose employment was as well-known as that of a nurse or a washerwoman'.

Having decided she was guilty of giving something to Solomon Taylor in the face of the court's verdict, its editorial spoke of her medicine chest in terms of 'an assortment of poison – ointments, powders and the like – such as was discovered by Claudius in the private cabinet of Caligula'.

She was, the newspaper declared, 'an accepted and reputed murderess who walked abroad in a village unchallenged and un-accused, and all the inhabitants had seen her children buried without remark or outcry, though they were clearly convinced that there had been foul play'.

She was, the newspaper said, a 'noxious animal' often seen 'prowling' around the village, a 'professed murderess' so gratuitous in her art that mothers 'snatch[ed] their children out of her path' and 'locked their children up when she was seen about the premises'.

The Times was the newspaper that put a new spin on the drama with the claim that when Lydia Taylor and her mother summoned help, Sarah fled and evaded capture by the police for a while, although the paper offered no evidence to back up this story. It was subsequently repeated by others as fact.

Almost five years later, writing about her as she awaited execution in 1851, *The Times* said she and Mary May had committed a dozen or more murders each. Having escaped the noose in 1847, the newspaper declared she had resumed her profession as poisoner. 'In fact,' the paper stated, 'it is impossible to say what havoc may not have been wrought by a murderess in the full swing of her profession for four years together.'

*

For centuries, public hangings had been an expected and, in some quarters, welcome part of British life. During the eighteenth century, when there were more than 220 crimes on the statute book for which perpetrators could be sentenced to death, the number of hangings was running at about 100 per year. The traditional view was that the public nature of the punishment was a necessary deterrent.

The regime of harsh penalties dispensed in the eighteenth and early nineteenth centuries was dubbed 'the Bloody Code'. However, there was a growing appetite for change, and legal reforms introduced by 1837 reduced the list of capital offences to just 16. During the next 24 years only five people were hanged for lesser offences than murder. Sarah Chesham was the sole woman among that unlucky handful of people who, having not been convicted of murder, might reasonably have hoped for a reprieve. In 1861, a decade after her death, the list of crimes for which people could be hanged was reduced to just four: murder, piracy, arson at a naval dockyard and treason.

There were always fewer women hanged than men. Of the 3,544 people hanged in England and Wales in the nineteenth century, just 172 were women (about five per cent). But there was a statistical glitch between 1837 and 1868 when women accounted for 32 out of 318 executions, just over ten per cent and the highest proportion ever recorded. Although Sarah was unlucky to face the noose, her fate reflected an upturn in the rate of punishment against women at a time when populist politicians had no hesitation in seeing poisoners meet their end at the gallows.

When she was hanged on 25 March 1851 outside Springfield jail, Chelmsford, she became the last woman in Britain to die for the offence of attempted murder. She followed in the footsteps of Mary May, the woman who had apparently implicated her as a ringleader of female poisoners two years previously. Her notoriety drew thousands who wanted to view the occasion, with one news-paper estimate putting the Tuesday morning crowd at 7,000 strong. A news sheet issued to mark the day described the scene as 'crammed to excess', with older people saying they couldn't remember so great an excitement during an execution. As was the custom, there were street vendors, entertainers, pickpockets and numerous children among the lively throng.

The gallows was set up at Springfield jail on the flat roof above the stone-built porter's lodge, which formed part of the prison's frontage. People could comfortably gather in the forecourt and be assured of an unimpaired view. Hangings had been carried out on the same site since 1827 and there were more than 40 in total before 1914, when the jail was requisitioned for wartime purposes and never used for capital punishment again.

For continuing to protest her innocence, Sarah was character-ised as belligerent in the press. 'I was innocent, though my neck be put in a halter for it,' she reportedly insisted. She refused to leave her cell for either exercise or prayer in the prison chapel, and this was generally taken as a sign of guilt from a public that valued repentance highly.

Sarah would not die alone. Thomas Drory, convicted of killing his pregnant servant girlfriend, was scheduled to share the gallows with her. Professor Taylor had also been involved in his trial, to prove that blood rather than berries had stained his trousers. Drory's motive was to sidestep the shame of an illegitimate birth and maintain his opportunity to wed a woman of a similar class to his own. The demeanours of the two were compared by commentators, and Sarah was once more found wanting. Drory had been visited at the jail by his family, including his ageing father, while Sarah spent her last days alone. Her isolation was generally taken as a signal of her unprofessed guilt.

Sarah's comparative composure, in contrast to his fearful trembling and calls to God, drew yet more criticism. The news sheet declared: 'Chesham still continued to maintain the same sullen indifference as to her fate but Drory was in a weak and evacuated state.' Yet this is likely to have been a case of giving the crowds the sensational story for which they yearned.

The executioner was London-based William Calcraft, who had begun his 45-year career as hangman in 1829. The first time he took charge of the gallows he hanged a woman wearing a straitjacket. Esther Hibber had been so violent since her conviction for killing a workhouse child she was considered a public peril. When the trap door opened there were chants of 'Good Old Calcraft' and he was given three cheers. This popularity wasn't to last, as he became infamous for using short rope lengths that resulted in the condemned suffering for minutes after the trap door was opened, being painfully strangled rather than having their necks broken. Smaller, lighter people suffered for longer than those with a greater bodyweight.

Calcraft also took to wearing flamboyant clothing, considered by most as inappropriate, and made coarse comments at the expense of the prisoners before him. Perhaps unsurprisingly, given the nature of the work, he drank heavily. Charles Dickens observed: 'Mr Calcraft should be restrained in his unseemly briskness, in his jokes, his oaths and his brandy.'

Still, Calcraft was quick to dispatch prisoners, as Sarah and Drory were about to find out. According to the *Huddersfield Chronicle*'s account, which appeared on Saturday March 29, Drory at least managed to get some sleep while Sarah spent her final night awake and in torment. Great importance was based on a condemned cell confession, so this was the kind of night that people who refused to repent should expect, the report decided.

When nine o'clock struck that morning, the appointed hour of the double execution, the prison bell began to toll. First to the scaffold was Drory, and at the sight of it he 'quivered in every limb and joint of his body and was obliged to be supported as he proceeded'. He was accompanied by the chaplain, who read solemn prayers to him rather than the burial service, a more usual choice. At the foot of the staircase leading to the gateway tower where the scaffold was sited, Drory was led into a cell to have his arms pinioned. Calcraft had invented a leather body belt that held a prisoner's wrists in place at their sides after more flimsy ties had left the condemned flailing as they were hanged. Before having his arms immobilised, Drory shook hands with the prison governor, a poignant act of normalcy before going to his doom. When Drory appeared on the platform, his head drooping and prayers issuing from trembling lips, the crowd descended into a hush. A white linen bag was pulled over his head and he was positioned by Calcraft.

Sarah followed in his wake. There was a short delay as prison staff persuaded her to begin her final journey. It's believed prolonged inactivity during her incarceration had caused her legs to swell painfully. The *Chronicle*, however, saw it differently: 'At first she seemed disposed not to move but on being told that she would be carried to the place of execution if she persisted she consented to walk there. Nature, however, and the terror of a violent and disgraceful death were too strong for her and she required the assistance of two persons as she moved forward.

'Without an instant's delay Calcraft completed his simple but dreadful preparations and then while with bated breath the thousands of spectators below looked on the bolt was drawn; a faint murmur of horror spread among the crowd as they saw the sentence of the law carried into effect, which was prolonged as the convulsive struggles of the dying man and woman were painfully visible. In Drory all signs of animation were extinct in four or five minutes but Chesham struggled for six or seven. They were both light figures and they "died hard".'

The newspaper commended the behaviour of the crowd as 'orderly and sedate'. It was composed in large part of rural workers, called 'smock fracked labourers' by the newspaper, 'spattered with mud and their steps heavy with the number of miles they had travelled'.

Then there came another telling insight into how working-class women were seen at the time: 'There were hardly any respectable people observable in the crowd but a most disgusting number of women. Some of these had gay flowers in their bonnets and evidently set up for the rustic Belles; others were mothers, giving suck to infants whom they carried in their arms; other were elderly Matron's presiding at the head of their families and from the elevation of the domestic Spring cart pointing out to their young daughters how they could best see the execution. With these exceptions the great assemblage in front of the gaol behaved itself with much propriety.'

When both bodies were finally still, the crowd moved off towards town like a raggle-taggle parade, with orange and cake vendors shouting their wares and children at play. Lurid news sheets were already on sale, some containing ballads devoted to the criminals. One of Sarah Chesham's published 'lamentations' went like this:

For a paltry sum of money

She did her lawful husband slay

And for no other cause but lucre

Did she take his life away.

Back at the jail, where a black flag was now flying, the bodies were left dangling for an hour before being taken down.

Drory was buried within the precincts of the jail, which was the only option for convicted murderers. However, Sarah's son Philip came to claim her body. As her crime wasn't murder he was entitled to take it for burial in their home village. Although the local priest refused to read a service or allow her to be buried in consecrated ground, her family had a grave dug at Clavering and hoped that a Christian burial could still be arranged. According to reports, 150 gathered to watch her being interred.

Even now she wasn't given the chance to rest in peace. In mid-April the *London Evening Standard* reported that her body and coffin had been taken from the resting place chosen by her family. Its eventual destination is unknown. Her remaining family, thrust into the eye of this storm, picked up the pieces as best they could. Daughter Harriet, who was already married, emigrated to Australia with her husband Nathan and brother George. It seems George died the same year they arrived. Philip was convicted of theft and imprisoned in the summer of 1851. However, he did go on to marry and have a daughter, who he lived with in old age.

Calcraft went on to carry out the last public hanging at Newgate jail, in 1868 – of Michael Barrett, who had been convicted of being behind a terrorist explosion in Clerkenwell that killed a dozen people – before that year's Capital Punishment (Amendment) Act put capital punishment behind closed doors.

Sarah Chesham is credited with a greater legacy still, one that changed the face of British society. After seeing how the country had become swept up in her story, Parliament decided to act, in the hope of stemming the apparently infectious nature of poisoning. In 1851, it passed the Sale of Arsenic Regulation Bill, trusting it could stop would-be poisoners in their tracks. The law required those who sold arsenic to keep the names and addresses of buyers in a register that became known as a 'poison book', and with it the quantity sold along with the purpose for which it was intended. Nor were shops supposed to sell to strangers or anyone under the age of 21. Further, it required arsenic to be dyed with soot or a vivid indigo so it could no longer be mistaken for food, if it was sold in anything less than 10-pound quantities. Those who ignored the new regulations risked a £20 fine, equivalent today to about £1,600.

Although it all seems like a collection of common sense measures, the Victorians were notoriously reluctant to introduce regulations for fear of stifling innovation and commerce, so the Bill's adoption was no mean feat. It was partly the result of a campaign by Dr Jonathan Toogood of Somerset, who began pressing for the new rules after Sarah Freeman was convicted of murdering her brother Charles in Glastonbury with arsenic bought at the local chemist's shop. She was also thought to have killed her husband, who was in a burial club, as well as her mother and son. Although she protested her innocence, she was duly hanged. Toogood wrote to *The Times*, saying: 'Scarcely a week passes in which some instance [of poisoning] is not brought before the public.'

George Howard, the Earl of Carlisle, clearly viewed arsenic poisoning as a working-class crime, which, as such, deserved special punishment. Speaking in support of the Bill in the House of Lords, he said he felt there was a mysterious horror attached to the use of poison, which 'seemed to attract and fascinate a certain class of minds more than any other kind of crime'.

There was some criticism that the law directed its fire only against arsenic and didn't include the array of other poisons available at the time, including strychnine and cyanide, known as Prussic acid. Carlisle sought to defend the Bill by saying that the criminal classes always resorted to arsenic. He also thought that arsenic should be sold exclusively to male adults, as several 'deplorable accidents' had occurred from young children and female servants having been sent to purchase it. He didn't win on this point.

Even as the Bill was being debated, alleged poisoner Mary Cage was undergoing a trial that would lead to her execution. However, her story reveals how the public appetite for poison cases was at last ebbing away. Her husband James Cage had fallen ill in the spring of 1851, with pains so tormenting that he had reportedly gouged strips of flesh from his stomach and tore at his itching gums as he tried to alleviate the pain. Within two weeks he was dead.

His coffin was about to begin its funeral procession to the church when the Reverend Charles Shorting dramatically halted the event, having heard that Mary had purchased arsenic in a nearby town prior to James's illness. The marriage had not been a happy one. Mary had already left James – who had a reputation for violence and a conviction for assaulting his wife – but returned when a teenage daughter fell pregnant. Mary never admitted guilt, but a post-mortem revealed the presence of arsenic and it took a jury at Ipswich just 22 minutes of deliberation to find her guilty.

Already there were marked changes to the way public hangings were conducted, although it was only a matter of months since Sarah's death. A description of the execution appeared in the *Suffolk Chronicle* in August 1851 and revealed that most houses in the vicinity drew their blinds or closed their shutters. Black drapes on the scaffold, which restricted the view of onlookers, added solemnity. The crowds that gathered were notable for the presence of members of the Young Men's Peace League, who were distributing news sheets of their own to passers-by entitled 'A Few Reasons for the Abolition of Capital Punishment'.

Gradually, the number of poisoning trials began to diminish. While 17 women were executed for poisoning crimes between

1843 and 1852, only ten were found guilty of murder or attempted murder by poison between 1852 and the turn of the century. The number of cases at the Old Bailey fell from 17 between 1849 and 1858 to seven in the subsequent decade. Even so, the concerns continued well into the second half of the century. In 1862, Professor Taylor told one murder trial he was convinced that cholera was still being blamed for deaths brought about by poisoning and that he had personally known of eight cases when this had happened. For him, there was still substance to the moral panic, even though its tide was receding.

*

Shortly before her death Sarah Chesham was seen as a monster, a woman who had killed her husband and sons, as well as the children of others, as a pleasurable pastime.

As neighbours, newspapers and nationally regarded politicians united against her, the accusations were repeated and elaborated upon until they became accepted truths. In newspaper columns she was referred to variously as 'a wicked wretch', 'a professional murderess' and 'a butcher of human beings'.

Sarah cuts a lonely figure in history; there's no evidence of anyone speaking out on her behalf before she went to the gallows. Decades later, however, Roz Powell stepped forward to take on the mantle. Having found Sarah in her family tree, she was at first bemused at being related to a convicted killer, then outraged when she investigated the circumstances of Sarah's supposed crimes.

Rather than a watertight legal case with stress-tested evidence, she discovered 'hearsay, nasty gossip and contradictions'. According to Roz, from the moment Sarah's sons died in 1845, she was doomed.

'I just feel so hurt, the way she was treated, and what she had to go through. It is so sad, and it should never have happened. And if I can clear her name, I'll do my damnedest to do it,' she said.

When barristers Jeremy Dein and Sasha Wass began their investigations, they quickly saw things from Roz's point of view and started to sense a miscarriage of justice. With historic cases like this, it's always vital to look at the cultural impetuses of the era, to see life how people at the time saw it and hear the mood music they heard. Sarah's case unfolded at a time when the hysteria generated by a wide-ranging moral panic over female poisoners was at its height in the heart of Essex. Jeremy quickly concluded: 'This corner of England was swept up in a sort of poison panic at the time. My concern is Sarah Chesham was a victim of that sort of phobia.'

Both Sarah's sons died from arsenic poisoning, and when Solomon Taylor and Richard Chesham then fell ill as well, observers jumped to a single conclusion – that Sarah had slipped something into their food. But historian Helen Barrell had another theory that she shared with Roz and her husband Steve: 'Perhaps arsenic had got into the family food by accident. Joseph and James were the ones who really suffered the most; perhaps they ingested the biggest amount.'

The next step was a series of inquests to investigate the cause of the deaths, which were not necessarily the sombre occasions they are today, Helen revealed. They were often informal affairs held in pubs and were open to all-comers. In Sarah's case, the largest single venue in the vicinity was chosen for the purpose. Helen explains: 'Inquests could be quite rowdy, and I think it was Sarah who shouted across the room, "You lie, neighbour!"'

Selecting an impartial jury was the first difficulty, because in a small town everyone knew each other. As it happened, it was the jury in her eventual trial that showed the vestiges of good sense, accepting that Joseph and James had died from arsenic poisoning but uncertain about when, where, how or by whom it was administered. Sarah was duly found not guilty, as she was in relation to Solomon Taylor's death. But while the relevant legal procedures were at an end, the frenzy about poisoners was not. When her husband died, Sarah was once again cast as a killer despite the lack of evidence. As Sasha pointed out, mud sticks and her reputation was now in tatters.

The intervention of London-based barristers at this point was a cause for concern for both Sasha and Jeremy. Documents from the National Archives that reveal what went on at government level to ensure Sarah faced a trial were proof, as far as Sasha was concerned, that they were taking matters back to front.

'They're saying, "We don't have evidence, we know she's guilty, we've got to stop her, what can we charge her with?" ... It's clear from what is being suggested in these documents that in order to get some evidence against Sarah Chesham, Hannah Phillips may be prepared to say more than she had thus far. So, it is almost a blueprint for creating evidence against a woman in respect of whom there is no evidence.'

According to Jeremy, the documents are shocking because they acknowledge that there was no evidence. 'The whole thing just escalated, and ultimately, without any proper evidential foundation, she finds herself on trial and convicted of an offence for which her life is taken away from her,' observed Jeremy. 'It's very, very concerning.'

To Professor Alfred Swaine Taylor, the small amount of arsenic discovered during the post-mortem of Richard Chesham was enough of a sign of sustained poisoning. So to better understand the role chemistry played in the drama, Jeremy and Sasha sought advice from Professor Andrea Sella of London's City University, who demonstrated for them the Reinsch test and Marsh's test. The result in the Reinsch test, which he undertook with an experiment and a control, did reveal the presence of arsenic, as expected. But, Professor Sella pointed out, the same response would have been recorded for other heavy metals, like lead, bismuth or antimony. 'The Reinsch test is a very useful test, but it's certainly not foolproof,' he told them.

The Marsh test is more robust but there are different issues with it. The test requires the use of sulphuric acid, but the quality of that varied at the time and sometimes it was itself contaminated with arsenic. So the results of the Marsh test could be accidentally affected by a contaminated acid, although this couldn't be discerned by the human eye.

Beyond the ambiguities of the tests lay the interpretation of their results. Jeremy and Sasha consulted Professor Atholl Johnston, from the clinical pharmacology department of Queen Mary's University in London. Professor Johnston cast doubt on the wisdom of linking the symptoms of TB and arsenic poisoning, as Professor Taylor did in court. He said: '[Richard Chesham] might well have had arsenic in his body but … one of the things that at this stage was not appreciated was that there is a normal level of arsenic in the body.' Any similarities were likely to have been brought about by the fact that Richard Chesham was on the verge of death, he said.

That no one was able to speak up for Sarah while Professor Taylor gave evidence, or challenge his statements, was to him a further issue: 'You are on a hiding to nothing if you are up against Swaine Taylor in 1850 and you've got no defence barrister or defence expert to question what he is saying. He was the man you went to for forensic toxicology at that stage, and his ability to convince juries was well known.'

From today's perspective, the lack of representation was a recipe for injustice, and Jeremy went as far as to label Sarah Chesham's 1851 trial as 'a sham'. His concerns were shared by Sasha, who, realising the scope for a qualified lawyer, called the absence of defending counsel 'extraordinary'.

It was Hannah Phillips's evidence that was most problematic for the two barristers, as she recounted conversations with Sarah about poisoning and even called her 'Sally Arsenic' in court, implying she was a professional poisoner. As Sasha explains, 'This was the sort of witness who probably had all sorts of baggage of her own and had a long history of a relationship with Sarah Chesham. All of this should have been challenged, no doubt could have been challenged, but was not challenged because of the lack of legal representation.'

The constant references to the deaths of Sarah's sons five years previously, and of Solomon Taylor in 1846, also meant that the 1851 trial often felt like all the offences were rolled into one.

When Roz visited Springfield jail, the site of Sarah's hanging, the injustice of her circumstances and the slow, lingering death she suffered after the noose was put around her neck spilled over into angry tears. Roz was unequivocal: 'In my mind, she was murdered. Right up until the very end she said, I am not guilty.'

Summing up before Judge Radford, Jeremy highlighted the lack of representation for Sarah that led to a singular lack of examination of crucial witnesses: 'In those circumstances, that the trial was nothing more than a show trial and that it was doomed to failure from the outset,' he said.

Sasha supported his submission, pointing out that the use of the term 'Sally Arsenic' during the trial implied to the jury that Sarah was known to be of bad character. It could not possibly be claimed that Sarah had had a fair trial, she said.

More than 150 years have passed since Sarah's skewed trial and her punishment, and when delving back into the past it's important not to make glib comparisons with today's more rigorous laws and tighter procedures. However, Judge Radford immediately pointed out that verdicts secured in unfair or unsafe ways should still be put under scrutiny: 'What was required here were the services of able senior counsel. Any such counsel had much material to work on, not least the inconsistent statements and fanciful embroidery to be exposed in the evidence of Hannah Phillips,' he said.

Despite his expertise, Professor Taylor should have been cross-examined to reveal the paucity of the toxicology results laid against her. 'I fear that Sarah Chesham's last trial was affected by prejudice and unproven allegations of which she had been cleared of guilt,' Judge Radford added.

More than 160 years after her shabby treatment at the hands of the law there was redemption as he declared the verdict against her 'unsafe'.

It was an overwhelming moment for Roz, who admitted she didn't know whether to laugh or cry but felt she would be getting Sarah's approval from beyond the grave: 'It's a mixture of emotions but at the end of the day, I'd like to think she's up there saying, "I'm glad you did it, because I am not a poisoner!"'

THE CASE OF
THE BATTERED WIFE

————————

EMILY SWANN

W hen a row broke out at the Swann household one midsummer Saturday evening in 1903 in Wombwell, Yorkshire, it was nothing unusual. Emily Swann had drunk too much beer, something she often did. William Swann, also drunk, raised his fists in fury and blackened her eye. Again, this was nothing out of the ordinary during a 22-year marriage that was beset by alcoholism, adultery, hostility and hopelessness. Domestic abuse had long been a grim hallmark of the unhappy union.

But this time things escalated. Instead of suffering the beating in silence as she often did, Emily, brimming with fury, flung a shawl over her head and went across the road to neighbour Mary Ann Ward's house, where a drinking party was in progress, to find her lover John Gallagher, whom she suspected would avenge the injury. 'See what our Bill has done,' she cried as she revealed her swelling face to a crowded room.

At the sight of the bruising, Gallagher, likewise full of drink, started issuing dark threats as he headed for the front door. He crossed George Square at speed, with Emily in his wake. Battering his way into the Swann household, he said: 'If you can't kick a bloody man, you shan't kick a bloody woman.' Then he set about William Swann with his fists and, by some accounts, a wooden chair. Nobody in the vicinity saw the violence unfold as the front door was shut. But some neighbours said they heard ominous thuds and could make out Emily's voice, urging Gallagher on with the attack.

After breaking four of William's ribs, he tracked back across the square, boasting of his exploits. But there was still a niggle inside about unfinished business, no doubt fuelled by alcohol. He had previously made threats against William's life and he couldn't resist the impetus to go back and, as it transpired, end what he'd started.

Back at the Swann household, for the second time in 30 minutes, there was another short but explosive spell of violence. This time Gallagher emerged with bloodstains on his face. The couple were seen holding hands briefly on the doorstep before Emily retreated inside and he left for a local pub.

Emily was too befuddled by drink to determine whether her husband was still breathing. Eventually she implored neighbour Mary Ann Ward to assist William, but only at the second time of asking did her neighbour reluctantly agree to become involved. When Mrs Ward arrived at the Swann house she found William lifeless on the floor, his head propped up by a cupboard door. Next to his body lay a poker.

Although the police station was only about 100 yards away, no alarm was raised for the time being. A doctor was finally called at about 8pm – some two hours after the incident started – and he estimated William had already been dead for about an hour. It gave Gallagher ample time to skip the area.

The only witness to the squalid scenes that unfolded in the Swann home that day was the couple's six-year-old son Ernest. He was no stranger to sudden bursts of ferocious violence, having often seen his mother sustain injuries at the hands of his dad. Although the young lad's account might have saved her from the scaffold, he was never asked to speak to the court on Emily Swann's behalf.

*

At the time of his death, William Swann was employed as a bottle blower at the Aldham Bridge glass works, which stood by the Dearne and Dove Canal. Both factory and waterway have since been consigned to history, along with much of the manufacturing that defined Wombwell in particular and South Yorkshire as a whole. But at the time heavy industry was rampant in the area and demand for specialist workers like William was high. Glass blowing, which needed considerable upper-arm strength, required a seven-year apprenticeship and was a job that tended to stay within families. William's income should have been steady and his prospects certain, but a long-standing taste for alcohol put paid to any hopes of that.

Standing at just four feet ten inches, the diminutive Emily Swann had nonetheless given birth to 11 children during her marriage, although only six still lived. Despite advances in science and medicine, infant mortality remained high in that corner of Yorkshire. With rent to pay, mouths to feed and a head of the household who was unreliable, Emily had to find a job. Before her marriage she had been a cotton and linen weaver at nearby Cawthorne, and it was to this now-struggling industry that she returned.

Inside the mills, life was noisy and dusty, not to mention hazardous, with workers losing digits and even limbs to the massive machinery. Women were the front-line workers at the mills but were paid substantially less than their male counterparts – and every penny counted for mill owners now that Britain was feeling the pinch from newly applied American tariffs. These import duties were imposed to bolster US industry by keeping its domestic products competitive against cheaper imports from the UK, where production costs were less.

Although they proliferated in other parts of Yorkshire, it wasn't mills that were the economic titans in Wombwell but coal mines. There were two in the heart of the town – Wombwell Main Colliery and Mitchell Colliery – and three more nearby. At the turn of the century, coal was king, as it powered steam engines in locomotives and ships as well as fuelling coke-fired blast furnaces, used in the production of steel. Without abundant coal, Britain would not have made such giant industrial strides in the last half of the nineteenth century. In addition to domestic use, the product of British mines accounted for two-thirds of the trade in coal globally.

No one knew it yet, but Britain was poised to yield her worldwide dominance to America and Germany as the age of steam was giving way to an era of electricity, and the first chill breezes of a downturn were starting to blow through the economy. But the optimism of a new Edwardian age wasn't yet dinted. A report made to the Home Office in 1900 about Yorkshire and Lincolnshire pits revealed that 79,000 people were employed below ground and 22,000 above, producing a mammoth 29 million tons of coal annually.

It was a tough existence, though. In 1901, less than 2 per cent of coal was machine-cut. That meant the bulk of the fuel that sent trains around a still-expanding railway network at home and ships across the globe was cut by hand. After descending in a lift to a gloomy subterranean corridor, the hewers at the coal face could sometimes stand tall and swing a pick axe but were usually on their hands and knees or even their stomachs. Working by the dim and eerie light of their Davy lamps, they filled tubs with chunks of coal they had prised away from the seam, which were taken back to the surface by wagons.

Of course, apart from being physically gruelling, working in the mines was a hazardous occupation. Ninety-six people died through-out the region in 1900, mostly being crushed after tunnel ceilings gave way. Although 17 men perished in shaft accidents alone, the Inspector of Mines described the figure as 'wonderfully low', given the number of men that travelled up and down each day. In addition to the range of injuries sustained by miners in the course of their work, they were far more likely to suffer from disabling illnesses like emphysema, pneumoconiosis (or black lung disease) and arthritis.

As a collier's daughter, Emily had hurtful personal experience of the horrors of mining. Aged just six, she lost two brothers in the Oaks mining catastrophe on 12 December 1866, which claimed 361 men and boys – Charles and Henry Hinchcliffe were among the 80 bodies never recovered from the mine. In some ways, the effects of the disaster upon Emily's family were less catastrophic than on other local families, who lost many more. Her father John and another brother, William, were not at work when the first explosion, caused by methane, occurred. Nor were they part of the rescue crews that died in a second blast. A relief fund established soon afterwards helped to alleviate the economic hardship in the family after two wage earners were lost. But the impact the grief had on her family and the wider community was immense.

The Hinchcliffe family recalibrated. Emily's 14-year-old sister had died from illness shortly before the blast, and so Emily was one of seven children now, rather than ten. Her mother Hannah, a weaver's daughter who could read and write, had plenty of tasks in hand to distract herself from mourning, though her husband John continued to struggle with breathing difficulties that saw him work less frequently down the mines. In the wake of the trauma of the disaster, Emily's youngest brother, also called John, became a shop worker rather than a miner. Nonetheless, Emily grew into adulthood with all the anxieties attached to the industry running through her core.

Although the Swanns didn't work at the pits, the overarching existence of the mining industry still had a huge effect on their daily lives. The economies of colliery towns may still have been relatively good at the turn of the century, yet sacrifices continued to be made for living in the shadow of the mines. Fresh air was hard to come by as smoke billowed out of assorted industrial chimneys. For example, Wombwell Main Colliery covered hundreds of acres and, beyond shafts, winding engines and locomotives to haul the coal, it also had 90 coke ovens in operation by 1897.

Once or twice a week the coke ovens were fired up, forcing impurities out of coal by baking it at high temperatures, leaving coke – almost pure carbon – as a residue, which was directed to steel manufacturers. When the ovens were alight, plumes of acrid black smoke charged with sulphuric acid enveloped the streets, obscuring any sunshine and blackening bricks, windows and roads. As early as 1879, this had been identified as a 'great nuisance' by one Dr Ballard when reporting to the government's medical officer, as it made homes and their occupants perpetually dirty. By now, that filth was some 30 years deep. But that wasn't all. Spoil banks, the heaped earth dug up as part of the mining process, also burned when hot cinders or furnace ashes were deposited on them. On these Dr Ballard observed: 'The smoke and fumes proceeding from a burning spoil bank are copious, very sulphurous and suffocating.' With the wind in the wrong direction, it made some homes unin-habitable, he declared.

Underground, the supplies of coal remained plentiful. Wombwell Main Colliery had three seams of coal to exploit and Mitchell Main had two. Although sons tended to follow their fathers into the mines, the town still couldn't provide sufficient labour to man the 2,000 jobs in both Wombwell mines. (Women had largely been stopped from working in mines by legislation in 1842.) There were also plenty more pits operating in the wider neighbourhood. Hordes of migrant workers were drawn to mining areas like South Yorkshire, having been enticed by the prospect of work at a time when there were no national welfare payments for the unemployed. Moreover, wages were generally good, with hewers among the best paid. A well-rewarded front-line miner in 1901 was receiving about 38 shillings a week, about £150 a day in modern values, which was several times the rate of pay an agricultural labourer might expect but also higher than policemen and clerks and on a par with skilled shipbuilders. However, there was an element of uncertainty about wages at the time. Despite the risks and the hard manual labour, miners' wages were sometimes cut by pit owners in the face of commercial competition. With only about a quarter of men belonging to a union, there was little workers could do about imposed reductions. Sometimes they went on strike and won a wage increase or improvement in conditions. But they might also find themselves locked out, with the bosses implacably set against them, and it wasn't unknown for them to return to work after a strike without any raise in pay.

Given all the above, it's not surprising that some of these migrant miners were hard-bitten, pitiless men coloured by the brutality of their everyday existence. Once such man was John Gallagher, the third person in the ill-fated love triangle, who, it turned out, was capable of killing a man with his bare hands.

Gallagher was from Middlesbrough, some 65 miles east of Wombwell. Little is known about his past other than that he was of Irish extraction and was discharged from the army after repeated wrongdoing. When he arrived in Wombwell, he became a lodger at the Swann house for several weeks. In exchange for his rent money he settled for surprisingly little in terms of space.

As industry mushroomed in Wombwell so did the number of homes, with lines of terraces, some better appointed than others, springing up to house workers. Although the era of council housing was underway elsewhere in the country, Wombwell residents were still beholden to private landlords. Any assistance in paying the rent was seized upon by hard-pressed householders, who shuffled their families into a smaller space to accommodate the house-guest – and that included the Swanns.

With William generally spending his income elsewhere, they were living in comparatively straightened circumstances. Every time he lost his job their home was put at risk, and they had moved so far down the housing ladder that they were now in a primitive and huddled-up back-to-back terraced house, usually the domain of workers paid far less than William. Still, there were hidden extras that more than made up for the lack of luxury as far as the new lodger was concerned.

Aged 30, Gallagher was a dozen years junior to Emily Swann, but the age gap didn't stop the pair becoming lovers. For Emily, the thrill of a newfound passion must have brought colour and energy to her life. It wasn't long before John found himself inter-vening between husband and wife as William lashed out at Emily. Although acknowledged as a bad penny, John had a degree of chivalry that refused to permit the doll-like Emily to suffer beatings at the hands of her well-built husband. The notion of having a champion living under the same roof must have been intoxicating for Emily, whose marriage to William had been so turbulent.

THE CASE OF THE BATTERED WIFE

After William discovered the liaison happening under his roof, Gallagher left the house but not the neighbourhood. He began lodging nearby with Mrs Ward and continued to see Emily on a regular basis.

*

On the day William died, virtually everyone drawn into the drama appeared to have been drinking, with the exception of the children. It was far from unusual for working people to take solace in drink. For Emily, there was not only the grief of losing five children in infancy – a large number even by nineteenth-century standards – but the routine drudgery that dominated her life.

Although she worked full time, she would have had a long list of chores to perform for her family, not least the arduous task of the laundry. Normally carried out on a Monday, this entailed heating water on a stove, emptying it into a tub and then bending over to scrub clothes in suds. Work clothes tended to be so filthy they were washed separately from other clothes, so at least two tubs of soapy water were needed. More was heated for rinsing. Once the clothes had dried – which was not easy in the winter – they would need ironing, and often repairing. Plus the cooking, cleaning and shopping piled up as the week progressed. As gritty grime made its way in through the doors and windows of houses in mining towns like Wombwell, the results of cleaning floors and clothes lasted for moments rather than hours.

Emily had four children at home: Charles, Frances, Ernest and Elsie. Two daughters, Eleanor and Annie, were already married. Her eldest daughter Eleanor had escaped much of the toxic atmosphere, having grown up with Emily's parents John and Hannah in Havelock Street, Barnsley, where in 1891 she was listed as 'a scholar', indicating that she attended school.

It's worth pointing out at this stage that Emily was among a number of those at the afternoon drinking session at the Wards' house who later signed police statements with a X. That meant that they could not read or write. From 1870 a series of government measures made education for 5- to 13-year-olds compulsory and introduced penalties for employers who used child labour. Emily would have been around ten when the new laws came into force, so she should have been swept up in its embrace, as would most of those drinking with her that afternoon who ended up as witnesses in the court case. Still, enforcement of education requirements was uncertain, especially in the early years, although it seems that at least some of Emily's siblings were educated. It's tempting to believe her schooling was overlooked during the years that her family returned to an even keel after the pit tragedy.

William and Gallagher both earned sufficient money to fund a drinking habit. Beer was threepence a pint – just under a pound by today's standards – and was sold at the public houses that proliferated on street corners at the time. Women were often not welcome in the male-dominated world of pubs. Those who preferred to drink at home brought foamy jugs from the pub and retreated to their back rooms.

This trio who drank too much, too often, were just a snapshot of the prevailing drinking culture. In 1901 *The Times* claimed that drunkenness was 'the most pressing of all the social questions of the day'. Beer drinking broadly reflected economic trends. When money was scarce, consumption fell, but as the economy soared so did the rates of drinking. Beer production in 1901 stood at more than 37 million barrels annually, outstripping the preceding years by a considerable margin and, as such, indicated a buoyant economy in those opening years of the century. At the time, beer was sold by the gill as well as by the pint – the equivalent of a teacup full or a quarter of a pint. This was the measure commonly bought by or for women.

In the nineteenth century, concerns about the rates of drinking and public drunkenness had escalated, resulting in the establishment of a non-drinking Temperance movement in the 1830s. However, this largely religious organisation had failed to make a major impact.

As society's nineteenth-century values outlived Queen Victoria by some considerable distance, there remained a narrative that framed alcoholics as wasters who lacked willpower. Habitually drinking to excess was something that could be overcome by gentlemen, it was thought, but against which women and the working classes had few defences.

Attitudes towards male drinkers were stirred up by public-health placards like the one paraded around Hampstead, London, in Edwardian times that claimed that, should men drink, 'the future of the race is imperilled' and that alcohol's first effect was to weaken a man's self-control, 'hence the number of crimes which occur under its influence as well as the spreading of vice and disease'. But it was women who were targeted when they were charged with offences linked to alcohol. Men and women who appeared repeatedly before the magistrate charged with public drunkenness presented a challenge – how was the law to cure them of their behaviour? In 1898, the Habitual Inebriates Act aimed to tackle the issue by incarcerating those convicted of 'habitual drunkenness' in a reformatory. Those with wealth were sent to private retreats; those without found themselves in a state-sponsored institution. Drinkers, particularly women, were sent to reformatories in droves – where they were deprived of liberty and family visits – for up to three years at a time, in the hope they would recover from their perceived weakness.

The gulf between the two was immense, as a report by the British Inspector of Inebriates pointed out. The average well-heeled (male) patient in a retreat was, apart from his weakness for drink, 'intellectual, gifted and the best of companions'. Alas, the inspector didn't have the same kind words for the inhabitants of the state's reformatories, especially women: 'Long neglect, years of unrestrained drunkenness, immorality, and filth, have between them created a class of person who is often on the borderland of insanity, generally degraded morally and physically, full of criminal tendencies, a curse to law and order, and a continual expense and charge upon the state.'

By 1904, women made up 91 per cent of reformatory inmates, while accounting for just 20 per cent of convictions for drunkenness. By 1906, nine of the eleven reformatories in England were exclusively for women, with the other two accommodating both sexes. Eventually, at the end of the Edwardian era, reformatories were replaced by lunatic asylums, with committed drinkers now viewed as feeble-minded.

Alcoholics of both sexes proved a thorn in the side of factory owners who wanted a sober, dependable workforce. Social reformers who were dedicated to improving slum conditions around Britain were likewise horrified by drunkenness. Thus, for all sorts of different reasons, the thought of beer-swigging among the workers filled the middle classes as a whole with unbridled horror, and this inbuilt intolerance offers another explanation as to why Emily and Gallagher were so reviled after William's death.

*

It wasn't the first time Emily, husband William and lover Gallagher had violently clashed. At some stage in the weeks after William found out about his wife's affair, Emily hit him with a poker as he walked through the front door – and it wasn't the first time she'd used a poker as a weapon. When William fought back, he was then set upon by Gallagher. About a month before his death, William was sporting two black eyes after brawling with Gallagher and took time off work. Two days prior to his death, when William discovered Gallagher at his home, he picked up a pint pot and hurled at it his wife. Missing her, the missile hit widow Mary Ann Ward.

Both Emily and Gallagher were heard freely making threats against William in the weeks leading up to his murder. Gallagher vowed to make Swann 'ready for a coffin', while, just a week before his death, Emily invited Gallagher to punch her husband. 'And I'll stand by and see you do it and think you do no wrong.' For his part, William told Gallagher: 'If you want her, take her.'

On the day of William's death, the drinking was inspired by Gallagher's impending departure. He had been paid off at Mitchell Colliery and was heading for Bradford. With cash in his pocket, he was buying the whisky and beer that everyone was enjoying at his landlady Mrs Ward's house. At one point, he asked her daughter Rose to fetch a jacket and waistcoat from the pawnshop on his behalf. However, the restored clothing was whisked away by Emily, who took them back to her home, presumably to entice Gallagher there for one last time. Alerted about the missing clothes Gallagher duly visited the Swann household and was halfway down the stairs when William arrived home. Although he wasn't working, William had been out since 9am – almost certainly drinking – and now it was 5.45pm.

On this occasion, it seems unlikely that the couple had been involved in anything more than a farewell embrace. According to Mrs Ward, they were away from her house for only ten minutes. But William's suspicions were understandably running high. He confronted Gallagher immediately, who sauntered past him with an insolent remark and went out of the front door. William then turned to his wife, who refused to answer when he asked if they'd been together upstairs. That's when he hit her.

After delivering two sets of beatings to William, Gallagher washed himself at the Wards and left, spending a short time in a pub before catching a train for Sheffield. Eventually Emily appeared at Mrs Ward's house and said to her neighbour: 'Missus, will you come to our house. I think my master's dead.' Initially Mrs Ward's son Edward told his mother not to get involved, unwilling for her to tangle with the unpredictable William. Finally she accompanied Emily to see William's body for herself.

*

There were just a handful of people who could give an account of events as they unfolded. Their first opportunity to do so was at William's inquest, held at the Horseshoe Hotel in Wombwell three days later. The Sheffield City coroner Dossey Wightman was in charge of proceedings.

In Gallagher's absence, Emily – wearing a black shawl and a thick bandage over her eye – had the opportunity to tell her side of the story without fear of contradiction. Having taken a blow from her husband she left the house as soon as she could, she told the inquest. Arriving at Mrs Ward's house, she had pleaded with an inflamed Gallagher not to get involved in the domestic argument, and, back at her own home, she tried to pull Gallagher off her husband, she insisted, and was struck on the chin by him. As for her husband, Gallagher 'struck him somewhere about the back of the neck and then started punching him', she said, before arming himself with a chair. When Gallagher left, she stayed with her husband, trying to lift him on to a chair and give him something to drink, 'but he sluttered down out of the chair whilst drinking the water'.

A post-mortem carried out by Wombwell doctor George Atkins found William had died from two clots on the brain, although he had suffered four broken ribs, a broken breastbone and at least 20 bruises. The injuries, he thought, were caused by a blunt instrument or a boot.

The inquest heard from two other witnesses, Mrs Ward and pony driver Walter Wrigglesworth, who had both been at the drinking party that fateful afternoon. Admitting she had been 'silly' with drink at the time, Mrs Ward's recollections were hazy, although she confirmed that Emily and Gallagher were lovers. A teetotaller, Mr Wrigglesworth said that Gallagher had returned from the Swann house with blood on his face.

Already the coroner had heard enough. After summing up everything the inquest had heard, he sent out the jury. They needed only a few minutes to decide Gallagher had murdered William Swann. For now there would be no charges brought against Emily, although public feeling against her was running high. A key witness and protagonist, she was kept under police supervision. Crowds gathered outside the pub at the end of the inquest and Emily was escorted home by officers to keep her from harm.

The following day, William's funeral, there was still more evidence of hostility. Outside the Swann home a large crowd gathered, made up mostly of women, the *Barnsley Chronicle* observed. In a bid to quell strident public sentiment, Emily raised her bedroom window to plead with the crowd: 'Let him go quietly.' However, she was forced to lower the sash quickly as she was subjected to a torrent of verbal abuse. It was apparent she would not be able to attend the funeral in safety. As the cortege left, her waving hand was seen poking out from behind a blind. Young Elsie was surely clinging to her skirts throughout.

At the front of the funeral procession were 30 workers from the Aldham Glass Bottle Works, with one bearing a small wreath.

Factory workers also acted as pallbearers. Behind the horse-drawn hearse, which was paid for by a well-wisher, there were some 40 mourners, including four of Emily and William's children and three of his brothers. Together they made slow progress along a route lined seven or eight deep. At the cemetery, the gates were closed so that curious onlookers couldn't ogle any further, while police were stationed at George Square in the vicinity of Emily's home to deter troublemakers.

The show of support was not because William was a popular man. It appears that neighbours, colleagues and family members had lost patience long ago with this garrulous drunk. But the fact that he was attacked and died in his own home chimed with many as an outrage. Being an older woman in an illicit relationship did Emily no favours as far as public perceptions went either.

*

Gallagher was on the run for two months before being caught in his native Middlesbrough after police were tipped off that he was visiting relatives there. Although he initially escaped from his sister's house just before three uniformed policemen knocked on the door, he was quickly tracked down to a remote cottage nearby and arrested. His capture came as something of a surprise to many people. As there had been no sightings of the fugitive, they assumed he had either died or skipped the country. Emily certainly must have been hoping for as much. But after police took a statement from Gallagher, which mentioned her wielding a poker, some officers unobtrusively slipped round to her house to arrest her.

Gallagher duly appeared in front of seven magistrates at Barnsley's court. With a tanned face, shabby clothes and unkempt hair it seemed as if he had spent the intervening months living like a tramp. Emily stood with him in the dock, wearing a black dress trimmed with beads, and a crepe hat.

After the brief hearing, both were dispatched back to Wakefield jail. Any attempt at subtlety on the behalf of the authorities was thwarted by waiting crowds, who, according to the *Barnsley Chronicle*, followed the suspects' cab 'helter skelter down Regent Street' as, flanked by their warders, the pair went to catch a train. By the time they arrived at the station there was a large throng on the platform. The police steered Emily and Gallagher to a railway bridge at one end of the platform to keep them out the way.

The tenor of the commentary in the *Barnsley Chronicle* illustrates how Emily was portrayed, with implied insults and criticisms familiar in coverage of women who were believed to have contravened social norms: 'Mrs Swann's face was absolutely impassive; it betrayed not a single sign of emotion – almost a callous indifference – and she lounged languidly against the handrail of the bridge until she, her companion and their guardians entered a third class smoking compartment bound for Wakefield. The blinds of the compartment were instantly drawn and thus shut out the gaze of an over-eager hustling crowd.'

At another committal hearing before the trial, one of Emily's sisters and her young daughter Elsie were in the courtroom. This time Emily was described as standing with folded arms 'half nonchalant, half defiant' – a show of bravado in front of a small child living without the benefit of a mother or father no doubt. It was more than three months before the stage was set for her final public performance, at the trial that decided her fate.

*

When Gallagher and Emily appeared at the West Riding Assizes held in Leeds on 7 December that year, theirs was by far the most notorious of the six murder trials scheduled. Neither had legal representation. Mr Justice Darling was presiding, famous for arriving at courts by horse, wearing a silk top hat with a liveried groom in tow. Among contemporaries he was thought to be an adequate lawyer blessed with a talent for words but nonetheless lacking the instinctive finesse of the best legal minds.

Darling ensured some lawyers were found but still, neither Mitchell Innes who represented Gallagher, nor Harold Newell, for Swann, were qualified as King's Counsel so they were outranked by prosecutor Mr Tindal Atkinson, who was. Both Emily and Gallagher pleaded not guilty to the murder charge.

When Mr Tindal Atkinson described the events that led up to their arrest, he talked in terms of 'the grossest brutality', outlining a story of drunkenness, menacing threats and unfettered aggression. Emily and Gallagher, who sat side by side in court separated by warders, listened intently as the case unfolded.

One witness, Alfred Harper, who was among the number of drinkers at Mrs Ward's house that afternoon, testified that he heard Emily say, about Gallagher: 'I hope he kills the bugger.' As for Gallagher, Harper said he pledged to finish off his adversary before going to Bradford. His version was echoed by the rest.

Mrs Ward – whose house was 18 metres from the Swanns' – was once again called as a witness, to recall what little she could of the evening William died. 'I had had some drink and it seemed to take my memory away,' she told the court, and admitted starting the drinking session at 10am that Saturday with whisky before moving on to beer. When she was asked how many people were drinking at Gallagher's expense at her house, she replied: 'As many as had a mind.' Ward went on to confirm that Swann and Gallagher were still lovers, with the miner visiting when William was working nights.

Her son Edward told the court that Gallagher tried a third time to enter the Swann house but found the door locked, revealing that Emily had barred his way. Later he said he saw Gallagher dance for joy on hearing Swann was dead, while insisting: 'I haven't bloody done it.'

The evidence of miner John Dunn, who lived opposite the Swanns, apparently offered much more clarity. He related the earlier incident, in which Emily had attacked William with the poker. Gallagher had been hiding in the kitchen until William fought back against his wife, and he emerged swinging his fists, Dunn confirmed. He also confirmed that the relationship between the Swanns had deteriorated. 'There was hardly a day [that] passed without quarrelling,' he said.

During Gallagher's first visit to the Swann house that Saturday, Mr Dunn said he heard Emily shout: 'Give it to him, Johnny.' Just prior to the second visit he heard Gallagher say: 'I will murder the swine.' His home was an estimated 16 metres away. Neither of the defence lawyers questioned whether it was even possible to distinctly hear what was being said at that distance, behind closed doors. Curiously, after being recalled by the judge before the end of the trial, he said he could not hear what Gallagher and Emily were saying as they stood on the doorstep, although he had heard what occurred inside the house.

Another miner, Thomas Beard, told the court he saw Emily say to Gallagher later that evening: 'You've done it.' Gallagher, he said, refused to return to the Swann house with her.

Police Sergeant Minty, called to the house the night William died, confirmed that both Mrs Ward and Emily were drunk that night. When he was at the house, Emily appeared distressed and cried: 'He is not dead, is he? He can't be dead.'

Although Mr Newell had hoped to call Emily's daughter Frances to the witness stand to testify that she was a good mother, Mr Justice Darling denied him the opportunity in order that the girl should not face distressing cross-examination, as well as believing the move would lead to a revelation of Emily's previous convictions to the jury. It was not the first time Emily had stood at Leeds Assizes accused of violence, and the judge felt that any reve-lation about her colourful history could influence the jury's attitude against her – and provide grounds for an appeal.

When it came to summing up the prosecution's case, Mr Tindal Atkinson told the jury in no uncertain terms that the use of threats by Gallagher and goading by Emily left them little other choice than to convict for murder above manslaughter. 'Although she may not have struck a single blow, the fact she was inciting him made her as guilty as if she had struck the blow which led to death,' he insisted.

For Gallagher, Mr Mitchell Innes said there was 'passion, excitement and confusion of mind'. He was, Mr Mitchell Innes insisted, 'besotted with drink' and 'inflamed with this mis-directed love for this woman' and went to the house to 'administer chastisement' in her defence. Although the pair were conducting an illicit relationship, it was not a tribunal of morals, he reminded the jury. Gallagher no more meant to kill William this time than he had on other occasions when the two had scrapped. Picking up a similar theme, Mr Newell called Emily 'reprehensible, wicked and sinful' but said there was no evidence of her inflicting a single blow. He advised the jury against convicting on 'intemperate words'.

For his part, Mr Justice Darling asked the jury to consider whether the threats made were idle ones or an expression of intention. An attack carried out on the spur of the moment was one thing, but a second visit lent a different meaning to events. Before the jurors retired, he too warned that instigators might also be guilty of murder alongside those who delivered the blows.

Emily and Gallagher were waiting for just half an hour to hear their fate. By 3.30pm a guilty verdict was returned for both, after a trial that lasted considerably less time than a working day. Accompanying the verdict, there was no recommendation for clemency, which often happened when a jury felt sympathy for an accused or saw extenuating circumstances. When she was asked if she had anything to say, Emily declared: 'I am innocent; but I am not afraid to meet death because I am innocent – and will go to God.'

After putting on the traditional black cap to pass the death sentences, the judge assured the jurors they had made the right decision. He pointed out that, having beaten William and wounded him, they withdrew, giving them time to calm down after any provocation. Still, they returned and killed him, proving it was not spur-of-the-moment, but a joint action by the pair.

For the first time, Gallagher's statement following his arrest was unveiled to the court. He claimed he hadn't delivered a single blow and that Emily, armed with a poker, was responsible for the death. Both judge and prosecution counsel had previously decided against sharing this revelation with the jury before a verdict against the pair was announced. This is accepted procedure. When two people are accused of the same crime it's usual for one to divert the blame, in the hope of securing freedom at the expense of the co-accused. As his statement wasn't supported by any other, it couldn't be given due weight in the case, for fear of blighting the trial.

When she left the court, Emily looked up at the public balcony and blew kisses to supporters.

*

What little we know of Gallagher's background prior to arriving in Wombwell comes from his criminal record. As a soldier with the West Riding Regiment, he was dispatched to South Africa several years before the outbreak of the Second Boer War in 1899, where he was stationed at Pietermaritzburg, in the heart of Zululand, which later became infamous as the site of a British-run concentration camp. Although Britain wasn't then at war, there were a number of uprisings to contend with and discipline was strict. In 1896 and 1897 he received a total of three sentences of hard labour in respect of one charge of disobeying orders and two of desertion.

With the outbreak of war came a period of greater tolerance from the British Army as it struggled to recruit soldiers, with those who volunteered from the urban poor that now proliferated in British cities often proving too sickly to serve. In any event, Gallagher stayed out of trouble until 1900, when he again deserted, this time from what was then known as Rangoon, the capital of Burma and part of the British Empire. Records suggest that he eluded justice for some time. Finally, after he was captured, the army, perhaps sensing victory in the Boer War, lost patience with Gallagher; they sentenced him to another term of hard labour and discharged him from the army 'with ignominy'. The only misdemeanour on his civilian charge sheet was one of drunk and disorderly conduct in March 1903, for which he was fined seven shillings and sixpence at Barnsley court.

Emily had a criminal record of a similar length. The most significant element was a six-month sentence of hard labour behind bars in 1901 – also handed down at Leeds Assizes – for attacking a neighbour with a poker. It was knowledge of this conviction that Mr Justice Darling was aiming to keep from the jury. The victim on this occasion was Eleanor Harrington, who, according to newspaper reports at the time, was disfigured for life. Perhaps bizarrely in retrospect, Emily had carried out the assault in defence of her husband, who she thought was going to be summonsed by Mrs

Harrington. Emily said she had acted in self-defence. Clearly, it was for her a household implement of first resort – although to the prosecution's regret there was no proof she wielded it against her husband on the day he died.

For Gallagher, hard labour probably meant splitting rocks or similar while for Emily it might have been silently pacing on a treadmill. They were among the last wave of prisoners to endure such mind-numbing tasks. The 1898 Prison Act finally decreed that jail terms were for inmate punishment and reform. Soon hard labour would be dispatched to history.

Further smudges on Emily's record include two five-shilling fines, in 1893 and 1898, for using obscene language. She was guilty of being drunk and disorderly in Barnsley on April 1902 and, a month later, there was another charge of using obscene language, attracting a ten-shilling fine this time. In November 1902 she was fined for soliciting, a quick route to getting extra cash used by many working-class women who were nonetheless not full-time prosti-tutes. The last two years of her life had by this standard been the most troubled.

But of the three, William Swann had by far the greatest number of convictions, with a dozen levied against him, beginning in 1887 with a fine of ten shillings for playing the gambling game pitch and toss. In no particular order, there followed a further charge under gaming laws, three relating to his behaviour after drinking, three for using obscene language, two for not paying maintenance for his destitute father and two assaults. For his first conviction of assault, in 1888 against one B. Harper, he was fined ten shillings. But it's the second that is most significant: in 1896 he was fined 40 shillings for an armed assault against Emily and bound over to keep the peace for six months in the sum of £10.

Here is nailed-on evidence that Emily was the victim of violent acts by her husband, one of an untold number of women of the era who were unable to escape from brutality at the hands of the men they married. Although we don't know the circumstances, for it to have reached the courts at all is a sign of how shocking the attack must have been. The fine is noticeably heavy, so events must have appalled magistrates who were accustomed to hearing about chaotic and even dangerous families. By comparison, in 1903 miner Frank Hibbert was fined just 20 shillings for an aggravated assault on his common-law wife Sarah Graham.

Domestic abuse was commonplace at the time, although its role in the Swann marriage leading up to the murder was barely mentioned at the trial. Laws preventing women being abused by their husbands first appeared in the 1830s, some 30 years after similar moves were made against animal cruelty and the formation of the Royal Society for the Prevention of Cruelty to Animals. There was some official recognition of their effect by the early years of the twentieth century and numerous women who had lashed out against a bullying husband had been shown leniency by the courts. On this basis, Emily was hopeful that she would win a reprieve from the death sentence hanging over her. Yet women were not necessarily cast as victims, as might happen today. Contemporary accounts showed how society looked differently at a crime that happened behind closed doors.

The diary of Yorkshire miner Joseph Knowles in 1886 offers an extraordinary insight. Knowles, also a music teacher and active in local politics, was a respected member of the community. One day he recorded how he grumbled after his mackerel breakfast had been ruined by his wife's cooking. 'She said that which caused me to shove her and her chair over. I was very sorry after but she drew my temper,' he wrote.

In Wombwell the following year, Isaac Hazelhurst, a 50-year-old miner, killed his wife by pushing her downstairs at their home. There had been a Sunday drinking session during which she had ended up in bed with another man. According to the *Barnsley Chronicle*, there was 'strong sympathy' for Hazelhurst, with most people quick to excuse his behaviour. One of his supporters opened a subscription, collecting money from sympathisers for him as he appeared in court. One local vicar, Reverend George Hadfield, stood in the pulpit not to denounce the killing of a woman but instead the habit of drinking on Sundays: 'One would think that those young men who spent their Sunday in such a sinful fashion would hardly dare to show their faces in the daylight ... They have disgraced themselves, their families and inflicted a stain on the district which years will not wipe out,' he raged.

It was a view echoed by many. The judge in the trial made it clear that he felt better efforts should have been made by those present to stop the row, but one local, a Mr Blackburn, told the newspaper that men in the district knew the wisdom of the proverb: 'Don't interfere between a man and wife.' Had they done so, they might have had to endure the ire of both. Still, the issue of public image was uppermost in his thoughts. 'It was unfortunate that thing happened as it did,' Mr Blackburn lamented. 'If it had occurred 15 yards further eastward it would have then occurred in another parish.'

And yet small but notable efforts were taking place to change a wilful public blindness when it came to domestic abuse. In the middle of the nineteenth century, political philosopher John Stuart Mill was a prominent campaigner against it, insisting the legal subordination of one sex to the other was wrong and inhibited human improvement.

Journalist Frances Power Cobbe shone a spotlight on the issue by interviewing women who had been attacked by their husbands, and in 1878 she produced an essay called 'Wife Torture in England'. In it Cobbe said that in many marriages there was a master/slave relationship between husband and wife. Indeed, when Emily sought help immediately after William's death, she called him 'my master'. But while newspapers of the era were filled with reports of marital violence, there seemed little appetite to address the issue. It was only in 1903 that Emmeline Pankhurst formed the Women's Social and Political Union to campaign for equality and the vote, taking women away from the margins of society and putting them centre stage. Until women were re-framed as equal members of society by law, they were still subject to being second-class citizens in their own homes. In 1910, one social worker wrote that 99 per cent of wife beating went unreported and women remained trapped inside miserable marriages, in which their lives were at risk. There were few options open to battered wives, especially those with children.

In 1857 the Matrimonial Causes Act had permitted ordinary people to divorce for the first time, where previously the process necessitated an Act of Parliament. However, the law remained weighted towards men. Women who were divorcing husbands on the grounds of adultery not only had to prove faithlessness but also further difficulties like cruelty or incest. Still, money – or lack of it – was why most marriages remained intact, although newspaper reports at the time revealed women were choosing separation and maintenance orders through the courts. Without funds from their husbands it was difficult to maintain a home and children. In 1903 the wife of Barnsley butcher Joseph Parker cited neglect and abuse when she applied for just such an order. She acted after Parker threatened to murder her. He was ordered to pay seven shillings a week to finance his family.

Despite the domestic abuse she suffered, there was no appeal made for Emily's life. Still, there was some sensitivity in government circles about what she'd been through. Reviewing Emily's case, Home Secretary Aretas Akers-Douglas was concerned that there would be an outcry if people thought an abused woman was going to hang. Accordingly, he sent a telegram to Superintendent Arthur Quest to inquire about William's character, asking whether he had been guilty of 'habitual cruelty'. Superintendent Quest had known Emily for some time, having arrested her after she assaulted Mrs Harrington with a poker in 1901. Here was a man ready to endorse all of society's misogynist prejudices against working-class women who stuck up for themselves.

William was, Quest conceded, a big drinker. 'Glassblowers are a class of men who from the nature of their employment imbibe very freely and the deceased man was no exception to the general description of them,' he said.

And he admitted that Swann thrashed his wife many times, 'Although I would not like to say that he has been habitually cruel to her,' he added. But then he put Emily in his crosshairs, saying that she had been a drunken, immoral woman for at least a dozen years.

'I think her conduct towards her husband has at times been most brutal and the wonder is that he has not killed her. He has frequently gone home after leaving work and found his wife drunk in the house and nothing prepared for him in the way of food. He has also been known to leave the house hours before the time he should leave to go to work to escape from her violence and bad temper.'

He had, he said, no hesitation in saying that she was much more to blame than her husband for their unhappy marriage. Furthermore, he claimed her own relatives had little or nothing to do with her on account of her vicious conduct. However, even if this had been true prior to William Swann's death, it certainly wasn't the case now, and Quest must have witnessed Emily's mother and sisters supporting her from the public gallery during the trial and at previous hearings.

He concluded the letter with the line: 'The feeling in the district is very much against the prisoners particularly against the woman. She is undoubtedly a very bad cruel woman.' While that may have been true in some sectors of society, it ignores the fact that some 50 people signed a petition to have Emily's death sentence overturned.

Although she may not have realised this chance of survival was being damningly dashed, Emily was entertaining other hopes. She was surely aware that Mary Stone, convicted of murder in July 1903, had had her death sentence commuted in August. Stone was a maid in Surrey who had re-ignited a relationship with an ex-boyfriend, William Tuffin. But Tuffin had married and he and his wife Caroline had a baby. Nonetheless, Mary moved into the Tuffin home in Thames Ditton, although it's not known if Caroline knew about her husband's affair with Stone.

By April 1903 Caroline had disappeared. Although Tuffin had told him that she died of natural causes, her brother called in the police when no grave for her was located. Inside the house, police made a grisly discovery. Caroline's dead body was in bed upstairs, kept behind a locked door with the bloodied hammer and hatchet that killed her. Inside the house the air was heavy with the foetid odour of death. Tuffin and Stone were found guilty of murder at Guildford Assizes. In the end, Tuffin alone was hanged for the crime, at Wandsworth jail in London

The previous year, two servants who suffocated an elderly woman during a robbery were reprieved. However, earlier in 1903 Amelia Sach and Annie Walters, so-called baby farmers, were hanged for the murder of possibly dozens of infants after claiming to the mothers they would find adoptive parents.

Statistically, the chances of Emily being taken to the scaffold seemed reduced, as the public appetite for hanging women, even behind closed doors, was waning. A later Home Office study backed this up, showing that in the 32 years between 1890 and 1922 only nine women were hanged. The list of women convicted of murder, excluding infanticide, numbers 23. Two were reprieved on the grounds of drunkenness at the time of the crime – although this was not a mercy shown to Emily – two were pregnant, one had dementia and one was insane. In the same period, more than 450 men were hanged.

There were issues with the trial that surely left Emily wondering about the competence of the British court system. With the exception of Mrs Ward, all the witnesses from the drinking party to appear in court against Emily were aged under 21. Could they have been caught up in the sensationalism of the case, lured by a moment in the spotlight to imagine rather than recall events? Emily felt 18-year-old James Dunn lived too far away to have heard any exhortations from her. She may have had a point. Next-door-but-one lived widow Fanny Caunt, who told police she was in her back kitchen with the door open on the night William died. Although she heard Ernest crying she didn't hear anything from Emily. Yet her version of events wasn't shared with the jury.

After the death sentence was passed, Emily's solicitors busied themselves on her behalf, collecting names for a petition and pointing out to the Home Office that one witness was never called to give evidence in Emily's defence. They were referring to Ernest, who saw his father's death. The police didn't interview him or call him to the witness box during the trial. Both solicitors and counsel, Mr Newell, interviewed him in October, some months after the traumatic event. Both times, the youngster insisted his mother did not strike his father and added that Emily was knocked down by Gallagher. After consideration, Mr Newell decided his memory might be branded unreliable during the trial.

But now the solicitors wanted it known that he had been living with sister Annie since June so had not been tutored by Emily. Also, they declared that her children were 'respectable and appear to us to have been well brought up', in the hope that the Home Secretary would give Emily credit for being a good mother.

Furthermore, there was a heartfelt petition from five out of her six children, with the name of four-year-old Elsie the only one missing, that hoped to find some favour with King Edward VII during the Christmas holiday. In it they insisted that Emily was indeed a good mother and put the blame for their ruptured existence firmly on their father – 'who by his drunken habits destroyed our home life and rendered us unhappy, causing our mother … to go out to work in order to keep our home together'. Although William earned good wages, they claimed he spent it on 'drink and debauchery' – here implying he used prostitutes – and they referenced his physical ill-treatment of Emily. Although she was drunk, there was no evidence she struck their father, the children said, while her ability to resist the attack was impaired by drink. They begged the King to exercise clemency 'and so spare us and unhappy mother the pain and misery of her meeting her untimely death at the hands of the executioner'.

An unknown hand at the Home Office referred the petition to Mr Justice Darling, adding a note that dismissed the claims that

William Swann had been brutal and that Emily had not been involved in the beating: 'The first statement requires much qualification and the second is contrary to evidence.' This was dispatched through the corridors of power unchallenged, even when it was universally accepted that there was no evidence that Emily had wielded a poker, or anything else for that matter. Accordingly, the Home Secretary turned down the petition, and a telegraph to the King also had no effect. Given the careless approach of the establishment throughout the case, perhaps it was no surprise that the pleas for Emily's life made by her children and wider family fell on deaf ears.

On Christmas Eve 1903, as other families were preparing for feasting and togetherness, Emily's family were in despair. Emily wrote a letter from her cell trying to comfort them, with her words taken down by a wardress. In it she referenced her forthcoming wedding anniversary, calling the nuptials 'a very unfortunate day for me'. Her married life had been hard and unhappy, she said. She asked sisters Elizabeth, Clara and Ellen to visit with her daughter Elsie, and sent best wishes to her sister Frances, who had been unwell. She also referenced the kindness of her sisters' husbands, giving lie once again to the idea that her family were estranged from her.

She had concerns too for her ageing mother. 'Do not mind, dear mother, what people say about me, if they had their sins written on their foreheads it would perhaps take a big Salvation Army bonnet to cover them.'

'I know it won't be a merry Christmas for you,' she acknowledged, and urged them to spend it in prayer. Her final thoughts in the letter were for daughter Elsie.

'I hope my daughter Eleanor will not forget that it is Elsie's fifth birthday the last day of this year. I hope she will not forget to give her a Christmas doll.'

On Boxing Day – on what would have been her parents' wedding anniversary – Elsie accompanied her aunts to visit Emily in Leeds's Armley jail. Her family didn't realise they would only be able to speak to Emily through the barred hatch in the cell door. When it became clear her daughter would barely be able to see her mother, let alone touch her, the youngster was left in the care of a guard near the prison entrance. Emily's mother Hannah, now in her eighties, was as devastated as little Elsie. She told one reporter: 'Eh mister, I've had a hard life [but] of all the trouble I have had this has been the hardest.'

Another letter written to one of her sisters four days later on the eve of her execution assured her family that she had put herself up entirely in God's hands: 'We are all sinners and I cannot help but feel they sinned greatly against me,' she said, adding that death would come as a 'happy release'. 'I would sooner die than spend my life in prison. I have children to meet and I have children to leave,' she added poignantly.

Attending her in her final days was her chaplain Henry Maunsell, who, after her death, confirmed she had not confessed, but rather felt that justice had been denied. She took particular exception to witness John Dunn's testimony. While she admitted being an accessory to murder in respect of her adultery, she consistently denied wishing her husband dead or hitting him with a poker. He passed on her final statement to the Home Office.

Maunsell relayed Emily's claim that, after her husband had hit her she went to Mrs Ward's and told Gallagher who was responsible, much as the court case heard. She insisted that, after Gallagher withdrew, she tried to get her husband to stand, but couldn't: 'At first she did not think her husband was so badly hurt – but on seeing his face change she thought he was dying. She thinks he died in her arms. She had tried to break off her connection with Gallagher but he had a great power over her because he was kind where her husband was cruel.'

One official prison visitor was also convinced of her innocence, he added.

As for Gallagher, who knew he had no hope of a reprieve, he also made a final statement, once again implicating Emily. It's an account that is barely credible, given all that was said at the trial. He claimed that when he went to the Swann house William squared up to him: 'He said, "You bastard I will stand the drop of York for you!" He there lifted up a quart jug and stuck me on the side of the face. Then gripping me by the throat and throwing me on the floor between the table and fire place. Then Mrs Swann came round the table lifting the poker and striking him on the right side of the back. Me and Swann then got up and he sat in a chair between the table and fire place. I said to him, "I am going away to day," and he said, "Good bye Jack."'

Gallagher had been receiving support from a Catholic priest and seemed as resigned to his fate as Emily was to hers.

*

Hangman John Ellis shared with Emily an expectation of a reprieve. Looking through the condemned cell window on the night before the execution he saw: 'a little, stumpy round-faced woman only four feet, ten inches tall and 122 pounds in weight. She was the first condemned woman I had ever seen and frankly I didn't think the authorities would allow her to go to the scaffold.'

Her face was a picture of 'utter misery' when her appeal for a reprieve was turned down. In his autobiography, he described Emily as 'coarse and rather vulgar' and compared her unfavourably with Edith Thompson, another woman who controversially met her fate at the scaffold in 1922. But he witnessed great fortitude from Emily and Gallagher as they made their journey to the gallows at 9am on the cold, raw morning of Tuesday 29 December.

Both wore their own clothes, save for the white linen hood that was pulled over their heads as they emerged from their respective condemned cells, where their limbs had been pinioned. Emily had been permitted a large glass of brandy beforehand to give her sufficient composure with which to make those final faltering steps unaided. There was a momentary delay before Emily's hood was lowered, enabling her to catch sight of Gallagher a short distance ahead of her.

'Good morning, John,' she called out, her voice ringing above the burial service being read by Reverend Maunsell at the head of the sombre procession. Momentarily surprised, Gallagher soon collected his thoughts and replied, 'Good morning, love.' Before they reached the steps of the scaffold she said: 'God bless you.'

Ellis took pride in getting the job in hand done quickly. The pair would barely have had time to muster another sentence before he positioned them both, put the nooses around their necks and drew the bolt on the scaffold's trap doors.

As always, their bodies were left hanging for an hour before being cut down. In a departure from tradition there was no black flag flying atop the jail. A crowd a few hundred strong had gathered outside, although there was nothing to see. They dispersed after the mournful toll of the prison bell confirmed the sentences had been carried out.

When they were finally cut down, the bodies underwent a post-mortem before being put in black coffins and buried side by side in graves lined with quick lime in the confines of the jail. An inquest into the deaths began at 10.15am, with the jail's medical officer confirming the deaths had been painless and practically instantaneous.

Although 30 executions had now been carried out at Armley jail, including five double executions, Emily was the first woman to die on a gallows there. It was the first time the death sentence had been carried out there since 1900.

*

Among the children Emily left behind was Elsie, days short of her fifth birthday when her mother was executed. It was pale, frightened Elsie who stayed inside a darkened house with Emily when father William's funeral procession left the house. Much later she was dwarfed by the majesty of a courtroom, watching her mother try to extricate herself from the clutches of a vengeful establishment. After that, she stood small and awed before the fearful edifice of Armley Prison, taken by her aunts to say a final farewell. The prison warder who took charge of her while Emily had her emotional final meeting with her sisters gave her a shiny sixpence to look after, presumably to distract the four-year-old from the intimidating environment of the jail.

The youngest of the Swann children, Elsie lost both parents in the space of half a year before it was possible to capture any treasured family moments that make a firm foundation for future life. Memories of her mother were mostly invested in a black and white photo, in which Emily looked small, unsmiling and even stern. From the day of the execution onwards, a dead, disgraced, hard-faced mother became her role model.

No matter how sensational the story, headlines eventually fade and the spotlight swings away. It's usually impossible to know just how the convicted's family members fare down the decades and, like everyone else, Elsie's teenage and middle years have been lost from sight. But thanks to Elsie's granddaughter we know how her life evolved.

Felicity Davis grew up with grandmother Elsie, her mother and grandfather in the coastal town of Scarborough. But despite the seaside setting, this was no idyllic childhood. Felicity suffered physically at the hands of her gran, who was swift to deliver back-handers for perceived misdemeanours. But it was the emotional abuse that scarred her. Not only was she subject to a torrent of insults most days, but there were inexplicably bizarre rituals that Elsie used to control the parameters of her life.

As a small child Felicity was made to walk across the room dozens of times while being scrutinised by her gran, who always told her she was doing it 'wrong' but never explained why. When she was older, Felicity became a sentry at the living-room light switch as Elsie had her turn it on and off at regular intervals – and again because the youngster was apparently carrying out the strange task incorrectly. Felicity, her mum and grandad, were all banned from using the bath, as Elsie didn't want the tub she used contaminated by them. With Elsie occupying an armchair in pride of place in the lounge, the others crept around silently for fear of incurring her boundless fury.

Their home remained without mod-cons; other families enjoyed new carpets, kitchens and washing machines during the sixties, while theirs was stranded in a dreary time warp. Elsie's vitriol was not solely reserved for family members. She would also insult neighbours with a volley of foul-mouthed accusations that left the family pariahs wherever they lived.

It was, said Felicity in her book *Sins of the Family*, like living with someone who was perpetually threatening to pull the pin out of a hand grenade. Even as a child, she realised her grandmother was suffering from a mental illness. But attempts to move Elsie from her home for treatment were thwarted by her husband, a kindly man who – to Felicity's eyes – seemed unable to free the family from its tyrant by sending her away.

As she emerged from childhood into adolescence, the domestic battles became more intense as Felicity began standing her ground or retaliating. All the while, she had no idea what lay behind her grandmother's strange behaviour and why her grandad and mother were apparently so accommodating. Respect and empathy for her gran were soon annihilated by the endless and atrocious behaviour. While there were veiled references by her grandad to a difficult past life, it was many years before Felicity – emerging from some challenging times of her own – looked in to Elsie's history. Horror-struck, she grew to realise the torment that great-grand-mother Emily had endured in her fruitless pursuit of justice, and she was delighted when barristers Jeremy Dein and Sasha Wass looked again at the case.

'Most certainly Emily Swann was the victim of a miscarriage of justice and there are many reasons for that,' she told them. 'I'm not so sure she had a fair hearing, especially as the jury came to their decision within 30 minutes, and I don't believe that she got fair representation.'

For the barristers, there was plenty to consider: the evidence given by neighbours, the swift court procedure and, crucially, the background of domestic abuse within the Swanns' marriage.

But first Felicity spoke to historian Lucy Williams about why Emily stayed in a difficult marital home and even resorted to prostitution, as her criminal record reveals. To some extent, Emily represents the plight suffered by countless thousands of working-class women at the time. Jobs for women were typically few and far between, Lucy confirmed, with long hours and low pay. Some, like Emily, occasionally fell back on prostitution to ease family finances, while for others it was a sustained activity to see themselves through economic hardship. No matter what their intentions, society judged prostitutes harshly and they were frequently prosecuted.

Emily was also contravening the social codes by taking a lover, despite the misery of her marriage. Lucy explained that, although it was difficult for women to leave unhappy homes, they were the object of criticism if they pursued any personal contentment. While it was not uncommon for people to notch up public order offences, the revelation of past criminal records served to confirm Emily's social profiling. The state had no compunction about making children like Elsie orphans because, said Lucy, '[Emily and Gallagher] would have been seen as some of the lowest people in society. Nobody's troubling themselves overmuch about making sure they get their story across or have good representation.'

Meanwhile, Sasha and Jeremy took another look at the attack itself, with both convinced that wild statements made by both Emily and Gallagher don't amount to proof of an intent to murder, especially given the mistreatment she had suffered at the hands of her husband. Furthermore, none of the witnesses saw Emily strike a blow in the killing – although there might have been a general feeling in parts of the community that she took part in it and was guilty. Only after Gallagher's arrest was she was charged by police.

But was there evidence that Gallagher and the rest of her detractors were right, that she did arm herself with a poker, as she had done previously, to take revenge against a brutal husband? Pathologist Dick Sheppard, who looked again at the injuries suffered by William, thought not. He explained that wounds from a poker would have been linear and probably parallel, while a blunt, heavy instrument wielded against a fallen victim would likely have fractured the skull. But there was no sign of injuries like this. Instead, he focused on the heavy boots worn by Gallagher that day. 'The injuries described would all fit with blows from a fist or kicks from a boot,' he explained, while the fractured breastbone was typical of a stamp on the centre of the chest.

Felicity consulted criminal psychologist Donna Youngs to find out more about how domestic abuse might affect a woman trapped in a loveless marriage, coupled with the combined pressures of motherhood, work and keeping house.

Emily was, Dr Youngs confirmed, suffering psychological and emotional stress, as well as being fatigued. 'Almost every basic human need is being threatened for Emily and [her] coping strategy might have collapsed,' she explained.

Counterintuitively, Dr Youngs said, stronger personalities, like Emily's, are dramatically affected when this happens, suddenly switching off from daily responsibilities like a light. 'She may be coping, coping, coping, then a very straightforward, very strong woman just suddenly can no longer cope. Cognitively, everything collapses,' Dr Youngs revealed.

And she cast fresh light on the evidence given by all the drinkers at the Ward home that afternoon, who spoke against Emily and Gallagher at the trial. Their statements were 'police-speak', according to Dr Youngs, who explained: 'When people are giving a truthful, natural description of what's happened, they begin with the most salient, intense, emotional component of the experience and there's none of that here, which makes me suspicious as to how much this is moulded by the police.'

It all confirmed Felicity's long-held suspicions that her great-grandmother was treated unfairly by society and the court system. Both Sasha and Jeremy were quick to contrast how the outcome of her trial would be different today because of the sustained assaults delivered by her husband. The law on provocation was different then, Jeremy pointed out; in those days there had to be a sudden and temporary loss of self-control in the face of provocative action, whereas now there can be a slower build-up. Demonstrably Emily had endured incidents of domestic violence and it was, he said, the basis of a legal defence. The two options that might be available today would be either 'manslaughter by reason of loss of control' or 'manslaughter by reason of diminished responsibility'.

Sasha termed it 'battered woman syndrome', which is considered part and parcel of post-traumatic stress disorder. The term 'battered woman syndrome' refers to those who feel unsafe and unhappy in a relationship but are unable to leave, not least because they fear they are the cause of the abuse. From the 1990s the cumulative effect of the violence they experience was recognised as a defence in the killing of abusive partners. Still, she had reservations about whether the legal process was flawed, given the way the law was applied at the time. The trial judge had even kept the fact that Emily had been prosecuted previously for use of a poker from the jury, despite Gallagher's statement, in the interests of fairness and balance. The barristers were united in concerns that the version of events offered by son Ernest Swann was not heard at the trial.

When it came to presenting today's case to Judge Radford, Jeremy pointed out that the evidence against Emily amounted to people hearing the threats she made shortly after being attacked. 'This is where the spectre of manslaughter becomes highly significant – that the type of comments that she is said to have made have to be viewed in the background of ongoing significant and violent abuse. It's our understanding that manslaughter was not left for the consideration of the jury and that the jury were therefore given one option, and one option alone, which was to convict this young lady of murder,' he said. Jeremy also argued that new forensic evidence reveals she did not brandish a poker against her husband, which is why the conviction against Emily was unsafe.

Despite misgivings about modern criticism levied at this historic trial, Sasha backed Jeremy on the issue. There was, she said, a well-documented history of domestic abuse that was noted at the time by the judge. While he then determined that did not explain a second attack on Swann, Sasha believed that, had Emily been tried in the modern era, the jury would be likely to look favourably on a defence against a murder charge because of the years that she had suffered from the physical outbursts of her husband.

After Judge Radford considered the case, he conceded that a 'partial defence' of provocation due to battered wife syndrome, reducing the murder conviction to manslaughter, might well have succeeded. But he believed the tempestuous behaviour by both William and Emily was properly highlighted in the trial. He found that the declared intentions of both Emily and Gallagher to kill William were clear and unequivocal, given the second visit to the household after a first beating had been administered.

'The defendants were properly represented and the judge appears to have tried the case fairly,' the judge said. 'The fact that the fatal violence was inflicted not in any immediate response to the assault on Mrs Swann by William Swann in my view made the defence counsel's plea to the jury at the trial – or any modern distillation reducing culpability to manslaughter only – a far from easy task.'

Accordingly, he found no reason to declare Emily's conviction unsafe.

For Felicity, it was the culmination of a decade spent investigating a family history kept under wraps for many years while its harmful effects spilled out into plain sight. For years she hated her grandmother for the sadistic cruelty that marked her childhood. But reading Emily's last letters had cast Elsie in a new light, and Felicity now understood the difficult journey she had faced growing up. Rather than seeing her as the wicked witch who stole her happy home life, Felicity could now picture Elsie as a vulnerable child who lost her mum in painful and public circumstances.

'Standing here now, I realise that I have been full circle,' she said. 'I shouldn't blame my gran for the way that she treated me because her mother was hanged. It helps me to understand that she was just a victim.'

Although the legal case was lost, it nonetheless highlighted a stark contrast between legal and social justice for Felicity, and unveiled Emily's story and its far-reaching consequences to a wider audience.

Her last task was to visit Armley jail once more to say a final goodbye to the dejected woman whose tumultuous existence at the turn of the twentieth century blighted her own life so severely 60 years later.

A CASE OF WICKED AFFECTION, PART 1

EDITH THOMPSON

I t is a few minutes before midnight, Tuesday 3 October 1922. The evening is clear and, although there's a three-quarters moon, the suburbs of East London are a dense patchwork of shadows broken only by pools of light from the 50 candle-power electric lamps on street corners. Six passengers alight from the 23.30 Liverpool Street to Ilford train, cross the track via a foot-bridge and leave via the York Road exit to head north up Belgrave Road. There's a party of four – a Mr and Mrs Clevely of Mayfair Avenue, Ilford, and their friends Miss Dora Pittard of Endsleigh Gardens and Mrs Jesse Secretan of Courtland Avenue. These four are leading the way while another couple, apparently not in their group, follow behind. Some distance further back there's a man on his own, walking in the same direction.

The pedestrians cross Northbrook Road and enter an estate of large, detached Edwardian houses with garden walls lining each pavement. Here the chestnut and sycamore trees block the moon-light and it is hard to see far ahead. When the lead party reaches Mayfair Avenue they pause and the gentleman begins escorting his wife and their two female friends to their respective front doors nearby. As he does this, the couple behind pass by, still proceeding along Belgrave Road.

A few steps further and this couple, now almost a mile from the station, approach the corner of Endsleigh Gardens. Suddenly an assailant leaps from the shadows, thrusts the woman aside and aggressively pushes her male companion further up Belgrave Road towards its junction with Kensington Gardens. A fight breaks out and the stalker pulls a dagger, repeatedly plunging it into his victim's neck and chest. The dying man, covered in blood, collapses onto a wall; a woman's voice screams: 'Oh don't, oh don't.' Moments later the alarm is raised, the woman runs towards Mr Cleverly and Miss Pittard screaming for help and a doctor. 'Oh, my God,' she cries hysterically, 'help me, my husband is ill, he is bleeding on the pavement.'

The three of them run to the door of a nearby surgery and raise Dr Maudsley. It takes him between five and eight minutes to reach the wounded man but only seconds to conclude that he is dead. At 12.40am Maudsley telephones Ilford police and three constables are despatched in a police ambulance.

The dead man was Percy Thompson; the distraught woman his wife Edith. The attacker knew them both as he was their lodger, Freddy Bywaters. Freddy was particularly well known to Edith as he was also her secret lover. Within three months, these two would be found guilty of murder, sentenced and executed. Yet while the case against Freddy was clear cut, against Edith it was anything but. Almost a century on, the question remains: was Edith Thompson hanged because she was complicit in a murder? Or because she was an adulterous wife; a professional woman holding her own in a man's world; an artistic, mischievous character immune to the traditions of deference? Was she the victim of a moral panic about wives poisoning their husbands – which was just one of the dubious allegations flung at her. Was she hanged on the lie of being a dominating, duplicitous older woman who orchestrated her young lover's attack? Or is the truth that the judicial system decided she *must* be guilty, irrespective of the evidence – or lack of it – against her?

*

Edith Jessie Graydon was born on Christmas Day 1893 at her parents' rented terraced house – 97 Norfolk Road, Dalston, in the London Borough of Hackney. Her mother, Ethel Graydon, was the daughter of a police constable – an intelligent, tall, attractive woman with a hint of severity in her demeanour and a desire to 'get on', while her father, William Graydon, had good prospects as a clerk with the Imperial Tobacco Company.

By the late summer of 1895, Edith had a little sister, Avis, with whom she would go on to develop a close relationship founded on the older daughter's confident manner. The family flourished, money was put aside and, in the summer of 1898, William secured a mortgage for a new house on one of the burgeoning estates in Manor Park, East London. This three-bedroom terrace – 231 Shakespeare Crescent – would be the Graydons' home for the next 40 years. With three more children arriving – Newenham, known as Newnie, later in 1898, William, aka Billie, in 1900 and Harold, nicknamed Towser, in 1902 – it was a cramped but happy existence for Edith. The quiet streets became a playground for her and her siblings and the pupils of nearby Kensington Avenue Schools their extended family.

Among her brothers' friends was one Frederick Edward Francis Bywaters, known to all as Freddy. Born in 1902, he was nine years her junior and so barely worthy of a glance. At least, not yet.

The Bywaters occupied a different rung on Manor Park's social ladder. Their small family home – 72 Rectory Road – was on the same estate as the Graydons', but their economic prospects were very different. Freddy's father, also called Frederick, was in employment but his meagre wages had to be supplemented by Freddy's mother Lilian's part-time work taking in mending. With an older and younger sister (Lilian and Florence) and a younger brother (Frank), Freddy was brought up in a household where both money and space were tight. This didn't prevent him emerging as a bright pupil at school and an admired figure among his mates. Strong and daring, he loved football, swimming and cycling, and was no slouch with his fists – once taking on a tough lad from a rival nearby school in a street fight watched by dozens of boys (Freddy won, emphatically). Throughout his early years he was also a close friend of Billie Graydon and a familiar face at 231 Shakespeare Crescent. Yet such was the age gap between him and Edith that he was not yet 12 years old when she lost her virginity during a summer holiday in Ilfracombe, Devon, to Percy Thompson, the man destined to be her husband.

Percy was a teenager when his family moved to 87 Clements Road, Manor Park. He was also the man of the house; his father had been fatally injured while serving in the merchant navy and so while still a schoolboy he'd taken whatever part-time jobs he could to help keep his mother, younger brother and two sisters in reasonable comfort. In 1903 he left school aged 13 – then the legal age to begin full-time employment – and the following year was taken on by a shipping company. With this experience behind him he soon moved on to O.J. Parker & Co., a firm of shipping agents, where his role as junior clerk offered promising future prospects. It was this secure wage that allowed the Thompsons to move up from their insalubrious docklands home into the comparatively posh Manor Park district.

By 1909, Percy was part of the daily commute from East Ham station to Mile End, from where he could get a connection to his company's premises in Bishopsgate. Almost certainly, he would first meet the teenage Edith Graydon on a platform at East Ham, where she too would be heading for work in the City.

Edith's later schooldays were marked by outstanding work in creative writing and drama. She won several prizes for her essays and her Parents' Day performance as Hippolyta in an excerpt from *A Midsummer Night's Dream*. She later played the challenging part of Portia in *The Merchant of Venice*, which was also warmly received. These formative years gave her a lifelong love of the arts; between 1905 and 1913 she was constantly engaged in rehearsal of or performing in amateur dramatics. At family gatherings she loved nothing better than a game of charades, while the expansion in music-hall culture across the country fuelled her love of dance. By her teenage years, her father was helping

out at a highly respected local dance academy and her effort-
less fluidity on the floor meant she too was taken on the books.
Writer, actress, dancer – Edith Thompson lived every moment
to the full.

In 1909 she left school and, after a brief stint with a cardboard
manufacturing company in Southwark, began work in the clerks'
office of clothing wholesaler Louis London in the City, where one
of her closest friends, Bessie, was head clerk. But the firm had a
staid image and Edith wanted a more glamorous role in the fashion
industry. In 1911 she found it in Carlton & Prior, a wholesale milli-
ners close to Aldersgate Tube Station (now known as Barbican).
The 16-year-old girl quickly made an impression and was marked
out by the proprietors, Herbert Carlton and Miss Ellen Prior, as a
potential buyer.

She had also made an impression on 19-year-old Percy
Thompson. During their initial conversations – probably on the
tube – they discovered a shared interest in theatre and music hall,
and he persuaded her to join the Stepney Elocution Class, an
amateur dramatics society run by a local vicar. By Christmas 1909,
she had invited him back to the Graydon residence in Shakespeare
Crescent, where, in a man-to-man discussion with her father, he
revealed he was very fond of Edith and wanted to continue courting
her. Mr Graydon made clear that marriage was not on the cards
but, so long as Percy remained honourable, he saw no problem.
Edith's reciprocal visits to Percy's home were less genial; his invalid
mother appeared jealous and wanted her son to look elsewhere. It
was a forlorn wish.

Over the next four years, Edith's career blossomed. Aged just 19, she was travelling to Paris as one of Carlton & Prior's millinery buyers, a role which confirmed her bosses' confidence that she had a natural eye for fashion. In June 1914, with money flowing in, she and Percy decided to take a summer holiday with Bessie and her boyfriend Reg in the bustling North Devon resort of Ilfracombe. While this was her introduction to sex, and no doubt convinced Percy that Edith was 'the one', Edith was reluctant to commit. War was looming and, besides, she had her career to consider. But Percy was love-struck and persuasive, and finally, on 15 January 1916, Edith Graydon became Mrs Edith Thompson.

Just 26 days later, Prime Minister Herbert Asquith's Military Service Act came into effect, introducing conscription for the first time in Britain. Percy had enlisted with an infantry regiment, the London Scottish, and was deemed A1 at his medical. Yet before the month's end, he'd reported sick with 'heart trouble' and missed his regiment's posting to France. As the dreadful massacres on the Somme filtered through to an aghast public, Percy was given an honourable discharge on grounds that he was physically unfit for service, though army doctors never managed to diagnose a heart problem.

And so the Thompsons' married life got underway – first lodging with her parents in Shakespeare Crescent, then, from April 1917, in furnished rooms some 30 miles east of London in Westcliff-on-Sea. This arrangement, which reduced the risk of Zeppelin and Gotha air raids, worked well for a time, but the long journey to and from work and renewed public safety brought about by the end of the war, rekindled the lure of the city. By September 1919 the Thompsons had moved back to Ilford and the spacious home of Percy's sister and brother-in-law, Lilian and Kenneth Chambers.

They were paying guests but their salaries – particularly Edith's – allowed them to continue saving hard for their own home. In July 1920, that dream was finally achieved without the need for a mortgage. They paid £250 to become proud owners of 41 Kensington Gardens, which they duly named The Retreat after their old address in Westcliff. True, it had sitting tenants in the shape of Mrs Fanny Lester and her sick husband. And, yes, the Lesters paid a ridiculously low rent. But they could be eased out. In fact, Percy began eviction proceedings almost immediately, prompting Mrs Lester to wage a one-woman public-relations campaign to prove how useful she was: cleaning, shopping, doing the laundry – even cooking everyone's porridge in the morning. The Lesters managed to hang on for a further two years thanks to some nifty legal work by their solicitor.

*

Freddy Bywaters had left school in the spring of 1916 aged 13, just as the Thompsons began married life. He found employment as an office runner with shipping agents Charles Howard in Leadenhall Street before moving on to one of its competitors, Van Hopplers. But, despite his age, he felt a growing need to serve his country and, on 13 June 1917, a massive raid on the City by Gotha heavy bombers of the Imperial German Flying Corps only hardened his conviction. Leadenhall Street took a direct hit, killing the friend he'd met a few minutes earlier. Freddy was knocked off his feet, yet rather than seeking shelter he ran to find his sister Nellie at her workplace in nearby Aldersgate. He then escorted her home to their parents.

In the autumn of 1917, Freddy tried to join the merchant navy, only to find his mother had refused parental consent – probably because her husband was already serving king and country and she considered that sufficient for one family. This merely served to delay matters, however; the following February Freddy was hired by P&O as a deskman and four days later signed up as a ship's writer – essentially an administrator – aboard the company's troop carrier *Nellore*, bound for India. He saw out the final months of the war at sea and, while docked in China, learnt of his father's death from the lingering effects of a gas attack in France. It was a pivotal moment in his life. With the breadwinner lost, the family had to sell their Rectory Road home and use the proceeds to set Mrs Bywaters up as a costumier in the cheaper district of Upper Norwood. This was south of the Thames and far from his old Ilford haunts. It was also a time-consuming journey to the docks on the occasions he had shore leave.

It was on one such occasion, in January 1920, that a 17-year-old Freddy Bywaters decided to look up his old school friend Billie Graydon. Perhaps he'd heard on the docklands grapevine that Billie was on leave from the White Star Line, and here was an opportunity to catch up. Or perhaps he was simply looking for a more convenient address at which to lodge whenever his ship was in port. Whatever his motive, he paid three more visits to the Graydons in Shakespeare Crescent that January and proved a popular guest –

not least in the eyes of Edith's sister Avis. She may have been seven years older but the loss of so many young men during the war had made suitors hard to find. Freddy was charming, good looking and had already seen something of the world. He noted the signals from the sociable Miss Graydon and was happy to reciprocate.

Four months later, his latest ship, the *Plassy*, was in port for an eight-week refit and Freddy once again caught the train for Ilford. This time he got straight to the point. Could he be a paying guest for a couple of months? The Graydons were happy to oblige this young man whose company they had so enjoyed. By mid-May he'd moved in with his few belongings. And, almost certainly, it was on Friday 24 May that he became reacquainted with a face from his past – a figure he'd occasionally dared to admire. Edith Thompson always called on her parents every other Friday evening.

Tellingly, for the seven weeks Freddy stayed at Shakespeare Crescent, Edith visited *every* Friday. Percy would also be there, and there's no suggestion that Edith openly flirted with her parents' lodger. Both she and her husband appeared to simply enjoy his company. In any case, by early July he was off again, joining a new ship at Southampton, the *Cap Polonia*, for a voyage to Bombay. He would not return until the autumn of 1920 – a particularly interesting period in the friendship between Edith and Freddy.

When, in 1986, the official police homicide file on 'Thompson & Bywaters' was released by the Public Record Office at Kew, several telegrams emerged for the first time. While brief, Edith's messages in two of these offer a tantalising glimpse into a growing familiarity. The first, dated Wednesday 22 September 1920, was addressed to 'Bywaters. Stewards Dept. SS *Malwa*, Tilbury Dk' (Freddy had been assigned to this ship, and, while officially a writer, was also expected to assist with stewarding duties). The cable read simply: *Chief away today cannot come.* This suggests Edith had agreed to meet Freddy, perhaps for lunch, but that the absence of her superior at work meant she was too busy. The fact that she was arranging to see him away from her family is itself telling, given that he'd landed in her social circle just four months earlier. Had Freddy initially courted Avis Graydon but realised his stronger affections were for Edith?

The second telegram, dated Wednesday 13 April 1921 was addressed to F. Bywaters at Freddy's family home, 11 Westow Street, Upper Norwood. It was again only five words but the message conveys both concern and flirtatiousness. *Keep contents of mackintosh safe* it read. Safe from, or for, whom? The attentions of another woman perhaps? Edith signed it with Freddy's pet name for her – PEIDI – which would be meaningless to his family. She sent it to Westow Street realising that it would be forwarded to his ship, now the *Orvieto* bound for Fremantle in Western Australia, and that he would receive it on docking there. We know that Edith at some point learned of his previous dalliance with an unidentified Australian woman, and it seems that during the *Orvieto*'s voyage around the southern Australian coast he renewed this acquaintance.

Of course, the telegram to Freddy could be read as a straight-forward, friendly wish for safe passage on the high seas. But within a few weeks, as the murder trial would discover, Edith would be kissing him passionately and, later, writing a stream of love letters with unmistakeable references to sex. While Freddy was away on one of his P&O ships she would assuage her lovesickness by throwing herself into the West End theatre life, watching plays such as Clemence Dane's *Bill of Divorcement*, Robert Hichens's *The Garden of Allah* and E. Temple Thurston's *The Wandering Jew*. Here were works that explored adultery, sexual obsession, self-sacrifice and the dilemma of choosing love over duty – all themes that fascinated Edith Thompson more than ever. But she also embraced lighter theatrical melodrama, espoused in vaudeville and music hall, and had a voracious appetite for the fantasy worlds of romantic literature, plots in which beautiful women and handsome lovers indulged in secret trysts amidst a glamorous and wealthy lifestyle.

On Saturday 4 June 1921 the *Orvieto* docked at Tilbury and Freddy Bywaters headed straight for the Graydons' home in Shakespeare Crescent. By chance – or perhaps not – Edith and Percy Thompson were visiting, and the conversation turned to holidays after Freddy casually mentioned he could do with one. The Thompsons had already planned a break with another couple on the Isle of Wight and were taking Avis with them. Why didn't Freddy come along, suggested Percy, clearly believing that the youthful sailor and Avis were contemplating romance.

The holiday plans were agreed and on Saturday 11 June the six Londoners took a Victoria train to Shanklin. While awaiting a connection at Portsmouth they wandered down to Southsea waterfront, where Avis took a photo of the Thompsons and Freddy lying on the pebbles. In it, Edith leans towards her husband but she has her right hand resting on Freddy's hair. Freddy meanwhile is curled towards her, eyes closed, his face resting against her thigh. It almost beggars belief that neither Percy nor Avis detected anything of concern in a pose redolent with eroticism.

The Shanklin holiday was a great success. The visitors attended productions at the Playhouse, danced to bands in Rylstone Gardens and on the lawn of the Marine Hotel, and joined revellers at nightly concert parties in the Town Hall. Then there was swimming on the beach below the hotel – Percy excused himself on account of his 'weak' heart – and the occasional men-only pub crawl. Percy often returned the worse for wear from these drinking sessions, a source of intense embarrassment to Edith and Avis.

On the evening of Tuesday 14 June, Edith and Freddy found themselves alone. They kissed and he clutched her arms and wrists so tightly they were bruised. For her part, she ran her fingers through his hair. By the end of the week they had declared their love for each other – the start of an affair that she would document so passionately in a blizzard of letters to Freddy during his voyages away, letters he kept locked safely in his cabin. These would later form the main plank of the prosecution's case against them both. His replies never surfaced. Edith would claim she destroyed them for fear of discovery.

*

A lingering holiday kiss was one thing. But how to pursue a long-term *physical* affair? That was self-evidently impossible while Freddy was away at sea, and finding the time and privacy during his shore leave would inevitably be risky. There was an obvious solution and Edith seized on it. How would it be, she suggested to Percy, if after the holiday Freddy stayed with them? He was such a pal (that ubiquitous term beloved by the twenties flapper set) to everyone, especially Avis of course, and some extra money would be handy. Percy acquiesced. Freddy would stay for a week in their small spare bedroom as a trial period to ensure he got along with them and the Lesters. If all went well, he could stay on terms of 25 shillings a week, a modest commercial rent but hardly comparable to the Lesters' 30 shillings a *month*. Within 48 hours of the return from Shanklin there was a new lodger at 41 Kensington Gardens.

For the next three months, Freddy passed up any opportunities to go to sea. It meant he could meet Edith during lunch breaks and enjoy her company, albeit in Percy's presence, during the evenings. However, early in this new arrangement they had an argument, sparked when he spotted her chatting happily to an old male friend. For a couple of days they remained apart – he stayed with his mother in Upper Norwood – but on Friday 24 June they met for lunch at the Holborn Hotel and in a heart-to-heart exchange Edith laid bare her innermost anxieties, chief among which was her sense of being trapped in a futile marriage. Freddy was flattered that this attractive older woman saw him as her saviour. He promised to return to Kensington Gardens that very night. He also pledged to meet Avis off her train back from the Isle of Wight (she had stayed on an extra week) to explain that for the time being she and he could not be an item.

His secretive courting of Edith blossomed into a full-blown affair. On Monday 27 June, with the Lesters away on holiday, she took advantage of the day off she had booked, unbeknown to Percy, and arrived in Freddy's room with his breakfast. It was his birthday and she planned to offer herself as his present. Yet she still wanted to be courted and her lover's eagerness for sex resulted in her bursting into tears. She spoke of her unhappiness and her preference for suicide rather than life with her husband. But eventually she calmed down, promising she would not contemplate suicide for five years, and they made love. Over the next few weeks, the marriage of Edith and Percy Thompson would quickly fracture into recriminations and outright domestic abuse.

Things came to a head on the evening of 30 July, with the Lesters still on holiday. It seems unlikely that Percy yet suspected he was being cuckolded by Freddy, nor that he knew his wife and their lodger had spent the day together at Kew Gardens. But he must have noticed that Edith had recently become detached, even distant, from him and that she was defensive about criticism aimed at young Freddy. A row erupted between the Thompsons that simmered throughout the Bank Holiday weekend. An outburst of violence was then triggered by the non-appearance of Avis for tea on Monday 31 August.

Uncharacteristically, Percy seized on this as a way to taunt Edith about her family and specifically Avis; Edith responded by screaming at him. She remained exceptionally close to all her family, especially her sister. Although for obvious reasons court records cannot provide Percy's recollection of the moment, Edith's account was that her husband hit her several times before hurling her across the room. She crashed into a chair and fell on a desk, whereupon Freddy, who had diplomatically distanced himself from the marital strife, barrelled into the room to stand between them. He warned Percy to leave Edith alone and stop beating her – unless he wanted to fight with Freddy himself. Humiliated, Percy ordered him to leave the house, which he eventually did after talking to Edith.

That evening, according to police and court records, the three of them met, possibly in a local pub, for crisis talks. She claimed Percy told her: 'We will come to an agreement and have a separation.' She replied: 'You always tell me that when I mention the subject and later, when it actually comes, you refuse to grant it me.' In another exchange she said: 'Yes, I should like that but you make a statement and then whine back to me and retract that statement. You have done that before.' By the end of this bizarre confrontation it was clear to Freddy that his continued presence at 41 Kensington Gardens had become untenable. On Friday 5 August he packed his bags and returned to his mother's home in Upper Norwood.

Yet becoming an ex-lodger did not equate to being an ex-lover. Over the next two weeks, he and Edith met every day for lunch and on Friday evenings (when they knew Percy would be having his usual after-work drink in the City). At one of these trysts Edith handed back a cache of letters that the 'Australian Girl' had sent to Freddy and that she'd demanded to see as evidence of his commitment. She later described them to police as 'personal' rather than love letters and insisted she'd returned them because she had nowhere to keep them safe, other than her cash box at Carlton & Prior.

On the evening of Friday 19 August the game was finally up. It is unclear how Percy knew Edith had been meeting Freddy, and he may still not have suspected outright adultery. But he was sufficiently convinced of a romantic attachment to confront her. She denied it, but the following day posted Freddy a warning letter that read: 'Come & see me Monday lunchtime, please darlint. He suspects. PEIDI.' Darlint is an abbreviation of darlingest, Edith's favourite form of address to her lover.

Freddy obliged and reassured her that they would take greater care in future. But it seems likely he'd already decided a spell at sea was needed. He had no desire to stay with his family and besides that, where else could he go? For the next three weeks he and Edith met only intermittently and communicated by way of telegram: 'Peidi sends herself to other half no chance to write,' she cabled on Monday 5 September and then, two days later, simply: 'Yes, I do know. PEIDI.' The latter is possibly a reference to Freddy obtaining a writer's berth aboard the P&O passenger liner *Morea*, due to slip her moorings at Tilbury that coming Friday.

For the next year, the name *Morea* would occupy Edith's every waking moment. Her letters to Freddy would be cherished and saved by him to read on lonely nights at sea. His decision to keep them would see the lovers to the gallows. The letters would later be seized by police, allowing the prosecution to interpret and reinterpret the 'true' meaning of Edith's words.

Seventy of her letters survived; indeed the only ones unaccounted for were sent during Freddy's first voyage on the *Morea*.

Their existence is known only through a later letter, written towards the end of 1921. In this, a depressed-sounding Edith wrote:

> *I seem to be able to talk to you always & forever, but you, I don't know, you don't seem the same as when you were away before* [i.e. on that first *Morea* voyage between 9 September and 29 October 1921], *you did talk to me a lot that trip, but this time you don't seem to at all.*

Conflating the words 'talk' and 'write' was a signature aspect of Edith's letters, and she never held back in 'talking' about every aspect of her life – her thoughts, views and fantasies – in forensic detail. She included criticisms of books she'd read and plays she'd seen, as well as descriptions of summer fetes, gossip at Carlton & Prior and general family chat. She sought to create intimacy with her distant lover by recording her periods and apparent miscarriages and stating her disgust at the thought of sex with her husband. A repeated theme was her undying love for Freddy; she once recounted a dream about them having sex in bed together only for him to be chased downstairs by Percy.

These letters would usually be waiting for Freddy in whatever corner of the world his ship docked. Edith had become something of an authority on P&O's published shipping routes, and like some heroine from one of her romantic fiction stories, perhaps saw herself as the lovesick lynchpin of their relationship.

The return of the *Morea* to Tilbury on Saturday 29 October heralded 12 days of secretive meetings, clandestine messages and the painful masquerade of pretending to be friends, rather than lovers.

Edith knew Freddy would call at her family's home in Shakespeare Crescent on that first Saturday and contrived an excuse – she had to discuss curtains with her mother – to avoid difficult questions from Percy. Her family knew nothing of the affair, and so she and Freddy were restricted to politely shaking hands.

The following Monday she arrived at Carlton & Prior to find a parcel waiting; inside were Oriental silks, beads and a letter from Freddy recalling how difficult the Saturday evening had been. 'What I am saying,' he wrote '[is] don't let this make you too miserable chére.' Edith hurriedly dashed off a reply and got her assistant Rose Jacob to give it to a gentleman of a certain description waiting either outside Aldersgate tube or Fullers tea room.

The trysts continued but on Thursday 3 November, after the lovers had skipped work (there are no court records revealing where they went), Edith returned home straight into another row. Percy claimed he'd seen her with her 'sailor boy' at the station and sneered, 'He is no man or else he would ask my permission to take you out.' The following day Edith relayed these words to Freddy at a 5.15pm liaison at Fenchurch Street and he immediately vowed to confront Percy.

The following afternoon, Guy Fawkes Night, there were certainly fireworks at 41 Kensington Gardens as Freddy informed Percy that he *was* a man, he did *not* need permission to see a lady, Percy was making Edith's life hell and he should either seek a divorce or separate. Freddy eventually wrung a promise from Percy not to beat his wife again, although his rival's taunt – 'I have got her and will keep her' – must have cut deep.

Why would Percy not grant Edith a divorce so she could be with her lover? At the time divorce was rare and belief in the sanctity of marriage immense. Divorces were also costly and there was a significant amount of shame attached to them. From her correspondence it seems Edith herself had no appetite for being a divorced woman as the stigma was too great.

Freddy and Edith now had precious little time before the *Morea* sailed for Bombay on 10 November. He would not be back until 7 January 1922. According to police and court documents, the lovers met at some point that day and renewed a suicide pledge they'd already made to each other – namely that if they were not man and wife, or at least free to be together, within five years of that first kiss on the Isle of Wight then they would kill themselves.

Edith's letters to Freddy during this Bombay trip vacillate between self-doubt over her appearance, declarations of love, recollections of their sex sessions, castigation about his attitude to women and failure to 'talk' enough, and the revulsion of sharing a marital bed with Percy. One letter, sent to Port Said and dated December, recounted a row over his demands for conjugal 'rights'.

> *We had – was it a row – anyway a very heated argument again last night (Sunday). It started through the usual source, I resisted and he wanted to know why since you went in August I was different – 'had I transferred my affections from him to you'. Darlint it's a great temptation to say 'Yes' but I did not. He said we were cunning, the pair of us and lots of other things that I forget, also that I told lies about*

not knowing you were coming on that Sat. He said 'Has he written
to you since he has been away,' and when I said 'No' he said 'That's
another lie'.

According to Edith, her husband's sexual advances were
repelled until 2 January 1922, when, she later told Freddy, she'd
'surrendered unconditionally to him' in the hope that it would
defuse suspicion ahead of the *Morea*'s return to Tilbury. But there
was another reason. She suspected sex with Freddy two months
earlier had left her pregnant.

At their reunion on Monday 9 January she excitedly accepted
his presents of chocolates and violets – she would place the flowers
on her desk next to a figure of Kikazaru (the hear-no-evil monkey),
an earlier and much-cherished present. Once initial hugs and kisses
were over, however, she quickly moved on to pregnancy worries
and her attempt to trigger a miscarriage using a backstreet abortion
device. That she would even contemplate an abortion would once
again cast her as a moral reprobate in the eyes of the nation during
the trial. In fact, Edith appears to have miscarried at home on the
evening of Friday 20 January, the day after Freddy again headed off
to sea. In a later missive she wrote: '… something awful happened,
darlint I don't know for certain what it was but I can guess, can you,
write and tell me.'

The letters from Edith to Freddy during this voyage (from which
he returned on Friday 17 March) and his next (Friday 31 March –
Friday 26 May) would prove extremely useful to the prosecution
at the trial. As we know, only Edith's letters survived because she

destroyed his. But Edith's alone contained sufficient references to methods for ending Percy Thompson's life to offer a veritable goldmine of suggestive evidence. Eagerly taken at face value by the police and Crown barristers, the mention of poison and broken glass smuggled into food pointed to a conspiracy to murder or, at least, to hasten the end of Percy's life. Yet knowing everything we know of Edith's character, this assessment seems fundamentally flawed. Far more likely she was immersed in a fantasy – a fantasy that drew on the plots of her favourite plays and novels, that showed her far-distant lover how much she wanted him, that countered any doubts he might harbour and that was a cathartic release from her miserable marriage.

Throughout the spring of 1922 Edith pursued her thoughts with rigour. She wrote of a bad cold her husband had contracted and how a sleeping draught supplied by a friend had made him sick. What could be more natural, she asked Freddy, than death from an overdose of a drug he was known to use? She tells how she had tried to appear worried and frightened in front of her sister Avis, feigning fears that Percy might die: 'As I thought perhaps it might be useful at some future time that I had told somebody.' In the same letter she asked: 'How about cigarettes' (she believed smoking heavily was how Percy escaped military service) and then mentioned hyoscine poisoning, mooted in the suspicious death of a local vicar, Reverend Horace Bolding.

A later note acknowledged a promise from Freddy that he had 'secured what is needed' to solve their problems (this turned out to be quinine, the main ingredient of tonic water, usually only fatal in huge doses), while in a letter dated Monday 20 February Edith appeared firmly committed to a plot. She wrote:

> *Darlingest boy, this thing that I am going to do for both of us will it ever – at all, make any difference between us, darlint, do you understand what I mean. Will you ever think any less of me – not now, I know darlint – but later on – perhaps some years hence – do you think you will feel any different – because of this thing that I shall do.*

Three weeks later, inside a 2,300-word letter written between 10 and 13 March, she enclosed a cutting from the *Daily Sketch* reporting the death of a dancer, Freda Kempton, found dead in her Paddington flat. Headlined 'Dancing Girl's Mystery Death. Story of Dope, Drugged Drink, Night Club & Chinese Café', the story goes on to suggest that a poisonous cocktail of cocaine and cyanide could have been administered. The 'Kempton cutting may be interesting if it's to be the same method,' explained Edith.

Between 17 and 30 March, when Freddy's ship was back at Tilbury, they arranged regular lunch- and tea-time meetings, and he gave her the quinine. It seemed their conversations were occasionally strained; during one she demanded he hand over his letters from the 'Australia Girl' as a kind of love test and he felt hurt that she doubted him. Nonetheless, they had sex, probably at her friend Bessie's house, on his last night of shore leave. The following day he departed for a two-month voyage.

It was on this trip that Freddy received a letter containing a separate note on which Edith wrote: 'Don't keep this piece.' The note contained what the prosecution would allege was a 'passage full of crime' – how she tried to poison Percy's tea with quinine, how he told his mother the tea seemed bitter 'as if something had been put into it', how he boasted to his friends that he had 'fought and fought with himself to keep consciousness' and that he would 'never die, except naturally – I'm like a cat with nine lives'. Edith went on: 'I'm going to try the glass again occasionally – when it's safe. I've got an electric light globe this time.' This sounds ominous until you consider a later letter in which she claimed: 'I used the "light bulb" three times but the third time – he found a piece – so I've given it up – until you come home.' It seems far-fetched. The idea that Percy, following his bitter-tea comments, didn't mention the glass to family and friends, not even to Mrs Lester, who often did the household cooking, lacks all credibility. In evidence, Edith would claim her accounts of quinine and glass poisoning were made up. She thought it was what Freddy wanted to hear.

Further musings from Edith to her lover reflected her fears, and irritation, that he nursed doubts about their future. She quoted back one of his phrases '... the last time we met we were pals, weren't we Chere?' Why had he needed to question this? When he wrote of feeling despondent at her lack of results from the quinine powder and glass fragments, she replied that the failure put her to shame – further reassurance that she was desperate for them to be permanently united.

On 8 May she wrote to him mentioning digitalin, a drug derived from foxgloves, which she'd read about in the plot of Robert

Hichens's novel *Bella Donna*. 'Is this any use?' she asked. It certainly would be ... to Crown prosecutors.

*

On Friday 26 May the *Morea* again returned to Tilbury, heralding another round of secretive meetings and missives between the lovers. These culminated in a dinner together on the evening of Thursday 8 June, during which Edith told Freddy she was pregnant by him once more and, again, wanted a termination. The crux of this conversation was contained in a note she passed to him, and, whether or not her claim was true, it was an emotional personal drama to throw into the mix on his last night ashore. The following day he would leave for Australia, his longest voyage since the start of the affair. Did Edith want to use the 'pregnancy' as a means of locking him in? Was she concerned about the Australian girl? After all, she remembered him saying that he still 'had something in connection with Australia'.

Whatever the truth about the pregnancy, Edith had now embraced melodramatic fantasy ahead of a summer fraught with domestic rows and loneliness. The evidence for this is clear: in a letter written a few days later, dated 12 and 13 June, she told Freddy her husband had discovered they were meeting. In a fit of pique, he had confronted her father and the rest of the family in Shakespeare Crescent, and Mr Graydon was furious. He had vowed to talk to Edith about her responsibilities as a married woman. She knew it was true because Avis said so, although, Edith concluded, her father didn't mention it when next she saw him.

It wasn't hard for Freddy to see through this. Unusually, he'd received a letter from Edith's father, dated 13 June, in which Mr Graydon asked him to meet his youngest son Harold. Harold had found work at a café in St Kilda, Melbourne, and Freddy had taken a bag of home comforts aboard the *Morea* to hand over when the ship docked in Melbourne. The letter ends with warm wishes and the line: 'Well, I don't think I've much more news to tell you.' This was hardly the sign-off of a man livid at his daughter and her secret lover. In court the whole story would be dismissed by Avis as total fabrication: Percy had not confronted the family and so her father had never been furious with Freddy. Here was proof, the defence would pointedly argue, that nothing in Edith's letters could be taken as fact. It was just another of her fantasies.

On 20 June Edith left work to collect Freddy's latest letter, posted from the *Morea*'s brief berth in Marseilles, from a nearby post office. But she was disappointed. For the second time he'd put off writing one of the detailed letters she so cherished and merely promised to send one later from Port Said. He told her 'not to be disappointed' and to 'try to be brave', but in her response Edith accused him of having neither 'time nor inclination to remember England or anything England holds'. We know from later letters that Freddy was starting to question his affections for her, believing that a future together would be impossible. He'd certainly met Avis before leaving London. However, this postal tiff was de-dramatised in a letter from Edith two days later in which she apologised for her outburst.

On 15 July, the Thompsons and Avis headed off to Bournemouth for a fortnight's holiday. Knowing she would not be able to 'talk' to Freddy during this time, Edith launched into a long letter shortly before leaving, mostly a critique of Robert Hichens's novel *Bella Donna* and, to a lesser extent, another of his books, *The Fruitful Vine*. Part of her letter would be trotted out in court by the prosecution – if nothing else to show jury members Edith's continued interest in poison and murder plots. Notwithstanding the obvious point – the absurdity of using an accused's interest in dastardly fictional deeds as evidence against them – Edith's main interest in *Bella Donna* appears to lie in its eroticism. The story involves an older woman attempting to poison her younger husband with lead in order to pursue a smouldering affair with an Egyptian slave-master.

In her first letter to him after the Bournemouth holiday, dated Friday 4 August, Edith mentioned their earlier suicide pact – another melodramatic fantasy – writing that: 'Perhaps this coming year will bring us the happiness we both desire more than anything in this world – and if it doesn't? We'll leave this world that we love so much – cling to so desperately.' She also responded to a previous signal from him that he wanted time and space on his return from Australia: 'You say you won't see me – but I shall hope & hope & hope.' The following Tuesday, she finally received a letter, only to realise it had been written more than a month previously and was largely comprised of a discussion of *The Fruitful Vine*.

On Thursday 7 September, with the *Morea* only 16 days from Tilbury, Edith received an anonymous warning note at work.

It was addressed to a Miss P. Graydon and had been posted the previous day in the West End. 'If you wish to remain the friend of F. Bywaters,' it read, 'be careful. Do not attempt to see him or communicate with him, when he is in England. Believe this to be a genuine warning from A Wellwisher.' Edith feared this had been dictated by Freddy, since only he and she used the nickname Peidi, and had been sent via his mother to post in London as a clumsy attempt to disguise its origin.

She forwarded it with her next letter, dated 8 September, questioning whether he knew anything about it – 'I don't suppose you do darlint but I'm just asking. I'm sure if you had reasons for not wanting to see me – you'd tell me and tell me the reasons – you couldn't resort to letters of this description.' In fact, the note had been sent without Freddy's knowledge by his mother. Mrs Bywaters had long known of his affection for Edith and loathed her.

A few days later, Edith wrote again. With only eleven days to go before the *Morea*'s arrival, doubts about Freddy's commitment had clearly surfaced. She'd heard nothing from him since 28 July and now vowed to abide by whatever he decided for their future. She was already starting to become the 'dutiful wife' whose spirit was finally 'bent to the will of her husband'. Perhaps she knew such a statement would make him jealous. However, it is not clear whether he got this letter before writing one that she received on 20 September, in which he asked if they might be 'Pals only, Peidi, it will make it easier', while also admitting how jealous he was of Percy.

Edith's response came in a long letter written the following day, which would prove a hammer blow to her courtroom defence: 'Yes darlint you are jealous of him – but I want you to be – he has the right by law to all that you have the right to by nature and love – yes darlint be jealous, so much that you will do something desperate.' It would prove easy for skilled counsel to portray this as incitement to murder. Yet 'desperate', in this context, could just as easily mean fleeing abroad to start a new life. And on the very eve of the murder, Edith begged Freddy to help her do exactly that.

The *Morea* arrived in port late on Saturday 23 September, and so it was not until 5.30pm the following Monday that Freddy Bywaters met Edith Thompson outside Carlton & Prior and walked with her along Aldersgate towards the Royal Exchange and on to Fenchurch Street station. There had been no mad hugs and kisses – they were adhering to his 'pals only' plea – but when they found an unoccupied carriage on the Ilford train they shared a passionate kiss.

On parting at Ilford, Edith slipped him the 'do something desperate' letter written two days earlier. She then returned to Percy at 41 Kensington Gardens; he went to 231 Shakespeare Crescent with a message from Harold to the Graydon family. But later that night, back at his mother's home in Upper Norwood, Freddy wrote his most passionate declaration of love yet to Edith:

> *Darlint I felt quite confident that I would be able to keep my feel-ings down – I was wrong Peidi. I was reckoning on will power over ordinary forces – but I was fighting what? Not ordinary forces – noth-ing was fighting the whole of me. Peidi you are my magnet – I cannot*

resist darlint – you draw me to you now and always, I shall never be able to see you and remain impassive.

His mental state could not be clearer. He needed no encouragement from Edith to do something desperate.

Over the next week, the lovers resumed their London trysts. There were the usual snatched lunch and tea meetings, including tea at one of their favourite haunts, Fullers, opposite Carlton & Prior, on Friday 29 September. The following morning there was a daring open-air sex session in Wanstead Park, which Freddy mentioned in a letter later that same day, calling Edith his 'little devil'. He hand-delivered this letter during their late lunch together at Queen Anne's restaurant the following Monday, and she hurriedly read it on returning to work.

By the time she met him again, in Fullers tea room a few hours later, Edith had produced a reply in the form of an addition to a letter she'd already begun. It was her last known letter to Freddy before the murder and it would provide further ammunition for a prosecution intent on proving her active involvement in the crime. In fact, both in context and in key passages, it would be misunderstood – some might argue *deliberately* misunderstood – by the Crown.

The letter starts with Edith's familiar theme of joy at being with Freddy and the knowledge that he is her lover even when they are apart:

Darlint, we've said we'll always be pals haven't we, shall we say we'll always be lovers – even tho' secret ones, or is it (this great big love) a thing we can't control – dare we say that – I think I will dare. Yes I will 'I'll always love you' – if you are dead – if you have left me even if you don't still love me, I always shall you.

Further on she pleads with him to help her escape abroad:

Darlint its funds that are our stumbling block – until we have those we can do nothing. Darlingest find me a job abroad. I'll go tomorrow and not say I was going to a soul and not have one little regret. I said I wouldn't think – that I'd try to forget – circumstances – Pal, help me to forget again – I have succeeded up to now – but it's thinking of tonight and tomorrow when I can't see you and feel you holding me. Darlint – do something tomorrow night will you? Something to make you forget. I'll be hurt I know, but I want you to hurt me – I do really – the bargain now, seems so one sided – so unfair – but how can I alter it.

These are hardly the clear instructions of a woman orchestrating a murder – a murder now only hours away. However, the letter included two further lines that would be specifically cited as evidence of guilt. The first read: 'He's still well – he's going to gaze all day long at you in your temporary home – after Wednesday.' The Crown tried to portray this as a nod to Percy still being 'well' despite Edith's attempts to poison him. In fact, she would explain, 'he' was the much-loved hear-no-evil monkey that she kept on her desk at work. As for the 'temporary home' – this was an artist's drawing of the *Morea* that she planned to collect from a framing shop later that week and place alongside the monkey.

The second 'incriminating' line came at the very end: 'Don't forget what we talked about in the tea room, I'll still risk and try if you will – we only have 3 ¼ years left darlingest [a reference to their five-year suicide-pact countdown]. Try & help.' This, the prosecution would argue, was Edith urging Freddy to take the 'risk' of attempting Percy's murder. Wasn't the tea room Fullers, where the lovers had met after work on 2 October, the eve of the murder? Wasn't Edith making a final attempt to stiffen her lover's spine? Of course she was. It all fitted.

Except it didn't. The letter had been started *before* that late-afternoon meeting at Fullers and was completed even before it took place. The words 'Don't forget what we talked about in the tea room' referred to their meeting at Fullers the *previous* Friday, 29 September. Indeed, earlier in this same letter Edith had thanked Freddy 'for Friday – it was lovely'. She would explain that the 'risk' referred to running away with Freddy and perhaps finding a job abroad. That is what they'd discussed at Fullers on Friday 29 September. She was simply reminding him of it. Indeed, an undated note from her to Freddy, probably written the previous week, states that 'Perhaps I shall get my appointment in Bombay this time – I hope so I failed before.' It is not clear what she meant but it would seem to be a job application, either real or imagined.

*

We can be reasonably certain about the movements of the key players on 3 October 1922, because these were reconstructed in police interviews with help from witnesses. Yet, curiously, not *all* witnesses. Edith phoned Freddy at his mother's home on her arrival at Carlton & Prior shortly before 9am and confirmed a lunch date at Queen Anne's restaurant. She explained why she couldn't get out of that evening's theatre visit with Percy – they were attending the Criterion with her aunt and uncle, Lily and Jack Liles-Laxton, to watch the farce *The Dippers*. The lovers agreed to meet again outside Fullers after work, but it could only be fleeting. They would have to have lunch the following day, his last before leaving again on the *Morea*.

At 5.45pm Edith met Percy and they headed for Piccadilly to meet up with the Liles-Laxtons outside the Criterion's pit entrance. Jack and Lily would later describe them as 'happy and in their usual spirits'. The foursome queued for a while before being joined at some point by Edith's old friends Bessie and Reg Aitken. Police records made no mention of the Aitkens attending the play, and the couple's presence that night did not emerge during the trial. The only evidence that they *were* there comes from a later report in *Lloyd's Sunday News* that was by-lined 'A Lifelong Friend'. This friend could only have been Bessie. Her somewhat gushing account was presumably ghost-written by a journalist.

Incidents of that last West End party come back. I see Edith Thompson as she sat in that restaurant, the centre of the party, its wit and its mainspring. Her eyes sparkle as she breathes in the atmosphere of pleasure and gaiety. I see her again as she stood outside the foyer of the theatre. I recall an episode that makes incomprehensible to me the murder which was to take place a few hours later. Another friend who was of our party said to Percy Thompson: 'Why haven't you a coat? You will catch your death of cold.' I forget what Thompson answered but I remember well the laughing remark of his wife: 'Oh, he's too mean to buy himself an overcoat! I have promised to buy him a dress overcoat but I won't until he gets a grey one I have asked him to buy.' A strange jest from a woman with murder in her heart.

It was certainly strange that Bessie was not considered an important enough trial witness, given that she was with Edith barely two hours before Percy's demise.

As the Thompsons were en route to the theatre, Freddy Bywaters was taking the District Line to East Ham and a dinner invitation at the Graydons' in Shakespeare Crescent. According to Freddy's testimony, Mrs Graydon hinted during the evening that she knew of Edith's affections for him, although she didn't directly name her daughter. Before leaving, Freddy told Avis he would take her to the cinema the following evening. This was surely aimed at providing a semblance of normality once the deed was done, because Freddy was already carrying the murder weapon – a double-edged five-and-a-half-inch dagger held in a leather sheath. According to his own testimony he told himself: 'I don't want to go home; I feel too miserable. I want to see Mrs Thompson; I want to see if I can help her.'

He left the Graydons around 11pm and was on a train from East Ham to Ilford by 11.15pm. His movements at Ilford station are unclear – his police statement says simply that he 'waited for Mrs Thompson and her husband', while in court he told the jury, 'When I got into Belgrave Road I walked for some time and some distance ahead I saw Mr and Mrs Thompson.' Most likely he waited at the station exit until they came out and then took a different route to theirs – probably via Beal Road and Mansfield Road – to intercept them in Endsleigh Gardens. And so we return to the moment Dr Maudsley phoned Ilford police to report the death of a man in the street. The time was 12.40am on 4 October 1922.

*

The doctor's call was taken by the senior night-desk officer, Sergeant Grimes, who immediately ordered PCs George Pearcey and Cyril Geal to join police ambulance driver PC Henry Palmer and head for the scene. They arrived to find a patrolling colleague, Sergeant Walter Mew, who promptly ordered Geal and Palmer to take the body to the mortuary while he and Pearcey accompanied Edith home. Mew recalled her saying, 'They will blame me for this,' although at this point everyone appeared to believe Percy had suffered a heart attack (in the dark, Dr Maudsley had not spotted any stab wounds, and Edith had not said anything). At around 1.45am, Sgt Mew called on Percy's brother Richard in nearby Seymour Gardens to break the bad news. Richard hurried round to Edith, whom he could see was 'overcome'. In his police statement, he recalled Edith telling him how Percy had suffered a seizure. He'd complained of a pain in his leg, then fell against her. She'd screamed for help but Percy was dead by the time a doctor arrived.

Edith was understandably in shock, though not so much that she was incapable of covering for her lover. But her words hardly mattered. At the mortuary, Geal and Palmer had undressed the body and seen the multiple gashes. This was no heart attack, they informed Sgt Grimes, back at the station. Moments later he called the duty inspector in K Division, Metropolitan Police, to report a suspected murder. Sgt Mew, meanwhile, had arrived at the mortuary and seen Percy's wounds for himself.

At 3am, Mew returned to Edith in Kensington Gardens to ask if she could account for them. He noted her response as: 'No, we were walking along and my husband said "Oh" and I said "bear up" thinking he had one of his attacks; he then fell on me and walked a little further; he then fell against the wall and then to the ground ... I did not see a knife or anything.' Edith had now blatantly lied to a police officer. The investigation was about to ratchet up. Events moved quickly.

At noon, Edith and her mother were taken to Ilford police station to assist with inquiries. It appears that at this point she had already dropped hints about Freddy's role to Mrs Graydon and Avis because, that same morning, Avis called at Carlton & Prior asking for her sister's assistant, Rose Jacobs. Avis told Rose to take a tin box from Edith's desk drawer (which she knew contained a photo of Freddy and three of his letters) and keep it safe at home. Rose complied but would later hand everything over to the police. Two of the letters from the tin would, crucially, be used by the prosecution to shore up the murder conspiracy theory.

Edith, meanwhile, was still insisting to police that she knew nothing of any street attacker. But already her position was unravelling. Percy's brother Richard had mentioned Freddy's name to the senior detective overseeing the inquiry, F. P. Wensley, claiming the young seaman was 'overly familiar' with his sister-in-law. Wensley wondered why neither Edith nor her mother had mentioned this man, despite being asked to suggest possible persons of interest. When he now put the name Bywaters to Mrs Graydon, she admitted Freddy had been at her house until 11pm on the night of the murder. Clearly he had to be considered a suspect.

Flying Squad and CID officers across London were ordered to watch Freddy's home in Upper Norwood, the Graydon's place in Shakespeare Crescent, P&O's City office and the *Morea* at Tilbury. At 6.15pm Freddy arrived at Shakespeare Crescent and learnt from Mr Graydon that Edith was still being questioned by Ilford police. Fifteen minutes later two officers were knocking on the door and he too was taken in.

After knifing Percy Thompson, Freddy had fled up The Drive, pausing only to drop his knife down a drain, and on through Leytonstone to Stratford. Here he'd hailed a cab to Aldgate, then another to Thornton Heath, arriving home in Upper Norwood at 3am. There was surely nothing to link him to the scene. Edith was the only witness, and although there were bloodstains on his coat they weren't overly noticeable. His day would continue as planned – a lunchtime shopping trip with his mother and a visit to the cinema with Avis later in the day. In a few more hours he would be on the *Morea*, bound for the Far East.

However, any hopes he may have nurtured about merely injuring Percy were dashed by the *Evening News*, which he bought at Mark Lane tube. The headline read: 'SHIPPING CLERK MURDERED: Midnight Mystery at Ilford'. The story would herald the start of a press frenzy, culminating in a scoop by *The*

Times: 'Murder in quiet Ilford residential road – Wife suspected of lying by police.'

At Ilford police station, Wensley immediately noticed spots on Freddy's coat and asked the police doctor to check whether these were dried blood. A crude test – wiping them with wet newspaper – was accepted as evidence that they were. Freddy was outraged that he could be considered a suspect but reluctantly agreed to give a statement, describing Edith and himself as 'good friends' and her home life as 'very unhappy'. He denied being at the scene of the attack – he had travelled straight to Upper Norwood after leaving the Graydons – and he certainly didn't own a knife. Yet his alibi would soon crumble. At 11pm that night, a detective saw Freddy's mother arrive home and was ordered by Wensley to get her permission for a search of his son's room. This turned up two long letters from Edith. One contained that fateful phrase: 'Yes darlint be jealous, so much that you will do something desperate.'

The following morning, police knew they were well on the way to pressing charges. Yet it would be easier if Edith and Freddy implicated each other. Divisional Inspector Francis Hall therefore sprang a calculated psychological trap – highly questionable under the Judges' Rules for holding suspects. He made sure that Edith knew for certain that her lover was in custody. Hall hoped the shock of this would prompt her to tell the truth about the attack. He was not disappointed.

As he escorted her through the station, he arranged for the library door to be opened just as they passed. Inside, Edith saw Freddy, accompanied by another officer, apparently about to leave.

The officer quickly shepherded Freddy back inside, but the staged encounter had worked. In evidence, Hall claimed Edith said: 'Oh God, oh God, what can I do? Why did he do it? I did not want him to do it.' And then, as though to herself: 'I must tell the truth.' Hall pressed his advantage home with an outright lie: 'It is no use your saying he did not do it; he has already told us he has. Go back to the CID room and think about it.'

Thirty minutes later Edith amended her statement to say that she'd seen Freddy Bywaters fleeing the scene. By 6pm Freddy was confessing to the attack.

His statement, which would be read in court, claimed he'd confronted Percy in Endsleigh Gardens and demanded a marital separation. 'We struggled. I took my knife from my pocket and we fought and he got the worst of it ... he never acted like a man to his wife. He always seemed several degrees lower than a snake. I loved her and I couldn't go on seeing her leading that life. I did not intend to kill him. I only meant to injure him ... I have had the knife for some time; it was a sheath knife. I threw it down a drain when I was running through Endsleigh Gardens.'

In fact Freddy would later freely volunteer that he'd been mistaken; he'd actually disposed of the knife in Cranbrook Road. This allowed the police to recover it and present it in evidence. The sight of its fearsome five-inch blade was not lost on the jury and effectively amounted to a free hit for the Crown.

At around 8pm on Thursday 5 October 1922, Freddy Bywaters and Edith Thompson were jointly charged with the wilful murder of Percy Thompson. The following day, the institutional mechanics of the criminal courts were cranked up: an inquest was opened; the accused appeared for an initial hearing at Stratford police court, then remanded to prison (Brixton for Freddy; Holloway for Edith); a further remand at Stratford Petty Sessions on 11 October.

At this last hearing, the lovers heard that only a few of their most recent letters had been found. However, that was about to change. The following day, Detective Inspector Alfred Scholes of the Port of London Authority boarded the *Morea* with a warrant to search Freddy's cabin. In a locked seaman's chest known as a 'ditty box' he found all of Edith's letters dating from 1921 (apart from the two already located at his mother's house). Looking through them, detectives felt they had all they needed to send their suspects to the gallows.

Over the next few days, Edith's solicitor, Mr F. A. S. Stern, was given the opportunity to read the letters. He knew he must try to present them as inadmissible evidence on grounds that there was no *prima facie* case against Edith. At the resumed inquest into Percy's death he succeeded – the coroner said their contents would be 'thrashed out' at a forthcoming Old Bailey trial, and the jury returned a verdict of 'wilful murder' against Freddy, with no reference to Edith. However, on 24 October, when Freddy and Edith were again arraigned in the dock at Stratford, prosecuting solicitor William Lewis managed to persuade the presiding magistrate, Eliot Howard, to admit them in evidence. This decision enabled a deeply flawed narrative, one that allowed the media to suggest a dominant older woman had coerced an impressionable young man.

At this resumed committal hearing, Howard was keen to paint Edith as a liar – hardly comparative to the crime of murder – telling Stern: 'She must have known perfectly well who did it, and again and again in the course of that night's detention she told different stories.' Stern replied: 'She told lies, admittedly, but that does not make her guilty.'

For the rest of that day and the next, Edith was forced to listen to her love letters – with occasional casual references to glass and supposedly poisonous substances – being made public. It was in the prosecution's interest to do so – after all, they had precious little evidence against her – but a key part of both Edith and Freddy's defence was that these passages were made up, elements of Edith's romantic fantasy world. Twice she collapsed in the dock, but Stern's plea for her to be allowed to wait outside the courtroom during the letter readings was summarily rejected. At the end, Howard adjourned proceedings for a further week and then, later, allowed two further weekly adjournments.

Finally, on 24 November, Edith and Freddy were committed for trial at the Old Bailey. The Crown was convinced it had a strong case that would be further bolstered by results from the independent post-mortem examination of Percy's body. This, surely, would prove Edith Thompson had administered glass and poison to her unsuspecting husband, just as she'd hinted in her letters.

In fact, the results proved nothing of the kind. Despite a forensic analysis of Percy's heart, stomach, intestines, kidneys and liver, there were no signs of any suspicious abnormalities. As the lead pathologist, Sir Bernard Spilsbury, noted in his report of

1 December: 'I found no indications of poisoning and no changes suggestive of previous attempts at poisoning. I detected no glass in the contents of the intestine.' At trial, this report would now have to be undermined by the Crown. The jury would need to be convinced that scientific evidence wasn't all it was cracked up to be.

In the run-up to Wednesday 6 December, the opening day of the trial, Edith held a series of meetings with her leading defence counsel, the formidable and newly knighted Sir Henry Curtis-Bennett. She was convinced she would be exonerated; justice would protect rather than condemn her because once the truth was presented in its full, emotive context, everyone would understand, and even Freddy would be cleared of the wilful murder charge, since he killed for love. Curtis-Bennett was aghast. She should not go anywhere near the witness box. Far better to let him deal with the letters (he would later insist he'd had 'an answer to every incriminating passage'). Edith, though, was unmoved.

*

And so it began. The scene in the world's most famous legal battle-ground – Court Number One of the Central Criminal Court, better known as the Old Bailey – saw Mr Justice Shearman begin proceedings with two legal decisions in the absence of the jury. Both went against Edith. Curtis-Bennett had argued that since the defendants faced completely different sets of evidence – he was active in the murder; she wasn't – they should be tried separately. When that failed, he pushed for the letters to be ruled admissible only if, during proceedings, the prosecution could *prove* she had been active in the murder. Again, Shearman turned him down.

The letters were, he said, 'evidence of intention and evidence of motive'.

Curtis-Bennett knew he had a fight on his hands. The judge was something of a moral crusader, a churchman who valued family and tradition above all. He disliked theatrics, was uncomfortable with female jury members (he addressed them as 'gentlemen') and often referred to a defendant's adultery as if this in itself were enough to swing a guilty verdict. Yet Curtis-Bennett was confident. His junior counsel, Walter Frampton and Ivor Snell, were highly regarded, while Freddy Bywaters' barrister, the urbane Cecil Whiteley, could be relied upon to land blows on the prosecution's case. The only danger was that Whiteley might try to save his client by portraying Freddy as a right-thinking young man who'd been mercilessly manipulated by an older seductress. Whiteley would surely have preferred this strategy, but his client forbade it. The prosecution on behalf of the Crown was led by the newly appointed Solicitor General, Thomas Inskip, backed by one of the Bar's sharpest legal brains, Travers Humphreys.

The jury of eleven men and a woman was sworn in and Inskip wasted little time in informing them of the letters. He was shamelessly duplicitous about the contents, claiming that 'There is the undoubted evidence in the letters upon which you can find that there was a pre-concerted meeting between Mrs Thompson and Bywaters at the place [of the murder].' In none of the 80 letters is there a scintilla of evidence to support this. But because less than half were submitted in evidence by the prosecution (some mentioned sex and abortion and so were thought to be too explicit for the public's ears), the jury could assume the defendants' meeting at 'the place' was arranged in some of the withheld correspondence. It was an evidential sleight of hand matched only by Inskip's presentation of the poison and ground-glass letters and newspaper cuttings. When he stated that 'a post-mortem examination showed that there were practically no traces of any poison,' it appeared he was being scrupulously fair to the defence. In fact he was deliberately dissembling. There were *no* traces of poison. Percy had never been poisoned.

For the rest of the day, and until 3.30pm the following day, the prosecution presented its witnesses – police officers, doctors, family members, the Thompsons' tenant Mrs Lester, and employees of both Carlton & Prior and Fullers tea room. Last to take the stand was the pathologist Sir Bernard Spilsbury, who comprehensively dismissed any hint that poison or glass had been found in Percy Thompson's body: 'I did not find any signs of poisoning, nor did I find any scars in the intestines. I found no indication of the presence of glass either in large pieces or in powdered particles,' he said. At this, Inskip announced he had no further witnesses. He believed in any case that his most potent evidence was about to be unleashed.

Inskip flourished four typed sets of letters to hand to the jury – one set per group of three – and assigned Travers Humphreys to read them aloud, reinforcing and emphasising certain phrases. The embarrassment and humiliation for Edith Thompson as she heard her innermost feelings exposed to the world can hardly be understated. The message to the jury was clear: she was the dominant personality in a murder conspiracy. Eventually, even the judge had heard enough and cut the readings short.

At 3.30pm, Freddy Bywaters' defence got underway. The tactics of his barrister, Cecil Whiteley, were simple: to present Freddy as a youth in love – a lad who well knew Edith's predisposition to the melodramatic and who regarded her mentions of suicide, poison and ground glass as part of the make-believe world she inhabited, constructed largely from the plots of her escapist novels. Freddy had seen the unhappiness she'd endured at Percy Thompson's hands and, on impulse, decided he could take no more. When he followed the couple on 3 October to confront Percy, his intention had been to demand a separation. Only when he believed his nemesis was carrying a gun (a recent addition to the defence narrative) did he brandish the dagger in self-defence.

Yet under cross-examination by Inskip, Freddy struggled to explain Edith's references to poison and glass particles, eventually dismissing the exchanges as 'a lie from her to me'. She was creating an imaginary act, one they did not intend to implement. Inskip then read out the contents of a letter, undated but thought to have been sent by Edith in November 1921, which touched on substances supposedly mixed into Percy's breakfast porridge: 'I had the wrong porridge today but I don't suppose it will matter and I don't seem to care much either way.' Then he read another letter dated 1 April 1922, concerning the noticeable taste of quinine – supplied by Freddy and described by him as 'enough for an elephant' – which she'd dropped into her husband's tea. Edith wrote of Percy's complaint about his tea tasting bitter, adding:

'Now I think whatever else I try it in again it will still taste bitter, he will recognise it and be more suspicious still and if the quantity is still not successful it will injure any chance I may have of trying when you come home.'

When Inskip pressed him on this, Freddy became agitated: 'She could not hurt herself with quinine.'

Inskip: 'You were playing with her ideas?'

Freddy: 'I was pulling her leg.'

As for Edith's admission that she wanted him to be jealous 'so much that you will do something desperate', he insisted he was not jealous, whatever he may have written to the contrary. When Inskip asked how he knew the Thompsons were going to the theatre, he said Edith told him during their meeting that same afternoon at Fullers. So why, asked Inskip, had he so emphatically denied this in his first police interview? Freddy insisted he'd not wanted to involve his lover in any way.

The sum of the cross-examination was that he'd lied to police. There was no evidence, other than his own, supporting the idea that he'd attacked on impulse (although this was probably his last chance to confront Percy before leaving on the *Morea*). As for his claim to have acted in self-defence, there were no grounds to believe Percy had even owned a gun. Nonetheless, Freddy had said nothing to assist the prosecution's allegation of a conspiracy with Edith. Quite the reverse.

Two sections of Mr Justice Shearman's abbreviated trial notes of Freddy's evidence are particularly illuminating, given his summing-up ahead of the verdict. The first touches on quinine: 'There was never any agreement between us that I should poison her husband. There was no agreement for any violence. I never believed she had given poison to her husband. It never entered her head. I had some quinine on board ship. It was in five grain tabloids. I gave her some of that quinine. I never gave her anything else. Nor any poison. Quinine has a bitter taste.'

The second section records Freddy's account of the final hours before his 3 October attack. In this he emphasises that he knew of the Thompsons' theatre trip only because Edith told him a couple of hours before it took place. Hardly, then, a long-planned knife assault. Rather, his decision had been made in the wake of a conversation that evening with Edith's mother. The judge noted Freddy's words as follows: 'I went to Mr Graydon's at Manor Park. I went there to get some tobacco – a special brand. I was there until 11pm. I was in the same room all the time. I spoke to Mr and Mrs Graydon, the son and daughter. I had a pouch with me. Mrs Thompson had given it to me. She gave it to me on the Monday. Both Mr and Mrs Graydon noticed it. There was conversation about Mrs Thompson. Mrs Graydon said to me: "You've got a new pouch. Is it from a girl?" I said: "Yes." She said: "I expect the same girl gave you that as gave you the watch." Mrs Thompson had given me a watch two voyages previously. I said: "The same girl gave it me." She said: "I can guess." I said: "I don't think you can." "I know who," she said, "but I am not going to say." She said: "Never mind. We won't argue any longer. She's one of the best." I said: "There is none better." '

This account by Freddy indicates that Mrs Graydon was well aware of his interest in *both* her daughters but particularly Edith.

Did he regard her words as a green light to pursue the married older girl? After all, she seemed to know how close they had become and appeared untroubled by it. Freddy never made this claim directly, although he stressed how the discussion had lingered with him.

This was noted by the judge, who went on to record Freddy's evidence that, after leaving the Graydons, he'd been thinking about Edith's unhappiness and wished he could help, how he'd not wanted to go home and on impulse decided to walk to Ilford because 'I knew they would be together and if I could see them it might make things better.' He said he had hoped to come to an 'amicable understanding' with Percy about a divorce. However, the reality was very different. After lying in wait for the Thompsons he'd grabbed Percy and pushed him along the street, swinging him round. He'd demanded a divorce or separation; Percy responded with: 'I know that is what you want. I won't give it to you.' Then, according to Freddy, Percy said: 'I've got her, I'll keep her and I'll shoot you,' while simultaneously hitting his attacker in the chest. At this point Freddy claimed he'd drawn his knife and began stabbing, 'Because all the time I thought he was going to shoot me.'

Freddy gave evidence for 90 minutes on 7 December and continued the following morning. Then, at midday, all eyes turned to Edith on the witness stand. After a few preliminaries, her junior counsel, Walter Frampton, handed her the 32 letters submitted in evidence and began taking her through them. The case against her would stand or fall by these letters. They did not connect her to the murder other than to confirm her affair with the killer, but the Crown was determined to glean from them proof of a plot.

Early on, Frampton tried to deal with the 'wrong porridge' phrase. What had she meant by it? Edith replied that she 'really cannot explain that', a damaging admission at face value. Mr Justice Shearman noted her full response as: 'We had talked about making my husband ill and I may have said, "I'll give him something one of these days." We were discussing my unhappiness and his treatment of me. I probably said I would give him something. He did take porridge in the morning. I never did make it. Mrs Lester made it.'

Is it possible she was telling Freddy she had taken the wrong porridge (i.e., porridge containing quinine) because she was hoping it might abort her pregnancy? If so, she could certainly not admit such an illegal act (which itself carried a maximum life sentence), especially in a courtroom full of men. It would destroy any last semblance of respectability.

Her words immediately after the 'porridge' reference were: *I don't suppose it will matter.* She was either saying that the porridge was not really poisonous, or perhaps that it would leave her unborn child unaffected. Either way, her words hardly proved she had the mindset of a determined husband-killer. They merely illustrated how implied meanings could be twisted.

Continuing his record of her evidence, the judge highlighted various phrases relating to bitter tea, quinine, crushed glass and the suggestion by Edith that Freddy should 'do something desperate'. There is also reference to ammoniated tincture – a readily available pharmaceutical drug to treat fevers, which contained quinine. Edith conceded she'd bought some but that Avis had thrown it away.

The judge's notes state that, according to Edith, the tea and glass incidents were imaginary – she'd never administered anything to her husband and she simply wanted to convince Freddy that she was 'willing to do what he suggested' to make Percy ill but 'not necessarily to take his life'. As for lying to the police about the attack, Edith insisted she had 'no idea' it would take place but afterwards decided to shield her lover by pretending Percy had been taken ill.

*

Much of Edith's evidence concerns her letter of 13 July 1922 about the plot of Hichens's novel *Bella Donna* and the relevance of its eponymous femme fatale's attempt to poison her husband Nigel in pursuit of a secret lover, Baroudi. Astonishingly, the judge would use this against Edith in his summing-up to the jury, even though Curtis-Bennett made clear that Edith's letter condemned the wife in scathing terms:

> *If she had loved Baroudi enough she could have gone to him, but she liked the security of being Nigel's wife – for the monetary assets it held. She doesn't seem a woman to me – she seems abnormal – a monster utterly selfish and self-living. Darlint this is where we differ about women. I usually stand up for them against you and in this case it's the reverse but honestly darlint I don't call her a woman – she is absolutely unnatural in every sense.*

Had the judge given due weight to this it would certainly have placed doubt in the jury's mind as to whether Edith was capable of administering poison – here she was stating unequivocally her repugnance at the idea.

Indeed, throughout her time on the stand, Mr Justice Shearman repeatedly seized on opportunities to undermine her. When Curtis-Bennett asks her to explain the 'five years', which crops up constantly in the correspondence, Edith said it was the time they agreed they would wait for her to secure a new job abroad. The judge immediately butted in: 'The other witness's story was that they wanted to commit suicide, and he said "Put it off five years," which seems to be the only sensible thing I have heard.' Clearly Shearman is unable to grasp that both interpretations might be true.

When, under cross-examination, Edith was asked whether she was suggesting it was Freddy's idea to poison Percy, she replied: 'I did not suggest it.'

Again, the judge jumped in: 'Give him something in his food; you answered my question a little while ago that it was to give him something to make him ill?'

Edith replied, 'That is what I surmised, that I should give him something so that when he had a heart attack he would not be able to resist it.'

This was a tactical mistake. She knew her husband was a hypochondriac and that the army had found no evidence of any heart condition. Had she emphasised the army medics' conclusion it would have shown the entire 'heart attack plot' for what it was – a baseless fantasy. Unfortunately, she was not given the chance to qualify her words because, again, the judge intervened: 'One moment. I do not want to be mistaken. Did I take you down rightly as saying, "I wanted him to think I was willing to take my husband's life"'?

Edith replied: 'I wanted him to think I was willing to do what he suggested.'

Shearman: 'That is, to take your husband's life?'

Edith: 'Not necessarily.'

She remained in the witness box for the rest of the day and then another hour on the morning of Saturday 9 December. Just before she returned to the dock, Curtis-Bennett asked why she'd written to Freddy in the way she did. 'I thought he was gradually drifting away from me,' she replied tearfully.

Curtis-Bennett: 'Did you still love him very much?'

Edith paused, eyes closed, face shivering: 'I did,' she replied.

And so, after almost four days of evidence, the trial moved to its endgame. The defending barristers went first with their closing speeches, followed by the prosecution and finally the judge, whose summing-up would be crucial. Freddy's barrister Cecil Whiteley knew his client's only hope was to crush the notion of 'wilful murder' and instead convince the jury to return a verdict of either excusable homicide or manslaughter. Freddy, he explained, was never influenced by Edith's letters – the supposedly relevant ones were in any case dated four months before the killing. In fact, he had been looking to cool their relationship. As Whiteley put it, far from a conspiracy to murder Percy, Freddy had been trying to cool his relationship with Edith. There had been little enjoyment in it except when he was home on leave and he recognised the 'impossibility of the situation'. Yet Edith was 'always holding out the hope that they might be able to join each other'. If the jury accepted that, until the evening of 3 October, Freddy had never intended to injure Percy Thompson, and that he had never agreed with Edith that 'any violence or anything else' should be done, then, said Whiteley, 'Your verdict, so far as Mrs Thompson is concerned, is "Not Guilty", and you will have to deal with the case as it affects Bywaters.'

Whiteley went on to defuse the significance of the knife as best he could. The prosecution had not proved that Freddy bought it specifically to do the deed. According to Freddy, he'd owned it for at least 11 months and it was perfectly reasonable for him to do so. There were few sailors who did *not* possess a knife, because they were often out and about in foreign ports. If the defendant's evidence was accepted, then he never intended to kill Percy Thompson that night. His aim was to 'make some arrangement with him' and it was only when he heard the words 'I will shoot you,' and saw Percy's hand going to a hip pocket, that he reacted. 'What was it that would flash through the mind of a man accustomed to visiting foreign countries?' asked Whiteley. 'It does not matter, I submit, whether there was a revolver or not. The question for the jury is, what did this man believe at that time?'

If Freddy indeed thought his life was in immediate danger then the verdict should be excusable homicide. If the jury believed that he did not start the fight with the intention of using the knife, but drew it 'in the heat of passion' as Percy attacked him, then the crime should be downgraded to manslaughter.

At 2.45pm it was Curtis-Bennett's turn. He roundly attacked the prosecution case as dishonest, reminding the jury there was no evidence to link Edith to the stabbing. She occupied a fantasy world, reflected in her letters, and it was all too convenient to dissect them retrospectively in search of guilt. In fact, if her words were taken at face value, it was clear the lovers were considering a suicide pact rather than murder. As to a plot involving poison or glass, the prosecution's own witness, a respected senior pathologist, had shown there was neither in Percy's body. It would have been a good end to the day for the defence had not the judge again stepped in, sternly warning the jury that they were 'trying a vulgar and common crime', not 'listening to a play from the stalls of a theatre'. With that, proceedings were adjourned and the jury, stalked by news reporters, were despatched to the Manchester Hotel, Aldersgate, until Monday 11 December.

That Monday morning, Curtis-Bennett again emphasised that the prosecution had nothing that linked Edith to the murder. His oratory was at its most potent when demolishing the relevance of her correspondence, and he used her 20 September letter, wanting Freddy to be jealous 'so much so that you will do something desperate', to illustrate his point. 'Start at the end of the story with the death and work back to that and you can make what is an absolutely innocent expression in a letter appear to be a guilty one,' said Curtis-Bennett. 'Work back, as the prosecution have done, from the tragedy and come to a letter written a fortnight before and because in that letter there is this phrase "do something desperate", that means the woman was trying to make the man return to England to murder her husband. Surely, if you look at the letters and all these references, they are absolutely consistent with the story that both Mrs Thompson and Bywaters have told. They are consistent with: "Take me away. I care not where."'

He then turned to the letter written on the eve of the murder, quoting the line: 'Don't forget what we talked about in the tearoom. I'll still risk and try if you will.' Curtis-Bennett told the jury: 'The suggestion of the prosecution – and they have no evidence at all of it – is that in that tearoom in Aldersgate Street these two people were plotting murder. There is not one scrap of evidence. But having put all those letters before you, and having created the prejudice those letters must create when first read without an explanation, the prosecution then say: "The night of 3 October Thompson dies, and don't forget what we talked about in the tearoom" and you … are urged to believe that they were talking about murder.' He pointed out that Edith and Percy had taken the 'the proper and the best way home' from Ilford Station to Kensington Gardens; she 'did not lure her husband into some dark by-way where a murder could be committed'.

*

In his summing-up for the Crown, Solicitor General Inskip again trotted out predictable lines: Thompson and Bywaters gave conflicting statements to police and so by implication were liars. It was possible that neither glass nor poison would leave any trace in Percy's body. The content of the letters proved the obviousness of a plot.

But Inskip had a problem with Edith's role. Her so-called incitement of Freddy had to be shown to subsist up to the time of the murder – not just in letters that were weeks or months old. In other words, she had to be shown to be encouraging it during the 2 October tearoom conversation. Clearly, Inskip could not prove this and the lovers had denied it in court. But Mr Justice Shearman was always keen to help. Here is the jaw-dropping exchange in which the judge effectively suggests, in the jury's presence, that Edith and Freddy were indeed plotting murder.

Shearman: 'If she was persuading him to act at 6 o'clock – half past 5 – when she parted with him upon that day, who can doubt when she saw him coming [at the murder scene], even whether she told him the place or not, that she was an accessory – not an accessory – she was a principal in this murder.'

Inskip: 'And even though the time or the place at which the crime was to be carried out varied, then I shall submit to the jury subject to your Lordship's direction, that she was guilty of murder.'

Shearman: 'I am glad of your assistance.'

The judge's subsequent summing-up was so redolent of bias and moral posturing that it seems remarkable members of the jury took a whole two hours to find both defendants guilty. He began by stating that, 'This charge is a common and ordinary charge of a wife and an adulterer murdering the husband. I am not saying it is proved but that is the charge.'

This immediately painted the defendants as guilty of an immoral act, namely adultery. The judge went on to express outrage at a phrase used by Edith in one letter, which he interpreted as meaning that marital love was meaningless. He had no doubt that the jury, and every proper-minded person, were filled with disgust by such an expression. The jury should also ask themselves whether they could believe the defendants' evidence that 'they were always talking to Thompson and saying: "Give her up".' But neither defendant had claimed this was 'always' happening. Indeed, given that Freddy was at sea for months at a time, it would have been impossible.

As to the murder itself, the judge made much of Edith's initial statement to police in which she claimed she had been senseless after being pushed over. How could she have been senseless when she was heard saying, "Oh don't"? The answer of course is obvious. She had said in her first interview that she naturally tried to shield her lover. That did not make her a conspirator. If anything, the words 'Oh don't' suggested she was trying to stop the attack. Yet Shearman instructed the jury that if they thought she'd witnessed the stabbing incident in its entirety – and had therefore lied about being knocked senseless – 'then from beginning to end there was a series of deceptions as to the real facts of the case.'

But it was in his assessment of the letters that the judge really sought to blow Edith's defence apart. He suggested that the absence of (proper) evidence made them all the more important – an extraordinary claim, tantamount to saying 'the Crown has nothing on this woman; we'll have to find something.' The letters, he said, were 'full of the outpourings of a silly but at the same time wicked affection'. They formed a very strong case that Edith was writing to Freddy asking for his assistance to remove her husband by the administration of poison. She was suggesting plotting and planning. Her explanation was that it was Freddy who made the suggestion. It was for the jury to say whether they believed that.

The guilty verdicts, when they came, offered neither defendant hope of avoiding the gallows. The foreman could have made a recommendation for mercy but chose not to. When asked if he had anything to say, Freddy replied: 'The verdict of the jury is wrong. Edith Thompson is not guilty. I am no murderer. I am not an assassin.'

Edith merely groaned when the question was first put to her but, after the judge had donned the black cap to pass sentence of death, the Clerk of the Court asked if she had anything to say in stay of her execution. This was code for asking if she was pregnant; the law did not permit the execution of expectant mothers. This time Edith threw up her arms exclaiming: 'Oh God, I am not guilty. Oh God, I am not guilty.' As Freddy was taken down she gripped the bar of the dock before being half carried by her escorting wardresses. Both would now occupy cells for the condemned – he at Pentonville Prison, she at Holloway – to await the result of an appeal.

The verdict won almost unanimous approval from the press, which the following day condemned Edith specifically and women in general. Leading the way was the *Daily Mirror*, which, in an editorial headed 'LOVE AND CRIME', observed that, showing 'admirable common sense' the judge had managed 'to strip the veils of false feeling off the plain vulgarity and to bring to earth the "flights of imagination" which had tried to make something romantic out of something very sordid'. The leader-writer went on: 'There are thousands of fiction-fed women who believe that, by some mysterious decree, there is a "right of nature and love" which is supreme over the "right by law". They are the Mme Bovarys of real life who regard it as impossible to love the man they have chosen to marry.'

The *Daily Chronicle* took the opportunity not only to condemn Edith's supposed glamorous lifestyle but also to take a gratuitous swipe at the French over their *crime passionnel* law permitting reduced sentences for crimes of passion. Only a British jury would have found the defendants guilty, the paper claimed, because 'the average English juryman, unlike the Frenchman, is quite unwilling to condone crime [which] sprang out of an overmastering passion of love or lust.'

The *Evening Standard*, while acknowledging that 'the Ilford case has many of the elements of epic tragedy', cautioned against leniency. True, it was 'unpleasant to hang a woman', but it would not be just for the Home Secretary to spare her and execute her younger lover who was 'probably of weaker character' and 'in the view of many acted under her influence'.

For its part, *The Daily Telegraph* insisted the probability that Edith was 'the leader in the deed' was considerable.

On Thursday 14 December the *Daily Sketch* began a petition seeking the reprieve of Freddy Bywaters that attracted a million signatures. The feeling among ordinary working people was that he should be saved; that here was a naïve, inexperienced boy who had become the puppet of his older lover. One of the signatories was Eliot Howard, the magistrate who committed Freddy for trial but now believed him to be innocent. The Graydons were also quick to add their names, although there was no move to include Edith in this appeal to the Home Secretary. Was this because her solicitor had assessed the public mood (as defined by newspaper editors) and feared opinion already ran too strongly against her? Who would sign to save a controlling, manipulative woman who had so cunningly led her young lover astray?

The following Saturday, 16 December, under the headline 'First Ilford Appeal Lodged', the *Chronicle* reported that Edith's legal team were citing three grounds – misdirection of the jury, lack of evidence to convict of murder and inadmissibility of the letters. Freddy's appeal was also underway, although his seemed a hopeless cause.

On 21 December the Court of Appeal announced its findings. No cause had been shown to interfere with the sentencing – the three judges had seen only a 'squalid case of lust and adultery in which the husband of Mrs Thompson was murdered in cruel fashion'. Crucially, they believed her letters *were* admissible and the prosecution was therefore bound to use them. The letters proved that Edith had been 'continuously' in touch with Freddy until shortly before the murder – evidence of a 'common design' – and that afterwards she'd tried to conceal his guilt.

At Pentonville, Freddy was stoic, while insisting that his lover was innocent. Even after the appeal failed, Edith had hopes of a reprieve. As the days passed and those hopes faded, she lurched into a state of collapse. There were more letters and visits from her family, who acted as go-betweens in communications with Freddy. Finally, the prison governor resorted to sedation to contain her suffering.

When the day of her execution came, she was carried to the gallows and supported, possibly on a chair, while swift preparations were made. To hangman John Ellis she looked dead already, even while she was in the condemned cell. Rumour has it that when the trap door was released blood rushed from between Edith's legs, a shocking sight for those in attendance. That might have been an undeclared pregnancy, as she had apparently gained a stone in weight while she was behind bars yet was barely eating, although it seems unlikely she would have been unaware of it and could have escaped the noose had she shared the information. It could also have been the result of any previously induced abortion or even the start of a period.

The circumstances of her hanging, her helplessness and hope-lessness, apparently had a profound effect on Ellis, who gave up the job as hangman later the same year, took to drink and finally committed suicide in 1932, by cutting his throat with a razor.

*

Almost a century after her execution, Edith Thompson's family finally won permission to re-bury her alongside her parents in the City of London cemetery. None of the mourners had known Edith, but there were cousins – distant ones – and other well-wishers outside the family who had been touched by her story. One of the leading mourners was Nicki Toay, whose grandfather was Edith's cousin. Since learning about the family link with one of the twentieth century's most sensational court cases, she had become among Edith's staunchest defenders and, like many, believes she was wrongly hanged.

Nicki sought a fresh examination of Edith's trial from barristers Jeremy Dein and Sasha Wass. Initially, Sasha believed Edith's response to her husband's death was suspect and that the catalogue of letters seized from her lover *did* point to complicity in the killing. The references to his murder were more than a passing comment, Sasha insisted, as Edith sent newspaper cuttings about wives poisoning their husbands and wrote at one stage: 'Darling, you must do something this time. I'm not really impatient but opportunities come and go. They have to because I'm helpless.' Sasha pointed out that while Edith's defence was pinned on the letters being 'fantasy', it was unfortunate that this fantasy had been fulfilled through Percy's murder. The case was not weak, and while it may have been tragic and unfortunate it did not equate to a miscarriage of justice.

For Jeremy, the correspondence was far less persuasive in confirming Edith's guilt. Even if the written word revealed dark inner thoughts, that didn't mean she had plotted the crime. The letters were 'ambiguous' and 'a cry for help'. Edith wasn't asking for her husband to be stabbed to death – Freddy had done that – and Freddy had made clear she wasn't involved.

With the letters a central plank in the case, Jeremy and Sasha decided to consult criminal psychologist Dr Donna Youngs. An illuminating tool in modern court cases, criminal psychology was in its infancy at the time of Edith Thompson's trial. However, Dr Youngs was now able to shed a different light on Edith's words. She was in no doubt that Edith, although an intriguing character, was both childlike and immature. One letter read: 'Three months from now is absolutely the longest I'm even going to try and imagine. I'm not going to look any further forward, and you're not going to either.' These were not the words of a mature woman, said Dr Youngs, but rather the way a young adolescent would frame issues. Nor was there reason to believe Edith was an older woman trying to manipulate a younger man – 'that's an utterly ridiculous characterisation of her'. The letters showed no 'genuine commitment' consistent with wishing to kill her husband and actually included one plea to Freddy not to do anything rash.

Consultant pathologist Dr Stuart Hamilton backed this view. Edith's references to quinine, ground glass and belladonna (deadly nightshade) were 'childish ideas' rather than credible assassination techniques. Finely ground glass would simply pass through the system, while larger shards, which could pose a hazard to the intestines, would cut the inside of the mouth and immediately alert a potential victim. Quinine was so bitter, he told Jeremy and Sasha, that it would be difficult to smuggle a significant amount into food or drink. As for belladonna, although a dangerous poison, it was commonly found as a murder method in contemporary literature, giving it currency at the time.

Yet despite the post-mortem examination failing to reveal any evidence of poisoning or similar, Sasha was still inclined to believe in Edith's guilt. Absence of evidence was not evidence of absence, and the jury must have concluded that she was deliberately encouraging Freddy.

Nicki was doing some research of her own to find out more about her doomed relative, and Professor Lucy Bland helped her put flesh on the bones. Vivacious and artistic, Edith continued to be known by her maiden name at work – a bone of contention for some, as Professor Bland explained: 'Huge numbers of men had died in the war, but there was still actually very high unemployment. So there was disapproval about a married woman still holding on to her job – she should be back in the home, looking after her husband, having children. So here you have a married woman earning good money, so she was seen as behaving rather inappropriately and having a rather fast way of living.'

That the *Daily Sketch* ran a petition for Freddy's reprieve and not Edith's was telling because it reflects the assumption that he had been led astray.

Nicki also met Professor René Weis, author of *Criminal Justice*, the most comprehensive book written about Edith Thompson. He became so close to surviving members of the Thompson family he was declared the heir to their family memorabilia; he showed Nicki Edith's necklace, a tray cloth she had stitched as a child, and an array of letters and photographs. One of the letters was written by Edith to Nicki's great-grandmother – who was Edith's godmother – just before she died.

'When I was told the result of the appeal yesterday it seemed the end of everything,' said Edith. 'I'm sure you never anticipated such an end as this for me.' Although she had always dismissed as silly superstition the saying that those like herself born on Christmas Day were unlucky, now she was not so sure.

As they took looked back from the twenty-first century into a different era, Jeremy and Sasha were seeking breakthrough evidence that might reshape the legal outcome of the Thompson case. When they scrutinised the judge's summing-up, they found it.

For Jeremy, the judge's harsh words about Edith's moral standards served to dehumanise the accused. 'They were stripped of their dignity long before they went to the gallows,' he observed.

And now Sasha herself was having doubts about the validity of the conviction, feeling an 'instinctive discomfort' about the judge's summing-up and that it would have compromised the pair's chances of a fair trial. When Jeremy laid out his objections to the conviction, mostly centred around the judge's summing-up, Sasha didn't oppose him

Judge Radford concurred with the barristers. Every defendant is entitled to a 'fair and just' trial, he said, which was as true in 1922 as it is today. Although he conferred respect to the trial judge, he declared: 'The summing-up in this trial failed to direct the jury properly as to key legal matters. It was, as a whole, fundamentally lacking in balance and fairness.'

Edith's conviction was 'unsafe and indeed unsatisfactory', he said, news that was a joyful relief for Nicki, who saw Edith as a victim of the age.

'Some people were still very much living in the Victorian era of "the woman must be at home, she must be a housewife, she must have children." This is not what Edith was doing at all – she was out having fun, she was dancing, she had a good career and she was earning good money. She was moving forward and I think that actually went against her in the court.'

After the hanging, as was customary, Edith was buried in the grounds of Holloway Prison. There she would remain until 1971 when, to accommodate structural changes, her body was moved to unconsecrated ground in Brookwood Cemetery in Surrey with four other women who had been hanged at Holloway. It wasn't until November 2018 that her body was moved for a second time, finally out of the clutches of the British legal system and into the arms of her family. In 1938 it had been her mother's dying wish for them to be reunited in death, although perpetual requests made to the Home Office had been ignored.

With its removal to the family plot in the City of London, Edith's body was also now in the company of others that lived outside society's self-imposed boundaries, including Joseph Merrick, also known as the Elephant Man, and Catherine Eddowes and Mary Ann Nichols, both victims of Jack the Ripper. The body of her husband Percy Thompson also lies in the same cemetery.

THE CASE OF
THE BOOT THIEF

————————

LOUIE CALVERT

Life had not been especially kind to Lily Waterhouse. Widowed and jobless, she survived in challenging circumstances as best she could. Her back-to-back terraced house in Leeds was furnished with boxes for tables and had bare walls and floors. The mattress wasn't set on a bedstead but was separated from the floorboards by a thin layer of newspaper. When she lay on it at night, she was plagued by the perpetual itch of scabies and lice, both of which infested her slight body. To correct a spinal deformity, she spent her waking hours clad in shoulder irons, which were both heavy and uncomfortable.

Times were tough in 1926, with simmering workers' unrest dominating the headlines as Britain struggled to regain its economic equilibrium, eight years after the end of the First World War. Lily, 41, was no stranger to the pawn shop, where she could exchange belongings for cash with the hope of redeeming items later when times improved. Like many others, Lily resorted to prostitution to help meet her bills. At times she was so hungry she was reduced to asking for food from strangers.

So when she found a lodger in the diminutive shape of 30-year-old Louie Calvert, it seemed some of her daily difficulties may have been alleviated. Apparently destitute, Louie had approached Lily in central Leeds, claiming she had nowhere to stay and nothing to eat. She was, she said, a separated mother of three, but none of her children were with her.

Initially the pair were good friends, with Lily rejoicing in some female company and the hope of some meagre financial support in terms of rent. The landlord was threatening to evict her from her run-down home whose front door opened directly onto the pavement of Amberley Road, and she knew that in her apparent state of extreme poverty her options beyond the immediate neighbourhood were limited. But within a fortnight, Lily noticed some of the few items she possessed had gone missing. Troubled, she then had what she described as a 'premonition' from her dead husband, George, instructing her to search Louie's bag. As her lodger slept, she crept into her room and opened the bag to find three pawnshop tickets, indicating that the items had been hocked for cash. One was for a gentlemen's black suit, like the one belonging to her husband that had recently disappeared. The other two tickets were for a black skirt and a pair of women's boots, which also matched the other articles that had vanished without trace. All the tickets were in Lily's name.

As Lily made sense of the revelation now contained in her hand, Louie awoke and events took a sinister turn. Immediately, Louie rose from her pillow and confronted Lily, her dark complexion glowing with menace. 'They are not yours and you must give them back to me,' Louie told her. Although Lily pointed out the tickets were in her own name, Louie – a far more forceful character – said that made no difference.

Lily put the tickets back in the bag and withdrew, shattered by what she'd discovered and reeling from the betrayal of her newfound friend. She confided in William Byrne, a benevolent 57-year-old Liverpudlian who ran a second-hand bookshop nearby. The kindly father of three had encountered Lily for the first time six months previously when she came to his shop desperate for a meal. Since then, he had employed her occasionally to run errands and regularly supplied hot tea, becoming a pillar of support. It was to him she had turned earlier that month when the Board of Health wanted her to have a sulphur bath as a treatment for scabies, and he supplied the necessary half crown to cover costs, taken out of money she had earned that he managed on her behalf. Now he quickly pointed out she should have kept the pawn-shop tickets as useful evidence. It was the same message that she got from police when, on William's advice, she reported the disturbing incident.

On Wednesday 31 March, Lily visited his shop three times: once in the morning in a vain attempt to sell him primroses, again at midday and then just before 5pm, when he gave her a cup of tea before she returned to her house. They had plenty to discuss – Lily had been to the police, where she had explained not only the circumstances of the missing items but that she was now terrified of her lodger. She told how Louie had threatened her, saying: 'If I get about you, you are a cripple and I will hurt you.' William and Lily shook hands as she left and she thanked him for the tea. It was the last time he ever saw her.

The next morning, when she failed to show up for an appointment made to begin proceedings against Louie, police were sufficiently concerned to check her home address. Finding the house locked, two officers asked neighbours if they'd seen Lily that morning, but no one had. Using a neighbour's key they went inside and discovered Lily's lifeless body in a small upstairs bedroom, fully dressed but for hat and shoes. The frugal furnishings in the room bore no signs of a disturbance, although the blinds were drawn.

Lily lay on her right side, with her body extended over two small mattresses – the cushions from a small, pull-out 'bed chair' – and her left leg flopping over her right. A piece of string lay across her feet and there was another similar length of string as well as a piece of tape near the body too. Lily's neck and wrists were scarred by marks, and there was a visible wound on the back of her head. Blood from it was saturating one of the cushions. Her thick hair had tumbled down, with hair grips that once contained it lost in the untidy mane. If the motive for the murder was theft, whoever killed her had failed to find the savings book hidden in her underwear, which showed she had £3, 19 shillings and 9 pence to her name – worth about £163 today.

The police began their detection work in the house. In an initial search, Detective Sergeant John Holland found it curiously under-equipped. There were no cups and saucers, while the only cutlery in evidence amounted to two tablespoons, one teaspoon, one fork and a breadknife. The china sugar basin was empty, while the only comestibles were a teacake and a currant square. It seemed the end of a bleak existence.

There was no service when Lily was buried in Beckett Street cemetery on 8 April. Without children to shoulder the cost, it's even possible the local authority paid for Lily's coffin.

*

Lily Waterhouse was one of eight children, and census records from 1901 reveal that, aged 16, she was living in Leeds with sisters Mary and Beatrice and brother Clifford. There was a man, railway engine driver John Hornshaw, listed at the same address as a lodger but he was known to be Clifford's father. It seems her mother was living miles away in Norfolk.

Ten years later, when the next census was taken, she had sunk from view, despite the considerable efforts made by the government to chart everybody's whereabouts on a nominated day. She wasn't always unemployed but when she had a job it was invariably a menial one. It's a safe assumption that she devoted her energies to keeping out of the workhouse, which might help to explain why in 1912 she married a man 22 years her senior. When mill hand George Waterhouse died in 1925, she fell into prostitution in an attempt to keep herself fed and clothed, and she had customers despite her parasite infestations.

It wasn't the only thing neighbours said about her when she died, however. She was known for wearing vintage Victorian underwear, although that was unlikely to be on account of any predilections of her customers. Thanks partly to the Suffragette movement, women in the 1920s had rejected corsets and bloomers and were wearing smaller, plainer knickers and petticoats than would have been considered acceptable by their mothers' or grandmothers' generation.

Lily also had a reputation as a medium. With vast numbers of lives lost in the First World War, spiritualism was popular, especially among bereaved women. She was known to hold seances, trying to contact the dead. Most, though, would just have regarded this as another one of Lily's eccentricities because, as one neighbour told a newspaper, 'She was a bit of a mystery.'

The police were able to chart Lily's final few hours based on sightings of her by her neighbours in and around Amberley Road. One saw her go into her home at about 6.15pm. But still more was noted that day about her female house guest.

Next-door neighbour Emily Clayton, who had known Lily for a dozen years or more, was aware of the existence of a new lodger and met her on several occasions. But, like Lily, she had no idea that Louie was an inveterate liar. Thanks to the embellished account given to Emily on the doorstep one day that spring, she believed Louie was from Manchester and had a poorly child in Leeds Infirmary who she was there to nurse. Louie had claimed she was waiting for a house on the newly developed Meanwood Estate in north-west Leeds to be cleaned, the cost of which was purportedly going to be £8. Her husband, who didn't know where she was, she said, was a travelling salesman for Jackson's Stores, an expanding chain of grocery shops. No one in Amberley Road was given Louie's surname, and even Lily didn't know it.

At 5pm that day, Emily had met Louie on the pavement outside their adjoining homes. On this occasion, Louie had a baby with her, whom none of the neighbours had seen before. Of course, Emily believed this was the child that had been in the infirmary. But while the baby was supposed to be several months old, she bore all the appearances of a newborn. Emily retreated inside, pondering the anomaly for a moment before continuing with chores. But before too long her attention was held by a rhythmic noise that seemed to emanate from next door, from behind the wall that adjoined Lily Waterhouse's small second bedroom.

'It was faint at first, then got louder and then fainter,' she told police. She described it as a tapping noise that seemed as if it came from the heel of a boot and estimated that she heard the unexplained sounds at about 7pm.

Later, she told magistrates: 'It was not the noise of a hammer I heard. It was not loud enough. More like the heel of a boot or something which had fallen … It seemed to be very cautiously done – as if they did not want it to be heard by anyone else.'

Outside, another neighbour, returning laundry worker Louisa Popple, saw Lily go through the arched front door of her house shortly before seven. Shortly afterwards, Mrs Popple joined Emily on the doorstep and also heard the same dull thudding. She likened it to the sound of someone hammering a bedstead. But neither neighbour could nail down precisely what it was they had heard, and it was curious enough for the incident to lodge in Emily's mind.

When Louie emerged laden from the house later than evening, she was immediately hailed by the inquisitive Emily, who had a barrage of questions. Was Louie packed up to leave the neighbourhood? Louie admitted she was going, although Lily had asked her to stay. 'I have left her in bed, crying,' Louie said. What were the strange noises that Emily had heard earlier? 'I have been pulling down the bed chair ready for Mrs Waterhouse.'

Although Emily had heard no sounds of sobbing, she may well have been unsurprised that Lily wanted another bed laid out as she was aware that her neighbour sometimes received male visitors in the early hours. Later, she told police that Lily used to like 'living on the town', referring to a fast-and-loose lifestyle. Emily also noted that the blind in the small bedroom was pulled down, the first time she had ever seen it so. It had been that way since mid-afternoon. She saw that the shutters were closed and the gas mantle was turned down just before Louie left.

In fact, the drumming noise heard by Emily Clayton and Louisa Popple was almost certainly the muffled struggle put up by their neighbour as she fought for her life. With her wrists and ankles most likely tied, all Lily could do was thrash around in the face of the muffled, murderous onslaught.

Neighbours had still more to report to police, suggesting Louie had returned to the property the following day. Steamroller driver David Darley – who had known Lily for more than a decade – noticed a strange woman in a dark coat and hat putting a key into her door at about 5.20am the next morning as he went down Amberley Road on his way to work.

Shortly afterwards, weaver Sarah Ann Dutton looked out of her bedroom window to witness a woman come out of Lily's house carrying a case, a basket and a bag, and head towards a nearby tram stop. Another weaver, Elizabeth Lumb, was on the tram that braked when the driver saw Louie running up Amberley Road. She and Louie sat on the lower deck of the vehicle as it trundled into Leeds. Mrs Lumb knew Louie and they greeted one another warmly. 'It's a grand morning,' declared Louie. 'Are you working?' Louie was wearing a scarf rather than a hat, Mrs Lumb told police. Two days later, Mrs Lumb would pick out Louie in an identity parade held at police cells – which were still then referred to by their old-fashioned name as a bridewell – with comparative ease.

Fitted together, the accounts revealed that Louie made a dawn departure from her own home across Leeds to return to the scene of the crime in order to liberate the few belongings of Lily's that she hadn't already purloined. She used the dead woman's bags to do so.

*

Louie Calvert was not pregnant when she first moved to Amberley Road. Yet when she left the property three weeks later, she was clutching a tiny baby that she called her own.

Louie was already a mother of two when she moved into Arthur Calvert's home at 7 Railway Terrace, Pottery Fields, Leeds, as housekeeper about a year before she met Lily. Annie, her eldest child, allegedly lived with Louie's sister in Dewsbury while son Kenneth was with her. Louie and Arthur – also known as Arty – had met in a pub, and he offered her and her son a room in his house at a reduced rate of three shillings and fivepence a week if she would also act as a housekeeper.

Later, Louie recalled: 'It was a poor home with only a table, bed and two chairs, yet we managed all right and I was glad to have a shelter of any kind over my head.'

THE CASE OF THE BOOT THIEF

The outlook improved considerably for Louie when she got a job at a mill, operating two looms in exchange for a wage of £3 and 17 shillings a week. Eventually, Louie and Arthur became lovers and they married in August 1925. The relationship wasn't entirely rosy, according to Louie. She claimed Arthur once hit her son, who fell against the fireplace fender and sustained a shocking head wound. After she took the child to hospital for treatment, the child cruelty office became involved and Arthur was apparently jailed. She herself bore a scar on her forehead caused by a bucket that he once threw at her.

The problems for Louie really started when she claimed to her husband that she was pregnant with his child when she wasn't. The pregnancy claim was likely to have been a trick that got him to agree to marriage, yet she certainly wasn't hoping to trap him into a long-term relationship on account of his wealth. Apart from a short spell as a night watchman, Arthur was perpetually unemployed, surviving on a small pension paid in recognition of an injury he sustained in the First World War. Three bullets remained lodged in his arm after the Battle of Passchendaele in 1917. Still, women like Louie operated on small margins and perhaps this regular income was sufficient to tempt her. They married in the industrial suburb of Hunslet, Leeds. Perhaps because she was a mother already, she assumed she would fall pregnant within a short time, and so didn't think anything of telling the man she wanted to marry her that there was a baby when there was not.

However, Louie – a slip of a woman – remained narrow-hipped and flat-stomached as the months rolled by. Eventually, her husband began inquiring about when the promised baby would arrive. In response she produced a pencil-written letter, purportedly coming from her sister in Dewsbury, inviting her there to have the baby. At the same time, she could see daughter Annie, the letter said. It was Arthur's first encounter of any kind with one of his wife's relations. In fact, the letter had been written by Louie herself as a route out of her dilemma. It offered an excuse to escape the confines of Railway Terrace and resolve the difficulties thrown up by a lack of pregnancy.

She didn't go far. Rather than Dewsbury, Louie headed for central Leeds, where she met Lily Waterhouse in Bond Street and pleaded for accommodation. Lily's home in Amberley Road was less than three miles from her own at Railway Terrace. Whether Louie considered the ample risk of being spotted by a friend or relative during the subterfuge isn't known.

Her next step was to advertise for a baby in the columns of a Leeds evening newspaper. In an age where shame was heaped upon unmarried mothers, the advertisement offered salvation for 17-year-old Myra Ward, from Pontefract, Yorkshire, a new mum in St Faith's mother and baby nursing home in Leeds. The era of legal adoptions was just a matter of months away – after 1 January 1927, all children given away by their mothers had to be registered, thanks to the 1926 Adoption of Children Act. For now, when Myra's mother spotted the advertisement it seemed like one mighty problem could be swiftly resolved. There's no doubt the family of this unfortunate teenage mum would have been relieved to pass on the burden that the infant presented to them and probably didn't make too many inquiries about what future awaited when they handed over the tiny bundle.

The baby's grandmother, Edith Ward, was told another set of lies by Louie, who claimed she'd had two children but both had died. This time, Louie posed as a hospital worker. When they met for the last time, as the baby was presented to Louie, Edith was told Louie and the baby were heading to Scotland.

Louie got custody of baby Dorothy May on Wednesday 31 March, the day of Lily's death. It was time for her to return home to show off her new daughter. To her obvious delight, she met friends as she made her way back across Leeds, who were keen to fuss over the baby. Back at Pottery Fields, her first port of call was the house of widow Leah McDermott, Arthur Calvert's sister who lived two minutes from his home. Louie arrived at about 8pm, to Mrs McDermott's great surprise.

When Louie had left the area some three weeks previously, there was no mention of a baby arriving imminently. She had told Leah she was going to Dewsbury because her daughter Annie had pneumonia. Now Louie appeared with a baby in her arms, claiming the birth had been 'sharp work'. She said her sister had given her ten shillings to return home with the baby. Louie had sent word back of the new arrival, but Mrs McDermott had burnt the telegram. Rumours had reached Mrs McDermott that her sister-in-law was in fact in Leeds all the while, but this Louie flatly denied. Louie then proceeded to her own home so that Arthur could meet the family's new addition.

The joy of the homecoming dissipated the following day with the arrival of the police. It hadn't taken long for them to realise that Louie Calvert was not a homeless pauper in Leeds as neighbours claimed, but that she actually had a Leeds address. Louie had left the letter she'd received in response to her newspaper advertise-ment, written by baby Dorothy's grandmother and addressing her by her full name, at Lily's house.

Detective Sergeant Thomas Sabey asked Louie if she knew Lily Waterhouse, and she admitted she'd been with her the previous evening. 'What is it, has she done herself in?' Louie asked. 'I wish I hadn't called there last night.' DS Sabey took Louie to Meadow Lane police station for questioning.

There's no record of the presumably bewildered response of Arthur Calvert – as a man whose life changed so dramatically, from being a new father to having a wife accused of murder, in the course of barely 24 hours. He too was taken to the police station but, due to the welter of lies told to him by his wife, he was unable to help much with the investigation.

Two days later, DS Sabey returned to the Calvert household and found cups, saucers and plates stored in a sideboard that matched the sugar bowl discovered at the Waterhouse home. He also found a decorative chocolate box that contained knives, forks, spoons and a mustard spoon, along with two whist programmes, both bearing Lily Waterhouse's name. There was a cot in the kitchen with sheets marked with Lily's initials. An unfamiliar case was also found. In his statement, DS Sabey remarked that none of the items were of great value, but Louie had clearly taken then from Lily's house, and the objects implicated her in the murder.

*

Police were soon in possession of the post-mortem results. Police surgeon Dr Hoyland Smith found a broad pressure mark measuring more than one centimetre (half an inch) in width around Lily's neck, level with her thyroid. The marks on her wrists led the surgeon to believe she had been tied up before death, with the bindings being released afterwards. There were palm-sized bruises between the shoulder blades as well as on her right shoulder, elbow and hip, along with more bruises on both legs.

On closer inspection, the surgeon found two injuries to Lily's head. Although the more serious of the two wounds was deep enough to expose the skull, it wasn't the killer blow. Rather, Lily died of asphyxiation caused by strangulation. According to Dr Hoyland Smith, there was nothing in that bare room which could have been used as a ligature to cause the mark that scarred Lily's neck. It means that the killer almost certainly used their hands. The blunt instrument used to cause the head injuries – which would most certainly have brought about concussion in the victim, rendering her senseless – was never found.

In his view, the killing had happened in the room where the body was found. Yet there were no signs of a struggle, which would have caused the bruising that covered Lily's body. 'Great force would be necessary to cause death from strangulation and I think great force had been used in this case,' he told police, although he thought that even a small woman like Louie could carry out the murder if she was standing behind a victim who had been concussed. Could Lily have been knocked out then tied up, police pondered.

Detective Superintendent Charles Pass interviewed Louie on Maundy Thursday, the day after the murder, and prior to her arrest. Louie insisted that when she had left the house at 7pm the previous night, Lily was alive and well. Having noticed her struggling to walk in boots that were too large for her, the detective questioned Louie about them. Lily had given them to her, Louie insisted, having one other pair of shoes and another pair of boots at the pawn shop. The scarf she was wearing was also a gift from Lily, she said. Louie denied any knowledge of Lily complaining about her behaviour to the police or of the existence of any appointment on the day after her death. All the items in the pawn shop were taken there with Lily's permission, she said. 'She has asked me to pledge them for money to keep going on …'

Lily was sitting eating the tea prepared by Louie before she left, she claimed. 'We parted on very good terms and she kissed me before I came away,' she told the superintendent.

It was at this point that a new dimension to the investigation arose. Just as she had mentioned the bed chair to Emily Clayton to explain the noises, Louie said she had put down the bed chair in the spare room, the cushions from which Lily's body was found on, because Lily was expecting a visitor. Louie named him as ex-soldier Fred Crabtree, who had been receiving treatment at Becketts Park Hospital, a military institution still busy treating soldiers with injuries sustained in the First World War. According to Louie's version of events, she had been drinking with Lily and Fred that Wednesday and he had brought more drink back to the house. A row broke out about who of the three were going to pair up, which led to a fight. Fred Crabtree was due to sail to Canada at the weekend, Louie said.

Instantly it sounded like another one of her tall stories. But there were two things that had been puzzling the police, even at this early stage in the investigation. Firstly, Louie was a tiny woman, shorter by several inches than Lily, who herself only measured about five feet two inches, and considerably lighter too. Did she really have the strength to kill another woman with her bare hands?

Secondly, the name Fred Crabtree was found on a piece of paper in Louie's bag, with an address that read 156 Logan Avenue, Winnipeg – obviously put there before her arrest and probably prior to Lily's death. Was Louie spinning more spurious falsehoods or was Fred Crabtree the real killer?

Police began searching for Fred Crabtree. They soon found a man of the same name living in Barnsley and working in Darton Main Colliery. He was a former soldier with the 14th Battalion Yorkshire and Lancashire Regiment who was getting treatment at Becketts Park Hospital after being shot in the right eye during the war. He received a pension of 20 shillings a week on account of his injury. He also had a sister who lived in Canada.

When questioned, Crabtree admitted visiting Leeds on Tuesday 30 March to attend an appointment at the hospital, making the 22-mile journey by train. Crabtree had lived alone in Waltham Street since the death of his mother the previous year. Still, his wasn't a hermit's existence. On his return from the hospital that Tuesday, he visited his niece Ida, went to the Spotted Leopard Inn and had supper with his housekeeper.

Then, on Wednesday 31 March he was up at 4am to prepare for his shift at the colliery, which lasted between 6am and 1pm. When he finished work, he visited his niece, after which he said he went back to his own home, where he remained for the afternoon. He was later seen there when housekeeper Ada Laws arrived at about 8pm. It seems inconceivable that he could have popped back into Leeds and then back again by train in the short window of time between the last sighting of Lily at 6.15pm and his housekeeper arriving at 8pm. He did arouse suspicion momentarily in the minds of detectives because he was sporting a facial injury. However, he explained that this was caused by a roof fall at the pit on Friday 2 April that was severe enough to end operations for the day. He told police he had never met either Lily Waterhouse or Louie Calvert.

Detectives inquired at Becketts Park Hospital, anxious that another man of the same name wasn't being overlooked. But hospital records showed that this was the only Fred Crabtree being treated there.

A letter from Winnipeg police revealed that inquiries across the Atlantic about a Fred Crabtree had drawn a blank. Although Logan Avenue was real enough – and there was a Salvation Army hostel nearby – there was no accommodation at that precise address. Immigration records, army service records and recent arrivals had been checked, without success.

Could someone else linked to the Leeds hospital have stolen his identity? In the mid-1920s the hospital, housed in a former work-house, was still treating hundreds of injured ex-servicemen. Police failed to look for fingerprint evidence in the room where Lily's body was found, although the first theft conviction won through the science of fingerprinting had been in 1902 and procedures had advanced since then. A handwritten note attached to the prosecution brief by police dated 4 May 1926 revealed that inquiries into Crabtree were not complete. The fact that no weapon was found could even imply that another person had been present, who disposed of vital evidence. But he's barely given a mention after that. The sliver of corroborating evidence found in Louie's handbag wasn't enough to persuade investigating policemen that Fred Crabtree from Barnsley was in the frame for the murder.

*

Although her story is blurred by her inventions, history still holds marginally more nailed-down details about Louie Calvert than Fred Crabtree. She was one of five children born to Annie and Smith Gomersall in Ossett, between Dewsbury and Wakefield in Yorkshire. After completing her education at 12, she became a weaver in one of the woollen mills that covered that part of the county. But she went off the rails, ending up serving a year-long borstal sentence after pleading guilty to stealing a purse, a ring and some money belonging to another mill worker, Mary Ann Carter.

Until 1902, young offenders like Louie found themselves behind bars with prisoners of all ages, experiences and dispositions. After that, the borstal system was created, with its emphasis on education and rehabilitation parallel with punishment. The experience didn't change Louie's ways, however, and afterwards she went to jail on numerous occasions, initially because she kept resorting to theft.

Police had difficulty tracking back into Louie's life, not least because she had numerous aliases. In total they discovered 11 convictions. Although the first seven charges against her – for theft, false pretences and home-breaking – were recorded in her maiden name of Louie Gomersall, one charge in 1924 of disorderly conduct appeared under the name of Edith Thompson, whose picture was in every newspaper and whose name dominated all the headlines when she was hanged for murder the previous year. Edith Thompson's story garnered enormous sympathy and became a cause célèbre. The same could not be said of Louie's public profile. For, while Edith Thompson was attractive and fashionable, Louie was hawkish and dirt poor. They were both motivated by grand passion, but while Edith's revealed itself in ardour, Louie's manifested in a violent temper.

By 1925, when the final three charges were brought, she was known to the establishment as Louie Jackson. In the space of a year, she was convicted twice on prostitution charges and once for disorderly conduct, being fined on each occasion. At times she posed as Louisa Jackson, taking the surname of a man she insisted was her husband.

Police took a clipped statement from Louie's sister Edith Birkenshaw, by now a farmer's wife in Ossett, where the family used to live. Edith was Louie's closest surviving adult relative, as both their parents were by now dead. She confirmed that Louie's daughter Annie was in fact in the Dewsbury Union Cottage Home, a workhouse, rather than the home of another sister. Although Edith and Louie's sister Hilda lived in Dewsbury, Edith confirmed that none of the three sisters were on speaking terms. She hadn't seen or heard anything from Louie for two years, except through an aunt, Mary Rayner, who earlier that year passed a letter to Edith from Louie announcing a pregnancy and the imminent arrival of a baby. Edith burned the letter.

All the information gathered by the police made it obvious that Louie should face a grilling. Given Louie's disposition, it must have been difficult for her to suppress rising rage when she was being questioned about Lily's death from 5.30pm on that Thursday until the early hours of Good Friday. She was charged with murder later that day and retorted: 'It is a lie.' She was at her Railway Terrace home when the murder happened, she insisted.

The case against Louie came speedily through the system of inquest and two police hearings. At her first appearance in the police court, the *News of the World* related what it termed 'the opening chapters in one of the most sensational murder cases of modern times'. At times, Louie appeared to relish the attention, although there was little indication she appreciated just how much trouble she was in. She became notorious at one of those hearings for changing her hat halfway through proceedings, replacing a mauve hat trimmed with flowers with a black one. In the subsequent hearing, according to newspaper reports, Mrs Calvert maintained a calm demeanour throughout the proceedings and occasionally laughed quietly at the remarks of the witnesses.

The fact that Lily's body was found without boots gained special traction at every appearance. Was it likely that any woman would give away her only pair of boots, prosecutors continually asked.

There were no impediments to stop her two-day trial opening at Leeds Assizes on 7 May 1926, in front of Mr Justice Wright, who would later become Master of the Rolls. Although she was a serial liar, the prison's medical officer wasn't unduly troubled by her behaviour. Howard Shannon wrote to the court of Louie: 'Her general behaviour and conversation has been quite rational and I have detected no indication of insanity.'

Normally, the British public would have lapped up every detail about a woman accused of murder appearing the dock. But this time a blanket of silence descended. By a quirk of timing, the trial took place during the General Strike, when the country was almost paralysed by industrial action. When 1.7 million workers downed tools on 3 May that year it wasn't only heavy industry and transport that were affected. Newspaper printers also left their posts, not least to prevent the government message about strikers being revolutionaries oft-repeated in newspaper columns getting into the wider public arena. With wireless broadcasts still in their infancy, daily papers were the only way the news travelled at the time.

The aim of the strike was to persuade the government to act on behalf of miners who were suffering wage reductions and worsening working conditions. Unions behind the industrial unrest knew the government was better placed to endure the shutdown than working people who needed their wages to survive. When middle-class volunteers stepped in to keep public transport running there was widespread recognition that the General Strike would have to end. However, by the time the workers returned to their posts on 12 May, Louie's trial was all over.

Without newspaper reports of the trial or the official transcript, which has gone missing, we are today reliant on the notes made by the judge to remind himself of essential points of interest. Much of what he heard was just as it had been initially told to the police, concerning Louie's movements both the night Lily was assumed to have died and first thing the following morning.

But there were a few other more unexpected contributions. Next-door neighbour Emily Clayton repeated in court the conversation she'd had with Louie and the noises she'd heard. It was the same story she told magistrates when the case was heard at the judicial stage prior to the Assizes. But this time there was fresh detail. Crucially, she added that she could hear a man's voice next door as she stood in her kitchen. Moreover, she said that on the previous Sunday at about 9am a man had knocked on her door asking for Mrs Waterhouse. 'He was tall, well built, said he had come from Becketts Park Hospital and was going to Canada the next month. He gave no name,' Mrs Clayton told the jury. With his cap pulled down over his face, she was unable to give a more detailed description of him.

Mrs Waterhouse spent most of her days away from home, said Mrs Clayton, although she had no idea where her neighbour went. 'I had an idea she was living an immoral life,' she said, adding that men used to leave the house in the early hours. Louie had confided in her that Lily was suffering from venereal disease, although police surgeon Dr Hoyland Smith declared this was untrue. However, mercury tablets, a long-standing remedy for syphilis, were found in the house. (Salvarsan, a more effective treatment, had been used to fight the disease for more than a decade.) He pointed out that there was a blood stain on the wall of the room in which Lily's body was found but no further smears or smudges elsewhere in the house.

Thus it seemed unlikely that she had been killed elsewhere in the house and dragged to the small room.

Detective Superintendent Pass reported Louie's insistence that Lily was fine when she last saw her. '[Lily] was all right when I left – I'll take my dying oath on that.' Then he related his conversation with Louie about Crabtree. The mysterious soldier had stayed the previous Sunday night, and came and went as he pleased at the house as he possessed his own key. Lily had asked Louie to fix the bed chair because Crabtree was expected again. 'If police raided she could say Crabtree was using the bed upstairs and she was using the bed downstairs,' Louie explained to him.

Louie came clean about 'adopting' baby Dorothy but insisted she had removed items from Lily's house the previous week, hiding the suitcase containing them in the arches of a suspension bridge. Given that many witnesses saw her with a suitcase immediately after Lily's death this immediately seemed a lie. But Pass conceded at the end of his evidence: 'Some of the things she said were true.'

Shoe repairer Thomas Mortimer testified that the boots worn by Louie to the police station did in fact belong to Lily. She had bought them some four months previously and had had them twice repaired. Mr Mortimer visited the mortuary to identify Lily as the purchaser of the boots. Waiting in the wings was Fred Crabtree, of Barnsley, ready to give his alibi. However, he wasn't called.

Defending solicitors and counsel decided against putting Louie in the stand. Working-class women like Louie who were coarse, unprepossessing and fell far short of the mark in personality and demeanour were thought to alienate juries. The expectation of women at the time was that they were caring homemakers. Anyone who didn't conform to the image provoked a generally hostile reaction.

Yet people also thought less of those who didn't take the stand to present their own defence as it almost seemed to imply guilt. It presented a quandary for solicitors, especially in capital cases. As the prosecution case pinpointed Louie's movements on the night of the murder and early the following morning, the defence had only limited means of extricating her from the scene.

Mr Justice Wright reminded the jury of what they'd heard in the prosecution case: 'You have to decide according to the best of your conscience and your judgment whether the circumstantial evidence which you have heard points with sufficient clearness to enable you to say that you are satisfied beyond all reasonable doubt that it was the prisoner who did this murder,' he said.

It was perhaps no surprise that, although there were question marks over the existence of Crabtree as Louie had described him and no sign of the weapon that was used in the attack on Lily, the jury found Louie guilty of murder and sentenced her to hang. Her instinctive response was to come up with another lie. She immediately told the court she was expecting a baby. (Down the centuries, pregnancy has been a well-worn reply to a death penalty, once dubbed 'pleading the belly'.)

A 'jury of matrons' was empanelled to examine Louie and determine whether she was indeed expecting a child. The 'matrons' – chosen because they had experience with pregnancy and childbirth – decided she was not expecting, a view with which

Dr Hoyland Smith concurred. (Two weeks later Louie began a period, a fact that appeared through a prison report sent to the government although not publicly circulated.)

When the lie about pregnancy failed her, Louie had to fall back on the scrutiny of the law. The Court of Criminal Appeal, established in 1907, had significantly improved the chances of anyone seeking to overturn a capital conviction. Prior to that date, the only grounds for appeal were on points of law. Now evidence and sentence were looked at by three judges – and Louie's counsel believed there was a chance of getting the death penalty overturned.

On 7 June, her counsel Mr E. C. Chappell contended that the evidence of Detective Superintendent Pass was not legally admissible because of the hours that Louie was subjected to questioning, contravening a long-held legal convention. She was examined and cross-examined 'to an unprecedented degree', Mr Chappell said. He also related another anomaly to the judges, the knocking sound heard by two neighbours and presumed to be Lily's muffled flailing as she fought for her life. In court, Dr Hoyland Smith said the convulsions of a woman being strangled would probably last a few minutes. But both neighbours were clear the sound they heard continued for about quarter of an hour.

The doctor also estimated time of death between 9pm and 5am, the earliest time being two hours after Louie was seen leaving the property. Although blood was found in the room, there was no sign of any weapon when one was surely used, and nothing to indicate that a struggle had taken place, with layers of dust remaining undisturbed. Louie was seen going into the house where Lily was lying dead at dawn, and she was demonstrably a liar, but that was not the same as committing murder – which should have been pointed out more forcefully to the jury, he insisted.

After Mr Chappell had spoken, the Lord Chief Justice Gordon Hewart, sitting with Justices Salter and Fraser, drew a line under the case, and did not allow an appeal. He began by questioning why Louie didn't take the stand when she was trying to prove her innocence. Louie had told one neighbour she was going to stay with Lily for three weeks. 'The jury might think that statement significant as [Louie] did stay for three weeks and at the end of that time Mrs Waterhouse was dead,' he said, implying the killing was planned. As for the criticism of Detective Superintendent Pass, Lord Hewart said the law was clear about the duty of the police and there was nothing to suggest that he went beyond what was reasonably expected of him.

The judge's summing-up was a clear statement, he went on, and the jury made their decision after hearing 'very cogent evidence'. For those reasons, the application for leave to appeal was turned down. Listening in the London courtroom, Louie wore an outfit of funereal black and stood throughout. Her face was pale as her fate was sealed.

*

On 12 June, Louie requested an exercise book in order to write her life history. She had stayed silent at her own trial and, thanks to the General Strike, any public conversation about her was kept to a minimum. Here she saw a chance to make her voice heard in the public domain, to speak on her own terms. Prison authorities tended to be generous when it came to prisoners with limited life expectancy and issued her with a buff-coloured book in which to record her thoughts. Over 29 pages, Louie describes in curious monotone how her 33 years had unfolded. Whatever her hopes to the contrary, prison authorities had no intention of circulating her words. What they anticipated was a piece of confessional writing, though it wasn't the candid disclosure to Lily's killing for which they'd hoped. Part of the narrative, however, turned into an admission of a second murder that had until now gone under the radar.

The revelation was buried inside the book, in a matter-of-fact way, and police investigations soon showed it was probably true. But investigations were not able to substantiate everything Louie said in her book, the only insight we have into her life prior to Lily's death. For example, there's no sign among official records of a marriage she describes around the outbreak of war. Indeed, when she later married Arthur Calvert she is described on the certificate as a spinster. But a century on, absence of evidence isn't perhaps the sole consideration. While the exercise book gives only limited understanding on why she chose a life of crime, it does lift a veil on a woman apparently capable of killing another for no obvious gain.

She begins her story with some verses of the kind that people once wrote on request in autograph books. Collecting autographs, not necessarily from celebrities but also friends and family, became popular in Edwardian times. Two of them seem particularly relevant, the first widely attributed to American writer and historian James Truslow:

There is so much good in the worst of us,
There is so much bad in the best of us,
That it ill becomes any of us,
To find fault with the rest of us.

The second is unattributed:

Live on what you have,
Live if you can on less,
Do not borrow either for vanity or pleasure,
For vanity ends in shame and pleasure leaves pain.

Louie describes her parents, Smith and Annie Gomersall, as 'humble'. Although the family lived in a mining community, Smith was a weaver. There's no attempt to blame her current difficulties on her childhood and when she speaks of her schooling it's with affection. She went to a Church of England 'Council School' between the ages of three and twelve. 'I had a very good school mistress and she taught me everything that was beneficial for me and at home I was taught as a little child to say my prayers at my mother's knee.'

She describes how her father read prayers and passages from the Bible both morning and night and how older sisters Hilda and Edith and younger brother Harold attended Sunday school. 'I was quite happy and contented with my surrounds and Mother never knew a moment's worry from any of us.'

Aged 12, she went to work at a blouse factory as a finisher, trimming off threads and sewing on buttons. After two years she followed her eldest sister into a mill and learned how to become a weaver. She was, she said, a quick learner and could operate a loom by herself within a fortnight of starting. Her first piece of work was a carriage rug, with nine different colours in it, made with five shuttles operating simultaneously.

For every 22 rugs produced, she would be paid 14 shillings. Thanks to her dexterity she could produce twice as many as that in a week and take home 28 shillings, which she gave to her mother. In return, she was given a single shilling as spending money.

Life was undoubtedly hard. She started work at 6am and had to walk for an hour over fields to reach the factory. At the end of a 12-hour shift she walked home again. Still, for six months she received no fines for lateness.

Then her eldest sister Hilda married and left home and, according to Louie, 'All my troubles began.' She said her sister continually bunked off work after her marriage and ducked out of the factory altogether, in the company of another married woman. While she was away, she expected Louie to keep her loom working.

'I did it at first but I soon got fed up with her always going out and I let her loom stand,' Louie says. As a result, her sister's output halved with the resulting fall in pay. Yet apparently it wasn't the errant sister who paid the price. At home Louie was blamed for taking her sister's wages, resulting in a thrashing from her mother. A resentful Louie was then sent to bed without any tea, despite her protests that no one at the factory was able to collect another person's wages without the presence of a doctor's note. 'It got to be a regular thing week after week so I ran away from home and told

Mother if she wanted any wages from me she would have to fetch them as I was not coming home any more,' she writes.

When Louie didn't come home that first Friday with her wages, her mother visited the factory on Saturday. She was shown the wages book that, Louie claimed, proved what had happened. This apparently fuelled her sister's ire and it seemed that she began tampering with Louie's loom. Louie was then allegedly framed for the theft of a sovereign from someone else's wage packet, which was recovered from the bottom of her bag. It was her sister's working partner who suggested the searchers might find it there. Louie was arrested and charged with theft. She spent three months in Armley jail, Leeds, before being sentenced to two years at a borstal. Eventually she was transferred to Holloway in London.

At first she appears to have revelled in the routine, clearing her cell out first thing in the morning before having breakfast and beginning to make dresses in the prison workroom. At 11am the prisoners changed into light clothing before doing an hour-long drill. This was followed by lunch (which Louie called dinner) and an exercise session, then she resumed sewing in the workroom until tea time. On three weekday evenings there was chapel followed by an hour of schooling.

Then Louie was assigned to the laundry and found herself doing tasks that she didn't enjoy. In her words: 'One day I was that fed up with [the officers] saying "do this, do that" I burnt some very delicate work with a red hot iron.' She was reported and punished, but not before she and three other girls 'had a real smash up' – presumably wrecking the laundry.

Louie was put into a straitjacket after striking a prison officer, then taken to the punishment cells, where she endured some wide-ranging retribution. First, she was put on a bread-and-water diet for three days followed by a week of close confinement inside a bare cell. She wasn't allowed to write letters home for two months and she also lost remission that would have shortened her sentence. It wasn't just her spirits that were depleted by the punishment regime but also her health. She caught pneumonia and was sent to the prison hospital. The experience was, she insisted, a sufficient deterrent to ever incurring the wrath of the prison authorities again.

When she recovered she was assigned to the farm and soon got 'brown as a berry' digging the prison plot. After her release, her mother said it looked as if she had been in a convalescent home at the seaside for a month, rather than in jail.

She went into service at Bramley, near Leeds, with only the benefit of a box of clothes given to her when she left the institution and a rule book to govern her behaviour. Each week, she had to report to the local police station. For three weeks she worked hard, attending church on Sunday. Then, she says, her 'daring spirit', rose up to envelop her once again.

'I robbed my employer of £50 and ran away to Blackpool where I had a good time and enjoyed myself for a month on the proceeds,' she writes. In modern times, the sum she stole equates to about £2,000, so it gave her considerable spending power. Most people would have been tempted to go on the run to escape justice. Yet afterwards she returned to Bramley to face the music. It seems she wasn't charged with theft this time but was sent back to borstal to complete her sentence and eventually returned to her parents again.

There followed a six-month spell working in a mill when she 'went straight', which ended when she was sacked after her boss was told she had been in jail. When other attempts to get a mill job failed because of her record, she ran away from home again and stole to support herself. As a result she went back to prison with a three-month sentence, this time with hard labour rather than any prospects of education.

'This was in the beginning of [the First World War] and we had to work hard in those days in the prison, making mailbags for the soldiers,' she writes. After release, her next job was as a ward maid in Leeds Infirmary, which she held throughout the war years, apparently without getting into difficulties with the law.

The account of her life from here isn't borne out by traceable records. She left the hospital job, she explains, to marry an army officer, Jim Jackson, who was subsequently sent to France. 'He was a good lad to me,' she says, admitting the couple lived on a generous wage. It's about this time that she gave birth to daughter Annie so he is presumed to be the father. Yet, by her own admission, neither marriage nor motherhood could change her ways. 'The love of daring and adventure was in me and I had not told my husband that I had been inside a prison. When he had been away in France about four months I got into trouble again and this time it was a hard sentence for me because I was confined whilst doing my sentence [away] from my little girl.'

It's not known whether she's referring to a three-month sentence she received at a Leeds court in March 1917 for stealing a dress or the one-month spell handed down to her in October that year at Bradford for taking a watch.

What she termed a 'daring and adventurous' streak might seem to others to be more of a perpetual impulse to self-destruct. Once again she was sent back to prison, dropping out of her husband's life for a while as she was too afraid to tell him where she was and why. 'You would have thought that this would have made me different but no, I had gone past that and prison did not bother me,' she writes.

In fact, her heart was so hardened that when she was released she abandoned daughter Annie with her mother. She told her mum she had a good job and would pay for her daughter's keep. After moving to Bradford, she did indeed get a reasonably well-paid job in the Osborne Hotel as a waitress and she lived in luxury, according to the notes in the exercise book. Although she sent one pound to her mother weekly, she didn't return home to visit. 'Once or twice I would write and ask how my baby was going on but that was all. I never bothered about her,' she says. It is this searing honesty that adds credence to the whole of her account.

After another spell in prison, she found a home near her mother and settled in just prior to a three-month home leave for husband Jim. As it turned out, it was his last. When he returned to a posting in India he was killed in an accident exactly one week before the birth of their son Kenneth.

When Kenneth was three months old, Louie was sent back to prison and her baby to a workhouse. More shockingly still, she discovered she was not Jim's widow as they were not legally married.

The wedding that she claims had taken place was invalid because Jim already had a wife. These twin blows apparently tipped her into some manner of mental-health crisis. 'I did not care whether I came out of prison dead or alive,' she writes. 'The doctor was very good to me. He got me to go to the workhouse to my boy but I only stopped there a fortnight. I would sooner have done six months over again [in prison] than be in the Union.'

She persuaded the workhouse medical staff to let her out of its doors, in order to find work and a home for herself and her baby. She spent a night covertly sleeping on an industrial canal boat with two other homeless women before the trio headed to a nearby fairground in the hope of getting some money. The other two were quickly arrested as pickpockets and received another three months behind bars. But Louie was diverted by the sound of the Salvation Army band and the tuneful hymn singing of one of its officers.

According to Louie, she was held spellbound then reduced to tears by an unseen force, which, she thought afterwards, must have been the work of God. A female officer comforted her as, tired, hungry and stressed, Louie wept. She then recalls a random act of kindness that changed the course of her life for a while at least, as she resolved to mend her ways. The woman whose singing had transfixed Louie ended up taking her home, where she provided her with a hearty tea and washing facilities before giving Louie a ten-shilling note and an address where she could find a bed for the night. It began an association with the Salvation Army – begun by William and Catherine Booth in East London in 1865 when they began a mission of 'soup, soap and salvation for the poor' – that lasted for a year at least.

Under its good influences, Louie got a housekeeping job with a widower who was happy to be joined by both her and baby Kenneth. 'The man was very good to us both and we always had plenty of good food and clothes to carry on with,' she says. It seemed that Louie finally had a chance to leave her headstrong waywardness in her past and bring stability to the life of little Kenneth. But the household harmony wasn't destined to last.

The body of John William Frobisher was found floating in the Leeds and Liverpool Canal by a policeman on 12 July 1922. He had suffered a severe head injury that left him with a fractured skull and, bizarrely, he wasn't wearing boots.

At his inquest, a Louisa Jackson came forward, explaining that she had been Frobisher's housekeeper. Neighbours corroborated her story, having often seen her in the street in a Salvation Army uniform. She explained the absence of boots in the house by saying she had pawned them, receiving three shillings and sixpence. Despite this jarring account and the strange circumstances in which his body was found, some 185 metres (200 yards) from his home in Mercy Street, the police mounted no further investigations and the cause of death was found to be drowning.

The housekeeper was, of course, Louie, using one of her aliases. It was only four years later, when she filled the pages of her exercise book with small handwriting, that the truth came to light. One night, according to Louie, Frobisher had come home drunk and used bad language in front of her son. When she told him to stop, he struck her. 'I started fighting back and struck him a foul blow which caused him to fall down the cellar steps and break his neck,' she wrote, with a calm clarity that gives no hint about her feelings.

Afterwards, she went back to Frobisher's house and lived there as if it were her own, though she was nearly rumbled by the arrival of his sister Sarah Ann Healey. When Healey asked where her brother was, Louie replied that he hadn't been home for a fortnight, then she produced a folded newspaper from a drawer containing a report of the drowning and said: 'What do you think about this?'

Together they went to the police and Louie was duly summoned to the inquest, which was taking place two days later on 21 July. She was given a dressing down by the coroner for not reporting Frobisher's disappearance sooner. But she had an instant answer for the disparity. He had gone out to seek work with a pound note in his pocket, promising to write when he had secured a job. That made the absence of his boots more mystifying still. When Healey later asked about them, Louie replied that he had left home without them. But still the inquest decided Frobisher had died from drowning.

Although the government was alerted to the confession contained in the notebook, it was decided not to take any further action against her. Thus no more details of the incident emerged. But the exercise book also contained descriptions of the night of Lily's death that varied from those that came out in court. Louie described why she left Railway Terrace – not to obtain a child but because she was weary of the way she and Arty were living, with her husband jobless, drinking and fighting. 'We have lived sometimes on the [Poor Law] Guardians and when we did not get any money from them I had to go out and get the money, fair means if I could and if not by foul,' she said.

She describes her time with Lily in stark terms. 'We used to go out at night and visit the public houses with the intention of [getting hold of] any men who had money and get them drunk, then rob them of whatever money they had left.' But they had become known to the police, so Louie decided to return home to her husband.

On the Sunday prior to her death, Lily brought home someone Louie believed to be an ex-soldier from Becketts Park Hospital called Fred Crabtree. On the Wednesday she died, according to Louie, all three of them went out for drinks before returning to Amberley Road with half a dozen bottles of beer and stout. 'Oh the drink, it is the ruination of everything, for we do lots of things in drink and temper that we are most sorry for after.'

Yet this was not a confession to murder. According to Louie, there was an argument that escalated when Lily lashed out at Fred Crabtree with her fists. The pair ended up rolling around on the floor, hitting one another. Louie claimed that she picked up a poker, the nearest thing to hand, to clout Crabtree so he would stop his attack on Lily, but he dodged out of the way and she landed the blow on Lily instead. According to Louie, 'She fell dead at our feet.'

By any stretch of the imagination, the next part of her story sounds far-fetched.

'He went mad then and got hold of her belt, strangled her and carried her upstairs. I got out and got home. God knows how I did it, I don't, but I managed to be all right and sane enough when I got there and my husband was glad to see me.'

For the first time she then mentions the baby, but she doesn't write about returning to Lily's house in the early hours of Thursday morning, then getting on a tram and speaking to Elizabeth Lumb. She claims she spent the day doing laundry before the arrival of the detectives at her home.

Dedicating the exercise book to the matron at Manchester's Strangeways Prison, Louie writes warmly of her treatment there. 'Whatever I have asked for I have been allowed to have in reason and the utmost kindness has been shown all round from the officers and all who have been in authority over me. The chaplain has been very good to me and attended well to my spiritual welfare and quite prepared me for whatever happens. Now I am waiting patiently for my reprieve if it is going to come and, if not, well God's will be done. I am ready to die.'

She said that what she had written in the exercise book was 'every bit true'. Alas, those who were told of its content at the Home Office were unconvinced. Louie addressed a lengthy and personal appeal to the Home Secretary, Sir William Joynson-Hicks, and, in papers kept at the National Archive for almost a century, the Home Secretary's response is revealed.

He asked the trial judge for a view and Mr Justice Wright had no hesitation in supporting the original verdict: 'The prisoner is a bad character, although the woman she murdered was also a prostitute, she seems to have befriended the prisoner with the result that the prisoner robbed her while she was alive then deliberately murdered her for the sake of robbing the rest of her small possessions.'

While the Home Secretary found the exercise book compelling, he declared that, although he was always reluctant to recommend capital punishment for women, he could find no extenuating circumstances to beckon him towards a reprieve. The theft and the killing were carried out 'with great deliberation', he said and he was settled on letting the punishment go ahead.

Yet there were issues that seemed to suggest some reasonable doubt regarding the verdict. No heed was given to a lack of motive. Louie had served time behind bars for theft before and the sentence held few fears for her. It seems unlikely she would become a killer in order to avoid a jail sentence. No forensic evidence pinned her to the murder, although Louie herself agreed that she was at the scene.

*

In 1926, there were 17 hangings carried out in England, with Louie being the sole female offender dealt with at the gallows. This compares to a murder total of 297 in England and Wales that year, down from 318 in 1925. These statistics immediately show how the chances of being hanged were low at this point, even for murder.

The reaction to the impending death sentence was a mark of how attitudes towards capital punishment, particularly for women, had changed. There was petition gathered in Manchester containing an estimated 3,000 names, which was spread around among significant government figures and also sent to Queen Mary, the wife of King George V. It read: 'We feel that in this 20th century after Christ's birth civilized men and women should not be called upon to suffer the awful indignity of the deliberate killing of a woman.'

There were also individual approaches, like the one from solicitor W. J. Wenham, who wrote an outraged letter to the government, protesting about the punishment. He expressed the 'amazement and indignation' that many in the heart of London's legal world were feeling at the absence of a reprieve and the political associa-tion of a 'ropes for women' policy, a perversion of the Suffragettes' motto and used by campaigners to halt female hangings, so recently renewed with the case of Edith Thompson.

'This letter is not stimulated by a sense of sympathy for the wretched criminal who will die tomorrow, but by a sense of what is in human decency due to those upon the electoral roll,' he said. All were then inadvertently caught up with this 'retrogres-sion into brutality'. He branded Thompson's execution as 'the blackest stain' upon a Conservative administration and pledged never to vote for the party again until hanging women had been abolished by law.

Only three women had been hanged in 20 years in England and Wales. And in that time, seven hangings involving women had been stopped. Nonetheless, by 22 June 1926, when it had become clear that she would not win a reprieve and that the king was not going to exercise royal prerogative, Louie became resigned to her fate. In a letter to her sister-in-law Leah McDermott she wrote: 'It may not always be dark for you. Hope for the best and trust in God. Do not worry over me as I am quite all right. I only want to see my sonny once more, to kiss him goodbye. Then I am satisfied.

'Tell Kenneth to be a good boy and then he will see his mother again in heaven. Tell him I am watching over him.'

Her son Kenneth was taken to Strangeways jail on the day before the execution by her husband and his sister. 'I've had a long ride in the train to see my mummy,' six-year-old Kenneth announced triumphantly to waiting reporters when he arrived.

Mrs McDermott described the moving reunion between mother and son: '[Louie] was just lovely. As soon as she saw her boy Kenneth she smiled and threw out her arms towards him. Drawing the youngster to her breast she smothered him with kisses. For quite a while she held her boy on her knee and chattered with him, answering his little questions quite cheerily. When he asked, "When are you coming home mummy?" she just kissed him on the lips and exclaimed, "Soon, my boy!"'

Mrs McDermott added that Mrs Calvert showed no signs whatever of breaking down under the strain and when asked to make a clean breast of her crime she once again firmly protested her innocence, saying: 'I haven't done it.'

The hanging was scheduled for 9am on Thursday 24 June, with Louie only the second woman to be hanged at Strangeways, after triple poisoner Mary Ann Britland went to the gallows there in 1886. While she waited for her final, short journey to begin, she resided in a specially built condemned cell, barely a stone's throw from the jail's permanent but concealed gallows. When the hanging party arrived at her cell door, just a minute before the appointed hour, the noose was revealed to her when the cell wardrobe was pushed to one side, to reveal a hidden route. Her executioner was Thomas Pierrepoint, the senior figure in a dynasty of hangmen.

Louie walked calmly and deliberately from cell to scaffold. There was no glimpse of that notorious temper as her limbs were pinioned and everyone in attendance paid tribute to her remarkable fortitude. After the trapdoor was released, the prison bell began to toll, informing the crowd of about 500 gathered outside that the sentence had been carried out. Still, people surged forward when two official notices were pinned on the prison gate: one to confirm that the hanging had been carried out and another by the prison doctor certifying that Louie was dead. At the same time, a service was held at St Jude's Church nearby, with pews packed by working people who were largely distraught by what was taking place.

After her hanging, newspaper reports portrayed two sides to Louie Calvert. The *News of the World* dubbed her 'the woman in black' because of the clothing she wore during her trial and related her 'taciturn and sulky' disposition: 'When standing her trial for murder her shifting black eyes were a psychological study. She seemed callous and indifferent and her hard, shot-featured face was the face of a wicked woman.'

But Leah McDermott's published testimony helped to balance the picture. 'She was the bravest women I have known,' she told reporters. She further outlined Louie's stoicism in one newspaper: 'She does not look like a woman who is to be hanged. She is bright and cheerful. I fully expected she would break down while we were with her but she behaved bravely. She looks well and seems to be much stouter than when I last saw her a few weeks ago. She takes a lively interest in life generally and seems totally unaffected by her position. She speaks well of the treatment given her by the prison officials and says she is having a quart of milk a day in addition to the ordinary rations.'

Even as she was hanged, there was still talk of a possible pregnancy that particularly exercised some MPs who were opposed to capital punishment. The inquest following her death conclusively gave lie to this rumour.

*

In 2019, a bunch of white and lilac flowers stood tall by a modest gravestone with no name. Instead, there was a number, C2710, and the words 'Rest in Peace'. Beneath it were Louie Calvert's ashes, alongside those of other convicted killers hanged at Strangeways Prison. Initially, Louie's body had been buried in an unmarked grave in the grounds of the jail. Building works carried out at the prison in 1991 led to her remains being exhumed and cremated at Blackley Crematorium in Manchester, with 62 others. At the time, not all the bodies could be identified, but that's not why those interred there are not named. The brutal anonymity is an extension of the punishment of those who've already suffered the ultimate sanction.

After the blooms had been placed in a weather-worn vase, two of Louie's relatives stood in silent tribute. Ninety years after her death, someone was at last visiting her final resting place. It was an emotional moment for siblings Sue Holt and Mick Walton. When she started investigating her family tree a decade ago, Sue made the shocking discovery that their great-aunt Louie was a convicted murderer. Louie's death – indeed, her very existence – had been brushed under the carpet by a family burdened with shame.

Now Sue and Mick were confronted with a dilemma. Was their delinquent relative wrongly convicted of a terrible crime and did she endure an agonising stay penned behind bars, marking off each hour as she waited for her unnatural end? Until that point, she was surely one of her era's overlooked women at the fringes of society, whose bad decisions took her down a path to criminality. Did she feel crime was her only real choice? Or was she a killer?

Louie was no stranger to telling lies. Untruths fell easily from her lips, creating for her a richer, more palatable lifestyle, if only momentarily in her own head. According to Louie, she had watched, terrified, as her landlady was strangled. Although there was only circumstantial evidence against her, jury and judge chose to jettison her protestations of innocence, deciding to believe she had toppled too easily from a life of petty crime into being a cold-blooded murderer. So had she cried wolf too often, leaving everyone convinced she was an abject liar when in reality she was every bit as much of a victim as Lily?

*

Only one picture of Louie exists, revealing that, although small, she had heavy features with bovine eyes, full cheeks and a thrusting lower lip. Her lips met in a thin line, disguising the fact she had already lost all her teeth. The darkly sullen expression of the photograph could be interpreted as that of an arch villain or of a victim cornered, sensing the weight of the establishment being brought to bear.

To get more of a sense of the woman and the unfolding events surrounding her life and death, Sue and Mick visited Amberley Road, now substantially redeveloped, and wondered, could one of their ancestors have killed here? They stood in the gateway of Strangeways Prison, looked up at its stark façade and pondered how a prisoner might feel going through the entry arch, some having seen liberty for the last time.

Reading newspaper accounts of her final meeting with son Kenneth was emotional for Mick and especially for Sue, who is herself a mother. But it would take more than empathy to disperse the dark clouds of suspicion that had gathered around this condemned woman. That Louie was wearing the dead woman's boots when she was taken to the police station casts serious doubt over her claims of innocence, both agreed.

To help put Louie's trial into context, criminologist Professor Helena Johnston told them that a string of previous convictions and two illegitimate children would have cast Louie as fitting the criminal stereotype of the era. 'Undoubtedly, that would have shaped how people viewed her in the trial in the courtroom and outside the court as well,' Professor Johnston said. She would have been considered devious and cunning, although it's important to bear in mind that Louie didn't have a single conviction for violence in her past, she added.

Mick was horrified to hear one of his extended family members being described by the judge in her trial as 'a low type'. 'She was a human being and she wasn't being treated like that, it was awful,' he said. With Sue, he remained baffled about the motive for Lily Waterhouse's killing. Louie had stolen on numerous occasions before and stepped up to face the consequences. Being a thief is not the same as being a killer.

The same issue was perplexing Jeremy, who was concerned that the complaint against Louie by Lily was taken by the police and prosecution for a motive. It was possible, he said, that they were 'barking up the wrong tree'.

In order to put Louie's own account of Lily's death to the test, Jeremy and Sasha met with forensic scientist Dr Jen Guest in a scale reconstruction of the downstairs room of the cramped terraced house where the killing took place. It's where Louie claimed to have brandished a poker and mistakenly hit Lily who was being attacked by Fred Crabtree. At the time, police found Lily's blood soaked into the upstairs mattress in the room where she was found. There were no apparent signs of blood elsewhere. Dr Guest admitted she would have expected to see more blood in the downstairs room and on the stairwell if Lily had fallen to the floor there and her body had later been moved, as Louie insisted it had. It was persuasive evidence for Sasha, who said Louie's version was 'completely unsupported by scientific evidence in this case'.

(To counter this, it's worth remembering that police at the time had a different set of concerns. They noticed that Lily's body was covered in bruises, as if from a fight, yet there was little sign of disturbance in the upstairs room where she was found – so little that no fingerprints were evident.)

If the story about what happened to Lily was made up, how much of the rest of the handwritten life story produced by Louie when she was behind bars, counting down to execution day, can be believed?

Clinical psychologist Dr Roberta Babb was called in by Sasha and Jeremy to find out more about the mind of the mysterious Louie.

She couldn't be sure whether the pages of the exercise book were furnished with the truth but said she thought that Louie wanted people to know who she was. '[The case] wasn't widely reported in the press,' Dr Babb explained, so little would ever be known about her life prior to Lily's death without the life story.

Naturally, both Jeremy and Sasha wanted to know whether the cogent and plausible words written by a woman who was faced with the premature end of her life were in fact a tissue of lies. It was a question that Dr Babb couldn't answer. 'We already know that Louie has lied before to get herself out of a tight spot,' observed Dr Babb. But despite that, she felt it had the feel of an authentic piece of work, written by someone who had accepted the severity of their actions.

This expert view was guarded and the lawyers were still left to decide whether the life story was written to trigger sympathy or offered real insight into what went on in Amberley Road on the night of Lily's death.

For Jeremy, there was another legal question to consider. After Louie failed to give evidence at her trial, did the judge deal with the issue fully and fairly in his summing-up? Today no one knows why Louie didn't take the stand, but the decision should not have presupposed her guilt, he said.

While Sasha was prepared to give that notion a fair hearing, she was already calling it 'a strong circumstantial case'. 'The fact that Louie Calvert was a woman who had fallen on hard times, who one might otherwise been very sympathetic to, does not alter the fact that she may also have committed murder,' she said.

Before Judge Radford, Jeremy gave the defence case first, pointing out that Dr Jen Guest did not dismiss out of hand the idea that Lily Waterhouse was killed downstairs, as Louie claimed in her belatedly given account of what went on. Indeed, if this was the case, she was not part of joint enterprise in the crime – this was murder by a different hand. More crucial still were flaws he identified in the judge's summing-up at the end of the trial.

Although the judge at the time had an obligation to give a balanced summing-up, he told the jury that 'the defendant has not thought fit to give evidence'. That was, said Jeremy, pejorative and unfair, and thus critical to the outcome of the trial.

Sasha reiterated the prosecution's case. Judge Radford heard that Louie had a motive to kill or at least badly frighten Lily when she discovered the police were getting involved following accusations of theft. Dr Guest had indicated the head wound – so severe it had cut through flesh to reach the skull – was bleeding profusely, said Sasha, yet there was no evidence of blood anywhere but in the bedroom. It was possible but unlikely that the fracas happened downstairs, as Louie claimed in her exercise book. 'The entire life story has to be set in the context that Louie Calvert was a consummate liar. The jury might very well have been slow to believe a word she said. Had this life story been advanced [in court or during an appeal] it is unlikely to have had any effect on the verdict of this case,' she told Judge Radford.

When it came to giving his thoughts, Judge Radford said that he found Dr Guest's evidence that she would have expected to see some blood downstairs and in the stairwell if the deceased had been moved persuasive. Meanwhile, Louie's credibility was very low, he said. Although there was some reference in an early police interview to Fred Crabtree, there was no proven involvement. While acknowledging her difficult background, Judge Radford said she had 'considerable motive' to carry out this violent attack. 'She was seen at the scene both on 31 March and 1 April, when she was stealing property of the person who was killed. She wanted to avoid being prosecuted for having done so in the past,' said the judge.

He had fully reviewed the summing-up given by the judge when Louie's trial ended. Trial judges at the time were permitted to comment in moderation, he explained, and he could find nothing 'improper' in what had been said. He ended by saying he'd seen no new material or fresh examination of the evidence yielded at the time that would lead anyone to sensibly conclude the original verdict was unsafe.

It wasn't the result Louie's great-niece and nephew, Sue and Mick, had hoped for. However, there are two sides to every story, Sue insisted, and for the first time Louie was better understood. While Louie's name had not been cleared, there was now at least insight into the life of a woman who fell at life's hurdles and empathy for her subsequent plight.

A CASE OF WICKED AFFECTION, PART 2

CHARLOTTE BRYANT

In the gathering gloom of an exceptionally cold and foggy December day, Frederick Bryant began writhing in pain. But the chill of the air inside and out of the rundown labourer's cottage was forgotten as the farm hand clutched his stomach and complained of 'a red-hot poker' thrashing about inside him. His breaths were laboured and his voice was hoarse.

It wasn't the first time Frederick had suffered from crippling acid pangs like these. Earlier that month and twice before in the same year he had been stricken by violent cramps that were diagnosed by visiting doctors as gastroenteritis. The conclusion that gastroenteritis was the cause of Frederick's volley of sudden illnesses was unsurprising, given the lack of refrigeration and food hygiene that prevailed in kitchens across the country. This time, though, nearly senseless with suffering, it was clear his case was critical. It was 1935, a dozen years before the National Health Service was established, bringing free treatment to all. Despite his lack of means, Frederick was finally taken from his dilapidated home in Coombe to the nearby Yeatman Hospital in Sherborne, Dorset. He died the following day, 23 December.

Dr Thomas McCarthy, a white-haired Irishman from County Cork who'd made Dorset his home decades earlier, was surprised at Frederick's sudden death. He'd had a nagging doubt about the man's violent illness the previous May. Gastroenteritis manifests symptoms similar to those of a hefty dose of the poison arsenic. There's intense gut pain, dizziness, bloody vomiting and a burning sensation through the body's core. Dr McCarthy was aware that arsenic was well known as the supposed weapon of choice for numerous female murderers, and he understood that Frederick's marriage was not a happy one. Now poisoning was at the forefront of his thinking.

After two hours' consideration, Dr McCarthy refused to issue a death certificate and asked a coroner to intervene.

Frederick's body was committed to an unmarked pauper's grave in Sherborne cemetery on 27 December 1935, with his wife in a widow's veil looking on, alongside his mother and siblings. There was a weighty silence between them all. By then, many of his internal organs had been removed for the purposes of a post-mortem and were speeding their way in two jars and a biscuit tin towards London for tests to be carried out by Home Office pathologist Dr Gerald Roche Lynch. They revealed much higher than expected levels of arsenic in the dead man's system. Armed with this information, police began an investigation, and six weeks later went to Sturminster Newton workhouse to arrest Frederick's wife Charlotte. Despite her denials she was charged with murder.

Charlotte's five children were taken into care. Two eventually faced her across a hushed courtroom, giving evidence that would help seal her fate. The shame of having a renowned murderess as a mother cast long shadows over their lives, while any memories of living with a loving mother ended abruptly here.

*

Charlotte Bryant was born in Waterside, Londonderry, on Valentine's Day in 1903, in the city's workhouse. Her illegitimacy was a matter of considerable and enduring shame to mother Sarah Reid, although she married Charlotte's father, carpenter John McHugh, three years later.

According to police, Charlotte was 'a headstrong, giddy girl who paid no heed or attention to the advice of her parents'. She didn't attend school, and ran wild and barefoot through the streets. In polite parlance, Charlotte – or Lottie, as she was better known – grew into something of a forces' sweetheart among the British soldiers based there at the time. Lottie had acquired a taste for alcohol and relished an active sex life.

Many, like Frederick, were First World War veterans who had been dispatched to fight during the Irish War of Independence, which started in 1919 and ended by treaty in 1921. That conflict was hotly followed by the Irish Civil War, with the newly formed government in the south fending off the Irish Republican Army, which wanted the treaty ripped up in favour of a united Ireland. British soldiers remained in the newly created province of Northern Ireland. The atmosphere was brittle.

This mattered little to Lottie, who, by all accounts, became distracted by the soldiers based at the Erbington Barracks on the east bank of the River Foyle without considering too deeply which side of the divide in the recent conflict they were placed. The eldest of four sisters born to the McHughs, raven-haired, full-lipped Lottie actively sought out the company and the favours of these smart, uniformed young men. In turn, they dubbed her 'Darkie' for her classically Celtic looks. One of the young soldiers who found himself captivated was Frederick. It's impossible to know if he was aware of other flirtations or whether he felt he was the sole object of her affections.

But Lottie was a Catholic and the rule of law on the streets where she lived was imposed not by the incumbent British authorities but by the IRA, whose commanders were enraged by her behaviour. They threatened to tar and feather her, a well-known retribution reserved for women who contravened the social code by fraternising with the British. Victims were snatched from their homes and usually tied to a lamppost in the street. Once they were immobilised their head was shaved and, together with their upper bodies, smothered in 'tar' – or a less dangerous equivalent, usually paint – onto which bags of white bird feathers were emptied.

The exercise in mob brutality acted not only as a punishment but also as a deterrent, warning other women of the dire consequences of consorting with soldiers. Even the sinister threat whispered in the community was enough to instil terrible fear in women like Lottie. She knew her best option was to escape the cloistered atmosphere of Northern Ireland as swiftly as possible. There was one time-honoured way of ensuring this came to pass.

With the end of his posting in sight, Lottie told Frederick she was expecting his child. Frederick was concerned enough to write to his mother, Arundell, who advised him that – if he was sure she was telling the truth – he should bring the woman home with him after he was discharged. When Frederick finished his tour, Lottie accompanied him back to England, although there's no evidence that she was pregnant. They married on 5 October 1922 at the picturesque fifteenth-century church of St Andrew's in the village of Mells, Somerset. If the church was an early introduction to life in Britain, then Lottie's heart must have soared. It had all the grace, elegance and refinement that chimes with English country living, and it was this existence that Lottie dreamt about. Inside the church when they wed was a newly installed monument dedicated to Edward Horner, who had died in the First World War after being shot by a sniper in France. Designed by Sir Edwin Lutyens, the man responsible for the Cenotaph in Whitehall, and sculpted by famous war artist Alfred Munnings, it is a striking memorial to the 29-year-old heir to the stately Mells Manor. Horner died of wounds in 1917, the year after his brother-in-law Raymond Asquith – son of the British prime minister Herbert Asquith – perished in France. A memorial to Asquith, also designed by Lutyens, is in the same church. Before the war both men had been part of a dazzling social set known as the Coterie, which indulged in wild parties fuelled by gambling, champagne, and drugs that included sniffing chloroform. Frederick had experienced the same war as Edward Horner and Raymond Asquith, but in vastly different circumstances.

The 1911 census illuminates his humble beginnings. At the age of 13, Frederick was assisting with cattle on a farm, working alongside his father. At the outbreak of war, he joined the 2nd Dorset Regiment and went to France before his nineteenth birthday. He spent some time in the trenches before moving around the globe at the behest of the British Army, visiting parts of the world he had only previously seen coloured in Imperial pink on a classroom map. After France he served in Mesopotamia and was in India when the war ended. He spent a short spell in Africa before heading home. Then he re-enlisted before his tour of duty in Ireland.

One legacy of this exotic overseas service was occasional bouts of malaria. According to his medical history, he also suffered 'a touch of stomach trouble from a whiff of gas on the Somme'. He'd had a foot injury and a hernia during the war years, making a good recovery from both.

For her part, Lottie had similar appetites to those young women in the notorious Coterie, in that she had a taste for alcohol and relished an active sex life. Her good looks had been widely acknowledged when she was at home in Northern Ireland and she used them to her best advantage, dreaming of a better future. But the rural existence she came to experience was a world away from that known by the chic, willowy socialites who frequented nearby country houses, secreted behind tall iron gates and high walls. With Lottie, Frederick had headed back to the mellow southern counties he knew as home, finding work relatively plentiful on the Somerset and Dorset border.

Lottie and Frederick's first son arrived in September 1923, 11 months after the wedding, and was christened Ernest Samuel. Four more children followed in total, although there was speculation as to whether Frederick had fathered them all.

Lottie found it difficult to settle into village life. The couple were compelled to move from one place after she was accused of stealing bread, and from another when she assaulted a neighbour. The woman claimed she had been knocked out cold by Lottie, having complained to Frederick about how she beat the children. Believing she had killed the woman, Lottie initially locked herself inside the farmhouse cottage they were occupying and refused to leave.

Then Frederick found work on a farm as a cowman at Over Compton, a village between Sherborne and Yeovil, in Dorset. But Over Compton – like their previous homes – had few attractions for newcomers like Lottie. Like many rural villages it was suffering from a general decline, with a dwindling population. There were fewer than 25 households, in which resided a population of about 100 people, with two-thirds of its men working on the land.

It didn't help that Lottie was illiterate and uneducated. (Later, at her trial, her own barrister acknowledged 'she is not very strong intellectually'.) But it was not her struggle to comprehend the world around her that was the primary problem. Lottie was a stranger, who looked and sounded different to locals. A strong Northern Irish brogue would have been enough to arouse considerable hostility at the time. There was plenty of anti-Irish sentiment washing about society. The two countries had of course had a complicated relationship for centuries, which had recently come to a head in events such as the Easter Rising of 1916, and the Irish War of Independence, which had spawned aggressively negative attitudes to Irish Catholics in Britain.

Lottie was destined to confirm every worst prejudice. She quickly tired of her husband's limited conversation and company. The eight-year age gap that once made him appear sophisticated now framed him as dreary and she became increasingly restive. Often, she found herself heading for the local inn to take solace in a glass or two of ale, escaping the numbing drudgery of childcare and household chores. And when money ran short, she resorted to prostitution, to help finance her drinking habit. Indeed, it was claimed she would bestow her sexual favours for the price of a pint. Fuelled by gossip and moral outrage, the small community united in opposition to her behaviour.

Even Frederick believed she was turning tricks. He reputedly once told a neighbour: 'I don't care what she does. Four pounds a week is better than the 30 shillings I earn as a cowman.'

Did he mean he felt defeated and betrayed by her actions? Clearly that's the inference drawn from the neighbour who reported his words. Yet he and Lottie were together struggling to survive in an era of depressed wages, and they had numerous mouths to feed. At the time, prostitution was often used as a backstop by married mothers to help put food on the table. Perhaps he accepted the harsh realities and even welcomed the extra income. Lottie was a woman with big dreams that didn't match up to her daily reality. Perhaps he had sufficient vision to see she was making the best life she could for herself and her children. If he felt empathy for her it certainly wasn't shared among those who lived locally.

Neighbours called her 'Black Bess' or 'Killarney Kate', names that suggested a seductress of dubious heritage and intent. In their minds she was already guilty of lax morals, which made her more likely to have committed a crime.

*

There's no dispute the Bryant family would have been struggling for money, not just to finance Lottie's drinking. Times were hard for virtually all working people in the thirties and many struggled to secure even modest accommodation. So, despite the confines of the farm workers' cottage where they lived, she also took in lodgers to help make ends meet.

But events took an altogether darker turn in December 1933 when Lottie encountered Leonard Edward Parsons for the first time. With striking blue eyes, a dark complexion and iron-grey curly hair, he was roguishly charming. By trade he was a hawker, selling items door to door. He went under several different names and initially the Bryants knew him as Bill Moss. An instantly besotted Lottie took him home to share the family Christmas dinner.

Before long, Parsons had moved into the Bryant home as a lodger. Lottie and he became lovers, scandalising the village. She regularly travelled in Parsons's car or alongside him in his pony and trap, helping him to sell linoleum door to door. He was also a well-known horse trader. Lottie clearly enjoyed his company, but she also seized the opportunity to earn extra cash for her family.

On one occasion Lottie even gathered up two of the four children she had at the time and went with Parsons to rented rooms in Dorchester. Ultimately she decided to return with the children. Once she was home, Parsons sent her a telegram asking her to meet him by the hayrick at Babylon Hill. Unable to read it, Lottie showed her husband and he got a local police constable to accompany him to the rendezvous. Yet no punches were thrown. In fact, she told police later, the three began living under the same roof once more with Frederick saying, 'Mistakes will happen.'

She claimed her husband welcomed Parsons back to the house that same night and he lived there virtually full time. His rent money of 15 shillings a week – to pay for washing, lodging and food – that was paid at breakfast time on Saturdays went to Frederick, she insisted.

The trip to Dorchester was just one of several Lottie took with Parsons – always taking two children but inevitably leaving others behind. They stayed together in Weymouth when her son George visited the eye hospital there, getting treatment for a cataract, as well as Yeovil, in either hotels or boarding houses. Using assumed names, the pair often left the premises without paying, leaving a trail of tall stories and small debts in their wake.

But bizarrely, they always returned to Frederick, with Lottie saying she had concerns about the two children she had abandoned to their working father. Frederick agreed to having them all back in the house, likewise to safeguard the welfare of the youngsters. There's further evidence that Frederick was tolerant, even welcoming, of his love rival for some time at least after that. The men played darts together at the local pub, the Crown Inn. Whatever promises she may have made to her husband after the Dorchester episode, though, Lottie was undeniably still in thrall to Parsons.

In the spring of 1934, Frederick was asked to leave his job by the farmer, who thoroughly disapproved of his domestic arrangements. It meant the family lost their home as it was linked to his role on the farm. After he secured another job, the family – with Parsons in tow – moved to Coombe, on the outskirts of Sherborne.

From March that year, Frederick worked for farmer Aubrey Priddle, himself a First World War veteran who had served in the Machine Gun Corps. Frederick received a wage of £1, eighteen shillings and sixpence a week, with three shillings immediately deducted to pay the rent of their semi-detached cottage. It was a two-up, two-down, ivy-clad house, with attic space used as a bedroom for the older children. There was an outside lavatory and washroom in a garden that was poorly maintained and strewn with rubbish.

Although there was evidence Parsons had at one stage hoped he and Lottie would run away together, his feelings towards her cooled. He already had a common-law wife, Priscilla Loveridge, and four children elsewhere in the county. He was obliged to pay £1, two shillings and sixpence for three of the youngsters each week, although the cash was rarely forthcoming and he was often being pursued by the police about unpaid maintenance.

And Parsons was not Lottie's only lover. At the same time as she was living with her husband and sleeping with Parsons, she was also having regular sex with local garage owner James Cutler

Slade. Later the 55-year-old businessman admitted to police he paid her anything between five shillings and £1 for what he called 'connections' – although sometimes he just parted with money in the hope she would not tell his wife of the relationship. In the course of four years, it's estimated he paid her as much as £400, more than £28,000 in today's terms. Police considered the arrangement to be tantamount to blackmail by Lottie.

One woman claimed that Mr Stichman, the manager of the Singer sewing-machine shop in Yeovil, also paid regular visits to the Bryant cottage, and another woman that she saw Lottie slip away towards the gasworks in the company of a man. Priddle received an anonymous letter postmarked 25 April 1934 about Mrs Bryant 'carrying on with men who pay her'.

In November 1934 Lottie gave birth to her fifth child, a boy who resembled Parsons. Within a year the relationship between Lottie and Parsons was over, at least as far Parsons was concerned. He had not been dutiful to his previous common-law wife, and he showed no signs of wanting the responsibility of Lottie and her children.

On one occasion, shortly before the baby's first birthday, Parsons became violently ill after eating breakfast at the Bryants' house. Later, when police were told about the incident, they believed it was probably a case of poisoning, possibly accidentally administered.

Parsons finally left the day after Pack Monday Fair, Sherborne's annual street fair held on 14 October 1935, without saying where he was going. No one knows if the bout of sickness helped make up his mind. As a result, it appears Parsons wasn't in the neighbourhood when Frederick died and that Lottie herself didn't know where her erstwhile lover was living at that point.

Now Lottie could be found in the company of Lucy Malvena Ostler, a newfound friend who had very recently moved into the district and became an occasional guest at the Bryant house. A widowed mother of seven children, she was in the Bryant household on the night Frederick became desperately ill.

Previously, Ostler had been married to Reginald Walter Ostler, a butcher who died of tuberculosis in September 1932. She got a weekly pension of 16 shillings. Like Lottie, she was renowned in the district for her barely hidden sexual exploits. When she was questioned about this by one landlord, Mrs Ostler boldly declared: 'I've got the name so I thought I would have the game.' She clearly had no qualms about living up to her reputation. Unlike Lottie, though, she had already seen four of her children taken away to Barnardo's Homes and was poised to lose the remaining three to the authorities. Negligence or immoral behaviour were the likely causes.

Lucy had not lost her looks, in spite of motherhood, although the same could not be said of her new landlady and friend. Initially, Lottie had been an attractive young woman. According to newspaper reports, Dr McCarthy described her at one stage as 'a Helen who happened to be born in the shanty end of Troy'. But ageing and motherhood hadn't been particularly kind to her. In December 1935, the same month her husband died, she'd had 19 teeth extracted, dental work that she was paying for in five shilling instalments.

*

Frederick's death soon became a high-profile case, and two Scotland Yard detectives were sent to Dorset to investigate.

One of the detectives heading for Sherborne was Alexander Bell. 'Alec', as he was known, was short, stubby and recognisable by his Aberdeen accent. Renowned for unmatched tenacity during investigations, he was a firm believer that criminals would be betrayed by their own mistakes. His unexceptional appearance helped him wring the smallest drips of information from those he interviewed, as he seemed more kindly and avuncular than perceptively clinical.

His first act was to have Lottie and her children removed to the workhouse in Sturminster Newton so he could conduct a thorough search of the house. Legislation passed in 1930 had signalled the end of the workhouse era, but five years on they remained a feature of the social landscape in the absence of any alternatives for those who lacked the means to live. They were now called institutions rather than workhouses, but they still remained shrouded in stigma and were seen as the last choice for the destitute. There followed some painstaking work at the cottage, with samples taken from all over the house and garden, to be sent off for analysis. Police also found the remnants of a branded weed killer tin. Was this the container for the poison that killed Frederick? Or was is a weed killer tin that had been cleaned out and was being reused for paraffin? While there was indisputable evidence that Frederick had suffered from arsenic poisoning, there was no definitive proof where the poison had come from or who had given it to him.

Understandably, there was considerable interest from the police in the victim's medical history. In the year before his death, Frederick had twice been taken ill with what was thought to be gastroenteritis. The first time was in May, after he'd eaten a meal that Lottie had cooked and left out for his lunch. Frederick was discovered by a neighbour, who induced vomiting with salt water and possibly saved his life. After a few days Frederick was able to return to work. A similar but less severe attack happened in August. Once again he made a full recovery. While the presence of arsenic was never proved on these occasions, Frederick's doctors readily shared details of the illnesses, and the two incidents formed a backdrop for the tale that finally ensnared Lottie.

With the groundwork completed, it was time for the police to interview witnesses who might shed light on how things were in the Bryant household in the weeks and months leading up to Frederick's death.

Frederick was a kindly man who was, by every account, devoted to his wife. It was said that he cooked on Sundays, cleaned the house, did the family's washing and was affectionate with his children. One abiding memory son William had was how, when he one day escaped the confines of the garden, his father whisked him to safety from the path of an oncoming herd of cows at Coombe. With Lottie unable to put pen to paper he also used to write to her mother Sarah three times a year, signing the letter on behalf of his illiterate wife.

Having returned from the horrors of wartime soldiering, there's little doubt he yearned for domestic harmony in idyllic countryside. Was it that fanciful quest that kept him in what appeared to everyone else to be a doomed relationship? Frederick's brother Alfred confirmed to police: 'He was fond of his wife and would not hear anything against her.'

Ultimately, the police were left sifting through a tirade aimed at Lottie, as everyone in the vicinity was quick to share her shortcomings. Frederick and Alfred's mother Arundell recalled how Lottie had made some big claims when she first arrived in England. There was furniture that she was having shipped over from Ireland, accompanied by a legacy that would relieve all their money problems. At first, Arundell believed the tales until, having lent the pair cash on the strength of the promises, she was forced to accept that they were a web of lies.

'Lottie was very impressive and would make people believe any story. She would tell it in such a way that you felt bound to believe her,' said Arundell. She recognised the malign influence Lottie was having on her son: 'Lottie appeared to have Fred in her power in a very peculiar way; she seemed to mesmerise him. He certainly knew of her doings with Parsons and must have heard of her conduct with other men. The only time he seemed worried was when she went away with the man Parsons, but then he only appeared to be anxious about Lily and the other child.'

Yet Frederick wasn't entirely blind to Lottie's flaws. Several years before his death he advertised in the Yeovil-based *Western Gazette* that he would not be responsible for any debts incurred without his sanction. It was clearly instigated by Lottie's profligacy, which he was unhappy about financing. But he was extraordinarily tolerant of her waywardness. While they were still living at Over Compton he showed neighbour Emily Tuck a message from Parsons, imploring Lottie to go away with him but to leave her children behind.

'Read this and tell me what you think of the bugger,' Frederick said, outraged.

'You are as bad as she is,' said Emily. 'You should have divorced her a long time ago.'

Despite promising her that he would no longer give Lottie houseroom he relented, and not for the last time.

Mrs Tuck, who lived in Over Compton, had a terse response when questioned about Lottie: 'I never had anything to do with Mrs Bryant and kept away from her because of her bad character and constant associations with men. This was constant gossip. She used to go down to the fields with the tree fellers. I know Mrs Bryant was an immoral woman and men used to visit her cottage. Her children have come to me and said they have been given money and told to stay out of doors for a while whilst Mrs Bryant has had a man in her cottage.'

Despite everything that was unfolding, life within the four walls of the cottage didn't seem to be a battleground. Alice Dumper, who worked for Lottie for a while, told police how Parsons was treated better that Frederick: 'I did notice that Mrs Bryant used to feed Parsons better than she did her own husband. She used to fry meat and bacon for him but I never saw her do this for her own husband. She used to give her husband bread and cheese and sometimes cold potatoes and cold bacon which had been left over from Parsons's meals. Mr Bryant never grumbled. Mrs Bryant seemed to be able to do anything she liked and her husband never interfered.'

Alice had a grudge against Lottie, who had called in the police when clothes allegedly went missing. Faced with investigating police officers, Alice did not miss her opportunity to take a sideswipe, implying a woman of Lottie's humble means should not be in possession of so much ready cash: 'I did hear that once when she went to a jumble sale she had seven £1 notes in her purse,' she told them. She confirmed that, as far as she knew, the Bryants didn't quarrel, nor did Frederick and Parsons.

The view of 24-year-old neighbour Ethel Violet Staunton – who was later called as a prosecution witness in court – seemed to resonate with most accounts gathered by police as they investigated Frederick's death. 'I was not very friendly with the Bryants,' she said. 'I was on speaking terms with Mr Bryant but did not have long conversations with him. He seemed a nice man, quiet in his manner, and he always seemed ready to do anybody a good turn. Mrs Bryant seemed to be a different type than her husband. She appeared to be more of the gipsy class and was friendly with gipsies when they were in this district. She used to shout and swear at her children and was lazy and dirty in her home. She seemed to be always out and left her husband and children to fare for themselves. She was sometimes away from her home all day.'

However, Inspector Bell wasn't inclined to have all the virulent nay-sayers on the stand in court, for fear of overplaying the hostility evident towards Lottie. For example, after taking three statements from 65-year-old Louisa Paull, he advised against using her damning words as part of the case, labelling her a 'garrulous old woman'.

Without particularly seeking to, neighbour Louisa Paull became a friend and confidante of Lottie when they lived in Over Compton, with Lottie probably attracted there by the travellers who habitually set up camp opposite the Paull residence. Mrs Paull was called 'Mother' by Lottie and Frederick, and 'Granny' by their children. She believed Frederick to be afraid of his wife. 'She had an awful temper. He wouldn't quarrel but would get out of her way, go off and let her have her own way. People used to tell tales about her, saying she was no good, but not knowing anything myself I wouldn't believe the stories,' she insisted, although she was aware of the relationship with Parsons: 'She used to tell me openly and often that there was no man like Parsons and that he was better towards her than Fred.'

Mrs Paull tried to dissuade Lottie, knowing that Frederick was a kind husband who never said anything against his wife. 'She said to me on several occasions that she would be glad if her husband was dead as she would have Parsons straight away as she loved him dearly.' In a later police interview Mrs Paull qualified her first statement. 'I now wish to say that I am not all sure she said the word "dead". She might have said "out of the way", which is the same meaning all the world over.'

But her loyalty to Lottie changed when Lottie advised her to get rid of her own sick husband. 'Back in the summer, Lottie came in here when my husband wasn't any too well with his heart trouble. We were talking about Parsons and Father (Mr Paull) shouted out that he didn't want that man's name mentioned in this house. Lottie then said: "If I was you Mrs Paull I'd get rid of him quick, 'cause the doctor would never know as he's got heart trouble." I said in answer, "They [men] ain't worth being hung for" ... She wasn't a bit the same towards Fred after Parsons met her and I never heard of Fred being [ill] before then.'

A fissure between Mrs Paull and Lottie and Mrs Ostler came after Pack Monday Fair, when the older woman told the pair they were 'worse than whores'. There was perhaps a surprising response from Lottie, in the form of a lawyer's letter. The two never spoke again.

Mrs Paull's daughter, Queenie Young, was also kept out of the witness box after her interview with Bell. She claimed Lottie had said: 'Parsons is a lot better than Fred and if I can't have him by fair means I'll have him by foul.' She alone among those interviewed by police claimed Lottie could read and write and was in letter contact with Parsons. But she also had another nugget of information for the police in their search for a killer when she recounted a conversation with the Bryants' latest lodger, Mrs Ostler. 'She said: "What do you think Mrs Bryant should ask me? If I knew what the best poison would be to give Fred."'

Afterwards, husband Ernest told Queenie not to see Mrs Ostler again.

In Inspector Bell's report on the case he admitted that Mrs Ostler had been worn down by some lengthy questioning. 'I spent about eight hours with her,' he recalled, 'and for some time her demeanour suggested that not only was she keeping something back but was involved.' However, he believed he had discovered the reason behind her reticence. Someone was threatening to tell police that she had killed her husband and his sister, both of whom she'd nursed until their deaths. However, Bell was satisfied both deaths were from tuberculosis. The Ostler family doctor also concurred. When Mrs Ostler was reassured on the issue she became 'spontaneous and convincing', according to Bell.

Unfortunately, none of this extensive interview was recorded. But the inspector kept faith with Mrs Ostler, showing a surprising partiality, and he later even attacked Lottie's solicitor Christopher Arrow for responding to 'rumours' about her. 'It is typical of him and his lack of principle that such a thing was put forward as a fact in an endeavour to blacken the evidence of such an important witness for the prosecution as Mrs Ostler.'

Parsons, meanwhile, was interviewed four times by the police. He told them that, during one of Frederick's illnesses, Lottie had said: 'I think I shall be a widow soon and if I am, will you marry me?' According to Parsons he demurred, saying he would never marry any woman.

Lottie's attitude to her husband following his death concerned some. According to Edwin Tuck, the Britannic Assurance Company agent who visited the house after Frederick's death, she seemed troublingly distracted. 'During the whole time I was at the house, Mrs Bryant showed no signs of mental or physical distress. I formed the opinion that she was rather a callous sort of woman. She seemed as if she was more perturbed as to what clothes she was going to wear at the funeral than she was over the death of her husband.'

After her husband's death, Lottie encountered Albert T. Brown, a former sergeant major who had recently become reacquainted with Frederick. According to Brown, she greeted him with the words: 'Do you know my old man is dead?'

'She did not seem to be the least bit upset,' reported Mr Brown. 'I must say that I was very much struck by the callous way in which she informed me of the death of her husband to whom she casually referred as her "old man". She was not crying and there was no signs of tears.'

Mr Brown told her there was no chance of a military funeral for Frederick because he had been out of the army for too long. He also recalled to the police how he saw Frederick again by chance after a 14-year gap after and ended up giving the Bryants a lift home.

'I expected to see a fit man. I was impressed by the way he huddled up in the corner of my car. He seemed to be in pain and I could see he was a sick man. I said to him, what's the matter with you? Mrs Bryant promptly replied, "Oh it's these war wounds, he suffers from his tummy." Knowing what I knew of Bryant I was surprised to hear this and said, "Oh, what a change." Bryant said very little. She did not give him a chance to say much but she forced the conversation. He was a hen-pecked man. I thought there was something funny as I did not expect to hear anything about war wounds or stomach trouble.'

At Marks & Spencer's the staff knew Lottie – a frequent and notoriously difficult customer – as 'the lady with plenty of mouth'. She was frequently vulgar in company, and was domestically and morally slipshod by the standards of the time – this didn't offer any proof that she was a murderer, but it gives us an insight as to why local people did not jump to her defence when the authorities cast their suspicions.

*

After a six-week investigation, the police decided they had collected enough evidence, and on 10 February 1936 Superintendent John Henry Cherrett of Sherborne police charged Lottie Bryant with the wilful murder of her husband. In response she said: 'I have never got any poison from anywhere and that people do know. I can't see how they can say I poisoned my husband.'

For Inspector Bell, it was remarkable that in his extensive inquiries he could find no one with a good word to say about Lottie. He branded her 'an inveterate liar', saying she seemed incapable of speaking the truth and displayed 'the typical low class cunning'. Still, he felt the contempt in which she was held was noteworthy. 'She is well known to many persons in the Sherborne and Yeovil [district] ... But it seems astonishing that not one of them can find anything in her favour.'

Even her mother was measured in her defence. Sarah McHugh heard her weaving tales but put it down to 'a giddy disposition'. 'She would tell these foolish stories to soldiers and other people who were strangers to her. She has no rich people and no one ever left her any money.'

Charlotte was certainly aware of her isolation, as a dictated letter sent to her mother in February proved:

I had your letter quite safe and sorry to hear you were upset but it could not be helped.

Do all you can do for me. I have no friends over here, only my solicitor up to now.

My husband's people have not been near me. We have not been speaking for the last six years and when he was ill during the whole nine months. I often sent for them and they refused to come.

I am quite well in myself and quite comfortable, thank the Lord. I had a nice letter from my eldest son this morning and it has cheered me up to know they are all well and in good health.

I hope you are all well at home. Do not worry too much about me – 'tis all in God's hands and God only knows I am innocent of all this.

In later letters she started to allude to the role Parsons had played in her downfall.

You must not heed all you read in the newspapers. There was a man lodging with us and they have arrested him as well. So I do not know if they thought there was anything between him and me but I know he was always asking me to leave my husband and I know he was a very bad man and always enticing me to leave my home. My husband threatened three or four times to take his life but then they were always getting about in the pub, drinking together.

[Parsons] took me away from my husband several times and threatened three or four times what he was going to do to me if I did not go with him. My husband knew everything about it and that was when he was going to do himself in.

*I knew I was doing wrong but I was ignorant and did not know an-
ything better for I cannot read or write and I was easily led. I wish
now I told all I knew in the beginning. I felt like telling the day I was
arrested only she got me to promise that I would not say anything.*

*Mrs Ostler gave my husband the medicine and I promised her I
would not say anything.*

After her arrest, Lottie didn't see her children until 20 March,
before a police hearing held prior to the trial, at which the array
of evidence was aired. The reunion, in a court anteroom, lasted an
hour and took place after a request made by Lottie's solicitor at a
previous hearing. She was visibly moved. When she took her baby
from the arms of a nurse the tot chuckled. 'Oh, my baby knows
me,' said Lottie. She nursed the little one while the other children
gathered around her. At the time, the youngsters were still living
at Sturminster Newton Institution, the same place as Mrs Ostler.

At this initial police hearing, however, it became clear that what
they had had failed to do was prove that Lottie bought arsenic at
any time, let alone near or during Frederick's illnesses. A Yeovil
pharmacist confirmed a woman had bought a tin of Eureka weed
killer on 21 December, but the poisons register revealed only that
it was signed with a cross, indicating the buyer was unable to write
their name. The mysterious buyer had given her name as Mrs
Austin from 390 Bristol Road, Sherborne. On investigation it was
found no such number existed and there was no woman living in
Bristol Road who was unable to sign their name. Police were sure

Lottie had visited Yeovil that afternoon, while her husband was ill and at home in the care of Mrs Ostler. It was thought significant, even though Frederick had been ill for a week previously. But in an identity parade, the Sherborne pharmacist failed to point out either Lottie or Lucy Ostler.

Despite an exhaustive operation by Scotland Yard working in conjunction with Dorset police, proof directly linking Lottie to the death of her husband was noticeably absent. However, great faith was placed in the existence of the burnt-out weed killer tin.

She was remanded in custody until her trial.

*

It had been five years since a murder trial was held at Dorchester's Shire Hall, and every day the public galleries were packed and the case relayed to a wider public by newspapers, who devoted numerous columns to a verbatim account of the unfolding story. There were tales of Lottie's infidelity, coupled with accounts that proved her unbridled ardour for Parsons in particular. She was at best ambivalent about the fate of her husband, while other evidence had it that she wanted him dead.

The case was heard over four days at the Dorset Assizes. Assizes were travelling courts that, until the system was changed in 1972, heard the most serious cases in the English legal system. It started on Wednesday 27 May, and with Mr Justice Mackinnon was presiding. With bushy eyebrows lying atop his notoriously penetrating eyes, Sir Frank Mackinnon was a 66-year-old judge with a passion for the work of Dr Samuel Johnson and other eighteenth century English writers. Sir Frank was unashamedly old school and, as such, had never owned a wireless. Most modern cultural references made during trials escaped him.

Wearing a black dress under a brown cloth coat with a fur collar and a brown hat, Lottie had travelled from Holloway jail in London, where she had been kept between committal and trial. During the trial, she stayed in a designated wing at Dorchester Prison. Quietly but firmly, Lottie pleaded not guilty when the charge of murder was put to her. It had already been decided that she was mentally sound, despite her glaring educational issues. She had been in hospital before the trial with otorrhea, a chronic ear condition, but was now returned to full health.

The case got underway after 12 male jurors were sworn in. Although a law had been passed in 1919 removing the bar that prevented women serving on juries, they were still in a minority. Jurors had to own land before being able to sit in on court cases – a rule that didn't change until the 1970s – and this obviously ruled out more women than men. Sometimes judges ordered that no women should sit on the jury of violent or disturbing cases, although it's not known if that was the case this time.

The prosecution's case was straightforward. Bryant had died after ingesting poison stored both in a tin and a bottle, and was highly unlikely to have taken either by mistake or to have committed suicide. Witnesses said there was weed killer in the house, although it wasn't used in the garden there and the former tenant confirmed he had not left any on the premises either. Lottie had apparently told her friend Lucy Ostler that said she hated her husband, and this was backed up by numerous comments illustrating her cold-hearted attitude towards him. Contrary to what she told police, Lottie appeared to be in love with Parsons. She had also discussed an arsenic poisoning case reported in the newspaper in August, as if her interest had been piqued.

After Frederick's death, there was arsenic on the lino and floor of the kitchen, in and around the fireplace and on the mantelpiece. It was found on the window ledge, on a tea tray and in two cupboards. In the sitting room it was on the floor, and under and in the couch. Traces were found in the bottom of a cupboard to the right of the fireplace and on shelves on the wall. But the vast majority was found on a bottletop in the kitchen cupboard, in the rubbish heap, in the remnants of a burnt tin and in ashes from copper. There was also a significant amount in the pocket of a blue coat that belonged to Lottie.

Lining up to deliver the prosecution case was Solicitor General Sir Terence O'Connor, the second-highest-ranking legal figure in England. He was assisted by another King's Counsel, with a third man as junior counsel. By any standards, the prosecution had some heavyweights in its corner.

But in his opening statement, Sir Terence conceded that all the evidence he had gathered to present to the jury was circumstantial. There was evidence of arsenic in the house but no convincing account of how it got there: 'I tell you at once that this is not the kind of case where I am in a position on behalf of the Crown to say that on a certain date and at a certain place this woman went and bought some arsenic, she took that arsenic home, she put it into her husband's tea or milk or whatever it might be, he consumed it, and of that consumption he died. The Crown is not in a position here to give you any such definite and convincing demonstration of how the death was brought about but the Crown is in a position to put before you a story of elaborate and continuous attempts over a period of seven or eight months to bring about the death of this man, attempts which in the end were entirely successful from the point of view, as the Crown says, of the woman you are about to try.'

He described Lottie as 'a woman with the strongest of human motives for destroying her husband in order that the marriage might be at an end'. Although her behaviour in and around Sherborne had been outrageous, he told the jury: 'We are not a court of morals.' Her conduct remained relevant, however, because, he said, 'Taken in conjunction with things she said about her desire to be rid of her husband and her desire to marry Parsons it does supply, if you are in need of it, a very strong motive in her mind for committing the very crime with which she is charged.'

Among the first to take the stand for the prosecution was Frederick's mother, Arundell Bryant. Although she confirmed that she and Lottie had not fallen out – 'We never had any words' – she told the court that she had never visited her son's home in Coombe nor had he been to see her where she lived in Yeovil, Somerset.

John Strickley, the tenant prior to the Bryants at the Coombe house, said the place had been thoroughly cleaned before he and his wife moved out. 'Everything was scrubbed out and cleaned, and every cupboard. The floors ... and everything was brushed down, cobwebs and all.' The prosecution wanted the world to know there was no arsenic accidentally left on the property. But he admitted leaving a few empty tins outside on the rubbish heap, which joined some left by a previous occupier.

Next-door neighbour Ethel Staunton confirmed it was she who took salt water to Frederick when he was ill in May. She found him 'shuddering and groaning' and holding his stomach at the foot of the stairs after hearing him call out to her through the wall. He was, she said, much better the following day.

Her husband, also called Frederick, followed her into the witness box and said that Frederick Bryant's lunch of meat, potato and peas had been left in the oven by his wife, who was away for the day. He also told the court of the doctor's anger in May when he found Lottie away and the house in a filthy state. As their father took to his bed, the children were at school in Horsecastles, some two miles from Coombe and a journey that all of them – even four-and-a-half-year-old William – used to walk. The youngsters had their evening meal that night with the Stauntons, Frederick said.

Staunton had been with Frederick Bryant on the morning of 11 December, when they were moving stones at the farm quarry for road building. As they were loading the cart, Bryant stopped to be sick, vomit that was green and frothy. Staunton also told the court about the impaired way Bryant walked before he died. 'He limped. He walked as if in pain all the time. He did not seem to have the strength in his legs that anyone else would have. They dragged along.'

Soon it was the turn of Dr McCarthy, who was with Frederick when he died. He said the possibility of arsenic poisoning being involved 'occurred to me within a minute or two of his death, while

I was standing there at his bedside'. Accordingly, he would not sign a death certificate. Although he had never seen a case himself, Dr McCarthy told the court it was 'possible but very improbable' that the violent illness suffered by Frederick was in fact dysentery, caught 16 years previously in India. However, he admitted that, although no expert, he would expect to find a blue or bluish-black colouring in the vomit of someone who had been poisoned with arsenic. When he arrived at the Bryant home the day before Frederick died, the patient was sitting up in bed, being sick. Dr McCarthy told the court that there was nothing out of the ordinary about the colour of his regurgitation and he confirmed that it was Frederick himself who delayed going to hospital, rather than any tactic by Lottie. When admission was suggested by Dr McCarthy, the sick man said: 'I don't think it is necessary. I shall be all right tomorrow.'

Dr McCarthy had also treated Frederick the previous May, when he saw no sickness but severe diarrhoea, with the patient complaining of cramp in his calves. At the time he gave the patient a morphia injection. There were no other similar bouts of illness in his medical records covering the previous eight years. He also saw Frederick nine days before he died, when he was 'very much better' than he had been on 21 December.

Dr John Tracey testified next, saying he saw Frederick on 11 December but that he had not considered the possibility of arsenic poisoning at the time.

The court then heard from another neighbour, who related behaviour by Lottie that made her seem hard and cold. Ellen Stone told how she visited the Bryant home both in May and again on

21 December to find Frederick in great pain. This time, she recalled, 'He was very sick and said he was dying. He kept asking for water and he had noticeable glassy eyes.' Meanwhile, Lottie called him 'a bloody fool' for eating bread and cheese the night before and sausages and bacon for breakfast, against medical advice. She was also keen to show Mrs Stone some new clothes she had received from her family as Christmas presents. She talked about Frederick being uninsured for funeral costs but being entitled to a military funeral, while he lay crouched on the shabby mattress in agony, in the same room and within earshot.

Described in court as 'a very kind friend to the family', Mrs Stone offered Lottie an Oxo cube for Frederick, which was in line with the doctor's advice. She left that day with Lily Bryant, who went to collect the stock cube, and Lottie who was heading to Sherborne for more medicine. After Frederick died, it was Mrs Stone who told Lottie to get a death certificate from the doctor and to visit the undertaker to arrange a funeral.

From the stand, farmer Aubrey Priddle hinted at his frustration with Lottie, saying: 'The woman was away too often to my thinking ... With a family of children and a man working all day long'. His wife Olive confirmed that she gave Lottie the empty weed killer tin found by investigators for use as a container for paraffin. Was this the tin that was found charred in the Bryant's garden? Neither defence nor prosecution counsels were clear.

But the headline testimony of the day came from Lucy Ostler, quizzed for 90 minutes by both counsels. She had been alone with Frederick on the day before he died while Lottie fetched medicine from the chemist in Sherborne. It was medicine he didn't take. As Mrs Ostler tried to administer some, Lottie insisted: 'You might just as well pour it into the bucket. Fred won't take that.' As a consequence Mrs Ostler poured the medicine away. She remained at the house for the night, sharing the Bryants' bedroom, and it was she who told the court that Lottie was up in the night helping her husband to swallow some Oxo.

Her relationship with Lottie was sufficiently close that she accompanied her to the hospital the day after Frederick's death. There, Lottie was told there would be an inquest, and Mrs Ostler had to explain what that meant. '[Lottie] said: "I suppose they will go to all the chemists to see if anything has been bought." I said: "If you can neither read nor write nothing can be found." She said: "If they cannot find anything they cannot put a rope round my neck."'

In further damning evidence, Mrs Ostler told the trial there was a weed killer tin in the kitchen cupboard and that, on Christmas Eve, two days after her husband's death, Lottie said, 'I must get rid of this.' Lottie implied to Mrs Ostler that the tin had been brought into the house by Parsons, and picked up two medicine bottles as well before heading for the garden. 'She went out of doors with them but I did not follow her out,' claimed Mrs Ostler. Lottie then said she was going to burn some old rags and rubbish in the washhouse. Later, when she went to retrieve a pram from the garden, Mrs Ostler saw the fire had indeed been lit. Two days later, Lottie complained that the fire beneath the washhouse copper would not burn properly, so Mrs Ostler went to shovel out the ashes. In the fire she discovered a burnt tin, which she said she dented with the shovel.

Mrs Ostler also said that back in October, she had been reading a newspaper report of a poisoning case, which she related to Lottie. 'She said: "What would you give anyone if you wanted to get rid of them?" I said, "I should not think of doing anything like that."'

Defending, Mr Casswell pointed out that Ostler herself was the only person who had seen the weed killer tin. She was also alone with Frederick before he was taken seriously ill. Mrs Ostler admitted she was frightened when she realised she could be implicated in his death. She burst into tears on the stand only at the suggestion of rumours that her husband's body was going to be exhumed.

*

On the second day of the trial, Leonard Parsons was the first witness, and he told the court how Lottie was aware there was weed killer in the house. He described how, back in August, Frederick was looking for a razor in the kitchen cupboard and his hand fell on an object on the shelf. 'What's this?' he asked his wife, who said it was weed killer. However, Parsons was forced to admit that he never saw the tin of weed killer himself. Frederick's lack of surprise that there was a tin of weed killer in the house might even suggest he had bought it himself, as police found evidence that he had intended to do so early in 1935.

It turned out Parsons was never moved to assemble his own shaving gear when he was living with the Bryants. 'If I wanted to shave I would simply say: "Is there any hot water?" Or it was suggested to me that I should shave nine times out of ten and they would find the razor for me. It was always put in front of me. The chair I was sitting on had always been treated as my chair.'

Indeed, on the day that the presence of the weedkiller was announced, Frederick – who habitually made him a cup of tea first thing every morning – was searching for the razor on Parsons's behalf. The razor was eventually found in the baby's pram. Clearly Parsons wielded some kind of hold over the entire household, not just Lottie. He admitted to using arsenic to remedy equine ailments but claimed he had trouble accessing it from chemist shops.

Afterwards, William Lord, a tin manufacturer, told the court the burnt tin, presumed to have contained the arsenic used to engineer Frederick's death, was similar to but not precisely the same as the majority of those made at his factory. It was impossible to say whether this was the tin kept in the cupboard, to which both Parsons and Ostler referred.

Continuing the prosecution case, Inspector Bell read out the statements Lottie had made to the police regarding her husband's death. The first started off with unvarnished truth about her husband's illnesses during 1935: 'They were all of the same kind. I can't remember the dates, only I handed the certificates to Mr Ballam the Relieving Officer, for groceries.' Two days before his death he was in the garden, sawing up sticks. They all went to bed about half past eight that night, when he appeared in reasonably good health, having recovered from the sickness he suffered the week previously. When he got up the following morning he was also apparently well, and it was only after he had some tea that he suffered a catastrophic relapse. But then came a series of statements that contradicted previous witnesses or would be quickly countered by others yet to take the stand.

Lottie denied telling anyone she was fond of Parsons or that she would not mind having another child by him, as Mrs Ostler had testified. It was, Lottie told police, just vicious gossip. 'I let people say what they like. I believe in letting them talk. I never got up in a temper about it. I told my husband what I had heard people saying and he said, "Send them to me and I will tell them different." [Parsons] was only there as a lodger. I have never carried on with him in a bad way.'

She claimed to have visited Parsons's previous lover, Priscilla Loveridge, in Weston-super-Mare at her husband's suggestion, having heard the deserted woman was making threats against her. However, the prosecution case pushed back against this as Lottie claimed to police to have gone once by train, when it was proved in court that she went twice and both times by car. Most likely she went in pursuit of Parsons, hoping to find him there.

Charles Leggett, employed by a Yeovil garage, told how Lottie had posed as a Mrs Parsons, on one occasion warning him against fixing Parsons's car because he would not pay, and on another organising transport to Weston-super-Mare. Colleague Ramon Jennings not only told the court he had ferried Lottie to Weston the next day, but said that during a café stop Lottie had pointed to Mrs Ostler and declared: 'She is lucky, she hasn't got a husband.'

Priscilla Loveridge and Lottie faced each other once more, this time across the court on the second day of the trial. Mrs Loveridge said she had four children by Parsons, and that she had resorted to law to get the maintenance money from him that she was owed. She didn't particularly welcome Lottie's unscheduled visits but she reserved her harshest criticism for Parsons himself. 'I was left with four children and expecting another,' she told the court. 'He is a fancy woman's man. I am not the only one he has treated bad, nor is Mrs Bryant. He is the sort of man who would break a woman's home up.'

Later that day, pathologist Dr Gerald Roche Lynch gave a detailed description of how arsenic kills to a courtroom enveloped in a horrified hush: 'The first symptom is generally a sense of faint-ness, depression and nausea, and very soon a burning pain in the mouth, throat, gullet and stomach occurs, which gets progressively worse. Vomiting soon occurs, which consists first of food but later of watery mucous, which may be blood stained. The nauseous, retching and vomiting goes on for a long time and are immediately exacerbated, that is, made worse, by any attempt to take anything by mouth, such as fluid, milk or water, which the patient of course naturally desires to take to relieve his thirst and pain in the throat. It may go on for many hours. [It is accompanied by] increasing cramp-like pain in the stomach from which the patient is writhing in agony, and patients have been known to describe as like a red-hot coal in the stomach. Eventually – which is a very variable time, from a few hours up to 18 hours – diarrhoea sets in. The purging continues at frequent intervals with great pain.

'By this time the patient has lost a great amount of fluid from the body so that he becomes shrunken and pinched, and at this time cramp in the calves of the legs occurs. This is a particularly painful and distressing symptom for the patient. The patient becomes collapsed and prostrated, and death generally takes place from heart failure. Consciousness is generally retained until the end.'

It would have taken anything from a few minutes to an hour for the first symptoms to appear, he said, arsenic taking effect at speed if taken in solution and on an empty stomach. After a meal, the first symptoms might not show for between one and two hours. He declared: 'I have no doubt whatever that [Frederick] died of acute arsenical poisoning.'

Most of the organs he inspected were pink, swollen and congested, and he estimated that Frederick's body had ingested some 4.09 grains of arsenic. As the fingernails had 300 times the expected arsenic content, Dr Roche Lynch believed he might have suffered repeated doses.

He tested dust and ash collected from around the house and garden. Of 146 samples collected at the house, 114 contained no trace of arsenic at all. While the ashes from the kitchen grate were normal, those taken from under the copper in the washhouse were 'excessive', as were those taken from a rusty tin on the rubbish heap. In effect, the tin comprised 70 per cent rust and 5.8 per cent arsenic. There was arsenic found on the top and bottom shelf inside the kitchen cupboard, but not on the middle shelf. Some was found in the left-hand pocket of one of Lottie's coats. None was found upstairs, or on the cutlery.

Given the relatively small amounts needed to cause suffering and death, the defence questioned whether Lottie had the skill to administer the tiny doses necessary to cause illnesses like those Frederick had suffered, but not death.

After Dr Roche Lynch produced a sample of arsenic dissolved in tea and an Oxo drink, proving it was impossible for the naked eye to detect, the case for the prosecution closed. Despite the shortcomings of the argument laid out by Mr O'Connor, it seemed to be striking a chord with the general public, some of whom gathered at the door of the courtroom when proceedings had finished in order to boo Lottie as she was taken back to jail.

*

It was now for the defence to show there was reasonable doubt as to whether Lottie had poisoned her husband, by undermining the evidence against her. Barristers hoped to demonstrate that she had everything to lose if her husband died, as she would be a widowed mother of five without a home or income. The relationship with Parsons was over. Most significantly, there was no conclusive evidence that Lottie had bought any weed killer or administered it.

The leading defence counsel was Joshua D. Casswell QC, who had served as a major during the First World War and became famous for getting £100 compensation from the White Star Line for several of the families of victims of the *Titanic* disaster in 1912. By the time he took on Lottie's case he was already known for being dexterous and able in the courtroom. On this occasion, though, he was far less senior than his opposite number.

As he opened the case for the defence, he acknowledged the gossip and 'a cloud of suspicion' that had enveloped Lottie in a town like Sherborne, where there was 'no place to hide'. But he urged the jury to remember that there were two sides to every story and that it was proof rather than suggestion that was needed for a conviction.

There must have been severe doubts in the hearts of her team about the wisdom of putting Lottie in the stand. She struggled to follow proceedings at times and had woven a tissue of lies that left her vulnerable to attack by prosecutors. Still, they had little choice, given the paucity of witnesses lined up to speak in her defence.

Initially, her evidence unfolded much as they hoped it would. 'I never had a black word with my husband all my life until Leonard Parsons came along,' she insisted. She had no recollection of discussing a poisoning case with Mrs Ostler in August. And she claimed she'd gone to Weston-super-Mare because she had heard that Mrs Loveridge was intending to visit her, demanding money.

As for Parsons, she had no idea why he had left. 'We had a few words in the morning and he asked for his clothes. I did not stop him from having his clothes and he took away my husband's boots with him.'

Lottie confirmed that on the night before Frederick died, Mrs Ostler had stayed over, saying: 'I would not think of leaving you in the muddle you are in.' However, she flatly denied giving her husband Oxo in the night. Her account varied substantially in fact and tone from that given by Lucy Ostler.

When she shared her concerns about being implicated after Frederick's death, Lottie claimed Mrs Ostler said: 'Mrs Bryant, you are not able to read or write; no bloody fools would give you anything. If they did they would be under a heavy penalty.' It was the doctor who was more likely to be in trouble, Mrs Ostler told her.

Lottie also denied there was weed killer in the house, saying there could not have been any without her knowledge. The fire under the copper was lit on Boxing Day rather than Christmas Eve, as Mrs Ostler had said.

Lottie said that while she was in Yeovil one day shortly after her husband's death, Mrs Ostler had cleaned up the house and was particularly sharp-tongued on Lottie's return. In response to Lottie's tears, Mrs Ostler had told her that all the grieving in the world wouldn't bring Frederick back. When Mrs Ostler went on to imply that she should thank God that he was gone, Lottie replied: 'I could not say that about my husband.'

As for the blue coat found to have arsenic in a pocket, she insisted it was not one she wore regularly. Trying on the coat in court, she proved it was uncomfortably small for her now.

Despite her protestations, though, Lottie's previous untruths surrounding her relationship with Parsons and her visit to Weston-super-Mare made her an easy target when it came to questioning by O'Connor. She agreed that her husband was an industrious man who treated her well and kept himself to himself. 'I had a good husband and I had no reason to get rid of him,' she insisted. 'Leonard Parsons knew I did not want him. I told him I did not want him and that I had a husband of my own that could keep me. He knew I did not care for him because I would not go away with him.'

But O'Connor quickly compelled her to admit she lied to the police about going to Weston, having told them she went just once and by bus. She also lied to the police about the contents of her husband's final breakfast while she told other people she was Mrs Parsons. At the very least it was difficult to separate fact from the fiction she told the police.

Lottie was followed on to the stand by two of her children. Lily, aged 10, said she had scraped out the ashes under the copper on Boxing Day, and found nothing untoward. Her mother then lit the fire. She also recalled an incident involving Parsons, who had bought back a bottle full of an unknown substance that 'fizzled up' when it was poured on to a stone. According to Lily, he told Lottie: 'If you don't look out I will ram that down your throat.' The implication was that Lottie lived in fear of Parsons, who had access to noxious substances and brought them to the family home.

However, her son Ernest, 12, did little to help Lottie's case when he said she asked him to throw away some bottles on her behalf after the death of his father – something she had denied.

Yeovil solicitor Christopher Arrow, who was acting for Lottie, told the court about an interview he'd had with Lucy Ostler. He claimed she said: 'Bryant was a man who had very little to say at times. Mrs Bryant never said she wanted him out of the way. I saw nothing unusual in their relations.' It was, she told him, the same story she had told the police. In fact, her version to the police cast Lottie in a far worse light and linked Lottie directly to the burnt weed killer tin. Talking to Mr Arrow, the tin wasn't mentioned. After she imparted her story to the police – during eight hours of questioning behind closed doors – the tin became a major piece of evidence.

In his closing speech for the defence, Mr Casswell said: 'It has been said that this was the story of an elaborate and continuous attempt [at poisoning] for a period of something like 12 months. I suggest that the evidence which has been called before you entirely fails to prove any such thing.' If Mrs Bryant had started an elaborate scheme to kill her husband, what could have prevented her giving a fatal dose in May, he asked. But on all the occasions he was ill, Lottie immediately sought help from a doctor. Rather than Lottie, it was Mrs Ostler who was alone with the victim when the fatal dose was likely to have been given, he said.

In response, Mr O'Connor declared there was no room for doubt on the cause of the preceding illnesses. Lottie's unbridled passion for Parsons and the evidence that revealed the presence of weed killer formed 'devastating links'. The tin was found on the heap where Mrs Ostler said she had thrown it, corroborating her evidence.

At the end of the trial, Mr Justice Mackinnon spent three hours summing up the content. He pointed out that Frederick had died of arsenic poisoning and that it was unlikely to have been a suicide. But it was 'infinitely more doubtful' that the arsenic was given to him by his wife. He raised the idea that her shortcomings as a housekeeper could have been to blame: 'It is physically possible that in some extraordinary way arsenic might have got into something he ate by accident. We have heard that this was a dirty house with a slatternly housekeeper. There again, if these three illnesses were due to arsenic it is inconceivable that any such accident should happen a second, still less a third time. If it was not himself or an accident then somebody else must have given it to him. The accused was the only person who was living in this house on each of these three occasions ...

'It was quite clear from Dr Roche Lynch's evidence that the battered tin once contained arsenic and more arsenic was found from the debris and dirt and scraping from that battered tin than from any other article he examined in the whole case.'

The jury took less than an hour to weigh up what they had heard. They returned to deliver a unanimous guilty verdict to a packed courtroom. Judge Mackinnon handed down the death sentence, his voice wracked with emotion.

As her chin sank to her chest, Lottie let out a sob. She was helped from the dock by two female wardens, although the court could still hear her cries long after she had disappeared from sight.

In a private note, written after the trial had ended, the judge said the case had highlighted 'the horrible ease with which a cheap weed killer can be used to take life.' The weed killer in question was 58 per cent arsenic and a tiny amount – less than a teaspoonful – would go undetected in food or drink but was enough to kill.

He reflected as he surveyed 'the ghouls in the gallery' that the case was giving them all the information they needed to commit murder.

*

Like millions of others, Professor William Bone, at the Imperial College of Science and Technology, read reports of Charlotte Bryant's trial. But it wasn't the series of salacious headlines that grabbed his attention, rather a technical element of the evidence given by Dr Roche Lynch. Specifically, it was the amount of arsenic that the Home Office expert said he found in coal ash that was of interest.

Bone, head of the chemical technology department, specialised in the study of fuel, and had been recently awarded the prestigious Davy Medal by the Royal Society for his 'pioneering work on combustion'. There was no simply better expert in the field. He wrote a letter to Lottie's legal team, revealing that the finding of 149 parts per million of arsenic in coal ash was not 'excessive', as Dr Roche Lynch had said, but comparatively mild.

Given Professor Bone's impeccable pedigree, this new information caused something of a stir. If he was right – and Dr Roche Lynch was wrong – then it meant there was no indication a weed-killer tin had been burned in that fire. If it had been, the levels would surely have been much higher. Doubt would inevitably have been cast on everything that Mrs Ostler had said about the presence of the tin and its fate, and the rest of the testimony given by her would have held altogether less weight.

In preparing for the appeal, the defence counsel's contention was that there was no proof Frederick's previous illnesses were caused by arsenic and that fact should have been better highlighted to the jury. This unexpected and seemingly crucial expert testimony from Professor Bone gave new hope for a retrial or even an acquittal.

This proved the cornerstone of the defence team's appeal of Lottie's conviction. The appeal took place at the Court of Criminal Appeal at the end of June, with the Lord Chief Justice Lord Hewart sitting with Justices Finlay and Humphreys.

A former journalist and member of Parliament, Lord Hewart was a distinguished figure credited with the phrase: 'Not only must justice be done, it must be seen to be done.' In 1931 he quashed a jury's guilty verdict in a capital case, the first time it had ever been done, after deeming the evidence used to prove the murder charge inadequate. So there were some grounds for optimism about the outcome of the case. But to temper that, he was known for making decisions too quickly and on insufficient evidence, and for taking sides.

Ultimately those weaknesses appeared to win the day. John Trapnell KC, steering Lottie's case this time, was on his feet for less than 30 minutes, outlining how the trial summing-up was 'defective', before the Lord Chief Justice cut in. There was a short conference between judges and barristers before the appeal was dramatically stopped in its tracks.

'The court is unanimously of the opinion that there is no occasion for the further evidence,' pronounced Lord Hewart. 'The application is of the objectionable kind which we foresaw in a recent case when in very exceptional circumstances we admitted further medical evidence. We set our faces like a flint against it. It would be intolerable if the court were to listen to the afterthoughts of a scientific gentleman in a capital case or in any other case.'

In his report of events, Inspector Bell said the Lord Chief Justice had insisted there was overwhelming evidence and that the judge's summing-up was both complete and meticulously fair. But, the detective conceded, a critical error had indeed occurred with

Dr Roche Lynch referring to the arsenic levels in coal rather than those of coal ash, where greater concentrations are to be found.

'On the whole, it seems that Doctor Roche Lynch was right from a comparative point of view but when mentioning about excessive arsenic was referring to coal when in fact he was dealing with coal ash in which the arsenical contents is greatly concentrated as compared with coal. It was clear that this was an important development which might have far reaching effect.'

Despite the fact there was no evidence that Lottie had bought arsenic, let alone administered it and burnt the evidence on the wash-house fire, the sentence of hanging still stood. It must have come as a body blow to Lottie, who sat in court throughout proceedings. Nonetheless, according to press reports, she showed 'extraordinary self composure'.

The issue haunted Lottie's defence counsel Joshua Casswell until his death in 1963. Later he wrote a book about his colourful career and in it he declared: 'I am still – even after all this time – not convinced that her guilt was adequately or properly proved.'

It wasn't the end of efforts to get a reprieve. Following the failed appeal, an attempt was made by the defence to have the case taken to the House of Lords but the Attorney General, Donald Somervell, wouldn't allow it. On 7 July, Samuel Silverman, elected as an MP the previous year and a fierce campaigner against capital punishment, asked Conservative Home Secretary Sir John Simon to comment on the disparity of representation in the original trial, with the prosecution comprising the Solicitor General, a KC and junior counsel while the defence was led by junior counsel. There was, he told the minister, 'public uneasiness' about the case, as there was 'a considerable danger of a miscarriage of justice'. Labour politician Sir Stafford Cripps, himself a barrister, also tried to get Sir John to declare a mistrial, but to no avail.

Lottie wrote to her mother, in a tone that sounded both desperate and resigned. Her concern for the children was now paramount.

Father Barney has promised me he will see they are brought up as Roman Catholic and the Governor here has had a letter to say that whatever my wishes are as regards the children they will be carried out.

I don't want anything to happen to the large photograph of their father, take special care of it, also there is a large one of him taken in India in uniform. You will easy know him as he is a servant of the police.

Ernie is 13 years old on September 22nd next,

Lily is 11 years old on November 1st next,

George is 8 years old on November eighteenth next,

Billie is 6 years old on April 24th next,

Freddie is 2 years old on September 24th next.

I can't say much more as I feel too full up about the children.

Reflecting on the lies she told at the beginning of the case she noted: 'I saved Mrs Ostler and injured myself. The inspector of Scotland Yard said the rights of the case would never be known and he is quite true.'

Father Barney, the priest who ministered to Lottie in the condemned cell, wrote to the Home Secretary begging for the death sentence to be commuted, citing Lottie's illiteracy as justification. 'Her illiteracy is a matter for compassion,' he wrote, 'in as much as her father being an invalid caused the mother to be the breadwinner and the accused had to stay at home and she was only spared to go to school sufficiently to be taught her religion.' He also questioned her motive, for she used to see Parsons whenever she pleased when her husband was alive.

But public sentiment was not on Lottie's side. On 12 July, the *Daily Express* declared: 'Charlotte Bryant will be only the third woman in nine years to be hanged in this country.' And with certainty it shared the prediction that, 'No reprieves are ever granted in cases of murder by poisoning. The crime is regarded as the most serious it is possible to commit against the community.'

Still the scramble behind the scenes continued, with Lottie's supporters trying to save her from the gallows, while establishment figures hoped to justify why her appeal had been so peremptorily closed down. As time ticked by, another barrister in Parliament, Denis Pritt, asked a question in the Houses of Parliament about the case in general and the appeal process in particular. In the absence of a pardon on this occasion, he wanted legislation to ensure that verdicts founded on allegedly mistaken evidence were subject to a mandatory inquiry on appeal.

Home Secretary Sir John Simon sensed there might be a furore in the offing. He had been trying to ascertain what had happened in the Court of Criminal Appeal, anticipating 'difficulties might arise' after persuasive expert testimony hadn't been heard at such a critical moment. However, he met with the Lord Chief Justice, who was adamant 'that right must be done'. He insisted the judges who sat on the Court of Criminal Appeal had read all the necessary papers and were satisfied that, even given the new evidence, there were no grounds for interfering with the verdict of the jury. No one could say whether the minds of the jury would be affected, he went on, but they should not have been. At the time, there was a strong feeling that judges and juries were beyond question. The fact that evidence was wrongly framed during the trial seemed to be of secondary importance to those involved at this level.

On Monday 13 July, Sir John met with Justice MacKinnon to hear his view. The judge who had presided at the trial said he had no doubts at all about the woman's guilt and called it a 'cruel and deliberate' crime. The ash analysis was, the judge insisted, quite a minor point introduced as additional corroboration. For him, it was the tin and the scrapings of the tin that were significant.

Finally, the Home Secretary decided there were 'no grounds at all for doubt as to the prisoner's guilt'. He felt the only result of Professor Bone's evidence would have been to show that the weed-killer tin had indeed been burnt on the fire or that a different, more noxious type of coal was responsible for the arsenic levels.

For good measure he added: 'The prisoner gave evidence on her own behalf and her evidence shows that though ignorant she is quite intelligent and shrewd. I can find no ground for interference with the course of law.'

It seemed there was no way the prevailing distaste for Lottie among society's upper echelons would change. A letter from the Chief Constable of Dorset, one Major Penfold, to the Home Office at around this time read: 'It seems that her whole character is one in which lust predominates to such an extent as to have deprived her of all other decent characteristics of womanhood.'

Within the confines of her small cell, Lottie began facing up to her fate. Under the wing of prison staff she began to learn to read and write. Having dictated one appeal to King George VI she painstakingly signed her name, perhaps the first time she wrote anything down: 'Sir, may I respectfully beg for your mercy in my case. The date of my execution has been fixed for Wednesday next, July the 15th and I am not guilty of the offence I am charged with. I humbly beg for the sake of my little children to spare my life. I remain, yours respectfully, Charlotte Bryant.'

But that unwritten rule at the Home Office, that poisoners should not be reprieved, held fast in Lottie's case, much as the *Daily Express* said it would. The prison was advised by telegram that the Home Secretary 'has failed to discover any sufficient ground to justify him in advising His Majesty to interfere with the due course of the law'.

In addition to her legal team, Lottie had doughty crusader Violet Van der Elst fighting her corner. Dubbed by Inspector Bell 'the notorious Mrs Van dear Elst', she was a tireless campaigner against the death penalty and was believed to have financed Lottie's appeal. The daughter of a washerwoman and a coal porter, Violet worked as a scullery maid before her marriage to a civil engineer, who died in 1927. She became a woman of independent means after inventing 'Shavex', the first brushless shaving cream. As an eccentric entrepreneur, she was the among the first women to race at Brooklands, at a time when motor cars were the preserve of a wealthy elite. Like many bereaved women between the wars, she was a keen spiritualist and also a fan of Shakespeare. After being widowed for a second time in 1934, she devoted her energies and her cash to campaigning against the death penalty as the issue had meant a lot to both her second husband Jean, a Belgian painter, and herself.

Dressed in black, she turned up outside prisons when hangings were scheduled, protesting her cause. In addition, she paid for brass bands who would strike up Chopin's 'Funeral March', men who paraded with appropriate messages written on sandwich boards and aircraft that flew overhead trailing a black banner. Sometimes she would ask her supporters to kneel in prayer, while at other times she led them in gusty song.

Her priority was to garner publicity, in her words, 'To draw attention to the barbarity of capital punishment' because 'no one has the right to take a life.' Using powerful language, she tried to evoke sympathy. Unfortunately, this often led her to exaggerate, a tactic that was quickly unmasked in the press. She also often lied about her age. However, her aim was to humanise those who were being hanged, especially if, like Charlotte, they were mothers or had suffered poverty or ill-treatment. Charlotte's case was among the first in her 20-year campaign inspired by the actions of the Suffragettes, who had engineered political change by attracting headlines and challenging the rules. Accordingly, she was loathed by the police, who insisted on branding her 'demented', and she had her own dedicated Special Branch file.

Her presence had a habit of causing chaos, which was what made her so universally unpopular with the police. On the night before Lottie's execution she held a rally in Exeter in the pouring rain and distributed pamphlets bearing the message 'The last SOS from Violet Van der Elst to save the life of an innocent woman'. A number were screwed up and hurled at her car as she drove away.

*

Before her hanging, Lottie spent almost six weeks in the condemned cell and her bobbed ebony hair turned virtually white. Staff recorded some of the conversations she had with them throughout her confinement. There was no doubt in her mind who had orchestrated her downfall.

'I never thought Mrs Ostler would have let me down like that after what I've done for her. I think it's awful to be taken off the earth when I've done nothing. She would have been starved if it hadn't been for me and yet she made it worse for me and she'll never have any luck.

'My husband and people in the town warned me of her. I don't care what happens as long as I see the children again. I had a husband and a good husband and I had no reason to do anything to my husband and Mrs Ostler knows that.'

Her version of events was that she had been shielding Mrs Ostler, who'd given Frederick the medicine during his final illness and lied in court having promised she would say nothing. She felt the trial had been unfair, possibly smarting from the vilification that was starkly apparent in the evidence.

After much agonising, she decided against seeing her children for a final time as she felt it would be too much for them to bear. It was a feeling echoed by her solicitors. The government had reluctantly given permission for a visit to take place but asked for it to be discouraged. Hopes that the children would be adopted in Ireland had been dashed.

The children were miserable. While she was in jail, Lottie's son Ernest had written a heartfelt letter, later published in the *Daily Mirror.*

Dear Mum,

When are you coming back to us. We all want you back. It has ben [sic] such a log [sic] time sins [sic] I had see you. [sic] Lily is ill. Peas [sic] come back soon.

From your loving son Ernest Bryant.

On the day after she was sentenced, he told a *Mirror* journalist of his turmoil: 'I cried myself to sleep last night. I could not help it. Only Lily and I know about it. The babies have not been told yet … Do you think if I wrote to the Judge he would let Mummy come home? She has been away for such a long time … I was all right waiting because I thought Mummy would be coming back in the end. I do not know what to do now.'

Perhaps inevitably, a certain closeness developed between Lottie and the female warders who looked after her around the clock. A small altar was set up in the cell, where she prayed with Father Thomas Barney, who recalled with her the tenets of the faith she had learned as a girl back in Northern Ireland. She spent a contemplative hour with him prior to her execution. When 8am approached, her hands were pinioned and she walked unaided the short distance to the gallows, with her emotions reined in, other than a few falling tears. Her lips moved in prayer as she listened to the consoling words of the priest who was at her side throughout.

Executioner Thomas Pierrepoint, Britain's hangman for 40 years, was awaiting her. Charlotte's final message of thanks, given via Father Barney, was to her solicitor Christopher Arrow and his chief clerk Archibald Emmens, as well as to the matron and 'wardresses', as female prison officers were then known, for their 'unflagging kindness'.

The charged silence within the prison walls contrasted sharply with the rowdy atmosphere outside. Although the hour was early, about 4,000 people had gathered. At least some of the crowd were there to protest against capital punishment, passing round hand-bills supplied by Mrs Van der Elst that read: 'Mrs Bryant is being murdered.'

Just 15 minutes before the appointed hour of the execution, Mrs Van der Elst drove her white Rolls-Royce – with her chauffeur in the passenger seat – through a hastily erected police cordon designed to keep traffic away from the jail. The vehicle was quickly swamped by demonstrators – although not all were on her side. People who vocally supported the death penalty had also made a prompt start that day. Police were quick to intervene, arresting Mrs Van der Elst, who subsequently drove herself to Exeter police court, where she appeared later that morning. It was one of 50 court appearances for her, in 15 years.

After official notification of Lottie's death was pinned outside the prison, there was a surge forward so that people could read first hand the grim news. 'Play the game, it is not a fair,' shouted one alarmed policeman as he struggled to control the heaving masses. Finally, eight policemen linked arms and pushed the crowd back. Afterwards, people slowly dispersed, with some heading straight for the police court to hear the case against Mrs Van der Elst.

She was furious after having her sanity questioned by the police during the hearing and she insisted she had a right to demonstrate. 'Every protestor expects to get arrested [but] I always say the state has no right to kill.' When she received applause for her outspokenness, there were warnings from an angry magistrate that the court would be cleared. A charge of breaching the peace was dismissed but she was found guilty of obstructing a constable and fined £5. Before leaving, Mrs Van der Elst also put £5 in the mayor's poor box and a further £5 in the police orphanage fund. She also announced that she was starting a fund intended to help all children of murder victims, which would care for Lottie's children. Her initial donation was £50,000.

Later the same day, around lunchtime, Lottie's body was buried in unconsecrated ground within the confines of the prison. Father Barney was in attendance and he told newspapers that Lottie had 'met her end with Christian fortitude'. She left a tiny estate, worth just five shillings and eight and a half pence and intended for her children, who indeed went to an orphanage together and spent the rest of their childhoods in care.

Lottie's story dominated the following day's papers. Even decades afterwards it was being revisited by newspapers, in increasingly sensational ways. During the sixties the *Sydney Morning Herald* produced the headline: 'The Vivacious Colleen: Trusting Cowman and "X" on the poison ledger'. The feature was written by a former policeman, who reported: 'I have heard it said by those of my colleagues at the Yard who profess to be expert in such matters that Charlotte Bryant was probably the most beautiful woman to be executed in England since Lady Jane Grey lost her head.'

It's not known what happened to Lucy Ostler after the case. But Parsons was quickly tracked down by a reporter and he related the sorry tale from his point of view. He said he had left the Bryants' home some weeks before the killing and, when he was arrested in Cullompton, Devon, he had no idea what had unfolded in his absence. Although he knew he was in breach of a maintenance order, he was taken aback by the way police treated him. He had never even heard of Scotland Yard. He insisted that he had helped police all he could. But his next words betrayed the nature of the man, as he implied that he too was a victim in this case: 'Now I am suffering for it. Whenever I try to sell a horse or anything else, people turn to me and say, you're the Parsons in the arsenic case. It makes things very difficult for me.'

The effect on Lottie's children was far more profound. Speaking in 1961, daughter Lily recalled what happened to them after that traumatic time. Aged ten at the time of her mother's hanging, she had been separated from her four brothers after the trial, as she was dispatched to a different orphanage. Although they wrote to each other for a while, united in the shame of being the children of a murderess, they eventually lost touch. They even changed their names to distance themselves from the notorious case. Still, throughout her young life Lily was subjected to abuse when people discovered her identity. Sometimes women spat at her in the street.

She was speaking out after barrister Joshua Casswell's book had been published, highlighting the analysis error by Dr Roche Lynch that may have led to Lottie's hanging. 'It's terrible to think my mother may have been hanged because of a mistake,' she added.

After the episode came to a close, Dr Roche Lynch asked for police permission to keep some of the samples used in the trial. Most were freely given but Inspector Bell kept the burnt tin – the item that so controversially damned Lottie to the hangman, for Scotland Yard's Black Museum. It was kept alongside an execution box, sent around Britain to facilitate provincial hangings, and the death masks of notorious criminals.

*

William Bryant, the second youngest, never knew his mother. Like his siblings, he was brought up in Muller's Children's Home in Bristol unaware of the dark shadows cloaking his past. His memories of his early years were fleeting and, if he was told about the fate of his mother, he certainly didn't remember it. Losing both parents in short order before his sixth birthday surely had an impact but it's not one that he could recall. So it was a shock when he discovered the grim story of his parents' unnatural deaths. For him, the first inkling of how they died came from a sensationalised newspaper account, likely to have been embroidered and embellished.

'The first I knew was when I read it in the paper in 1964,' he said. 'Up till then I knew nothing whatsoever. It was something completely out of the blue. I didn't really know how to react. For a while I couldn't really believe what I was reading.'

When he eventually passed the information on to his son David, there was a similar shocked response. At the wheel of his car when he was told, David nearly drove off the road he was so taken aback by the news.

With the bald facts about his distant past laid out before him, William realised there was a piece of the puzzle missing in his life, not just because he grew up without the love and guidance of parents.

Both men wanted to find closure by learning more about the circumstances of Frederick's death and Lottie's court case. Without it, they felt the family would be continually sucked into the murky mists of judicial history, wondering whether Lottie was wrongly condemned to the hangman's noose or was guilty as charged. Despite the fact he couldn't recall any bond between them, it was natural for William to hope that in investigating further, his mother's case would be found to be a miscarriage of justice. 'Although I never knew mother at all, I would like to think she was innocent. That would be a nice fairytale ending,' he said.

William and David clung to some facts that they believed amplified her claims of innocence. Before the safety net of the welfare state was installed, people without a steady wage risked homelessness and hunger. The levels of public assistance were pitiful at the time, and it was this that formed a powerful plank for the defence in the eyes of barrister Jeremy Dein. 'She knew she would be much worse off by killing him. She'd have lost her house and ended up in the workhouse,' he said. 'So there's no evidence of motive – in fact, the evidence militates in the opposite direction, and that's a matter of real concern.'

Sasha Dass likewise acknowledged that the 'love triangle' differed from those usually found in domestic crimes, as Frederick knew about the affair but seemed unconcerned. In court, Lottie stated the affair was over, so the motive tendered by the prosecution at the time – that she was still besotted with Parsons – didn't hold water. With vilification no longer permissible in proceedings, Sasha acknowledged the case against Lottie was 'very thin indeed'.

But what of the murder weapon? Naturally occurring in the earth's crust, arsenic is still found today in industrial processing, but access to it is severely restricted. Back then it was a different story, with arsenic still being routinely used on farms as a weed killer and for rodent control as well as in medicines, and it was thought to be a treatment for cancer. If it was bought in a tin it had to be coloured blue to flag up its hazardous nature, following a 1851 change to the law following the moral panic linked to poisons. Still, farmworkers like Frederick would have handled it regularly. Also, arsenic ore was used in the glove-making process and there were 70 glove factories in Yeovil at the time.

Yet a lurid history had grown up around the way it was used in crime, as medical historian Sandra Hempel explained to Jeremy and Sasha: '[It] generally was known as the woman's weapon of choice because it was seen to be rather duplicitous and sneaky, and there was a perception, certainly in the nineteenth century, that that's what women were like. And women were always in charge of the sick room and the kitchen, so would have had access to people's food and medicine, and they were also thought to be particularly prone to poisoning their husbands.'

Other countries perceived its use differently; in France, for example, it was called 'inheritance powder', used against relatives by those who hoped to be beneficiaries at their death. Perpetrators must have hoped the symptoms so mimicked those of cholera that evil intent would have passed unnoticed.

Accurately speaking, the white powder in regular household use in the 1930s was arsenic trioxide. Samples drawn from all over the Bryants' house showed the presence of arsenic at various downstairs sites, although there was none found past the staircase. By far the greatest concentrations were found in the burnt tin, which the prosecution said had contained weed killer.

Still, the good news for William and David was that there was still no proof that Lottie had dipped into the tin at any time.

From toxicologist David Osselton, Sasha and Jeremy learned that the evidence found by the police fitted with arsenic poisoning. Four grains of arsenic – the quantity discovered in Frederick's body – amounted to about a teaspoonful of arsenic powder, far too much to have been accidentally ingested.

Osselton reiterated the point that Dr Roche Lynch made in the trial about the presence of arsenic in Frederick's fingernails: 'Fingernails were analysed and arsenic was detected in them. Now that's an interesting point because fingernails grow quite slowly – about a third of a centimetre a month – so that could potentially be from earlier doses.'

For Sasha, this confirmed that not only was arsenic poisoning the cause of death but also that there may well have been previous attempts made against Frederick's life: 'The tin evidence is much stronger than I originally thought – it is now clear that it contained large amounts of arsenic. So all in all, the toxicological evidence leads me to suggest that the prosecution case is stronger than I originally considered it to be.'

Osselton's contribution left defence counsel Jeremy pondering the possibilities. 'I have to accept as things stand that aspects of his evidence reinforce the probability that this was a deliberate case of poisoning, but of course that doesn't rule out Lucy Ostler or anybody else.'

Overarching the trial was the antagonism felt towards Lottie by successive witnesses, some of whom had scores to settle. Even the police felt compelled to sift out some of the more malicious and possibly fanciful accounts of her for the purposes of the trial, even though they were keen to secure a prosecution.

The point was not lost on Jeremy, who felt it affected the fairness of proceedings. 'The starting point for me is that her character played a major part in the trial,' he said. 'She was portrayed as a low-life, someone without any morals, so by way of starting point, that is a really dangerous platform for the case to proceed on.'

The person who provided the link between Lottie and the presence of arsenic was Lucy Ostler. It was she who testified to seeing a tin in the kitchen cupboard. Parsons also said there was a tin of weed killer, but didn't see it with his own eyes. Underpinning her account, the prosecution insisted a tin that once held arsenic found on the property was almost certainly critical evidence.

As Jeremy observed: 'Lucy Ostler gave some very, very damaging evidence. She said that Charlotte went to the cupboard and on the bottom shelf she saw a tin marked weed killer. She said that Charlotte picked it up and said, "I must get rid of this."'

When he read further into historic papers, he wondered if had found something that signalled why she might have been prepared to lie in the witness stand. He was looking at Inspector Bell's report that revealed she spent eight hours with police being questioned about her movements and possible motives. Although Bell was satisfied Mrs Ostler was ultimately 'spontaneous and convincing', without knowing the contents of the interview Jeremy was less so. 'There's a stench about this. It probably wouldn't even be admissible in modern times,' he explained. The jury were in no position to assess her evidence because they remained unaware of this scenario.

Led through the evidence, Lottie's grandson David felt there was every chance the legal argument would now be viewed differently. 'The two things that really struck me was what I would call the lack of real hard evidence – it just seemed to be really circumstantial. I guess she was an easy target because she was illiterate, she was an outsider. It just looked like it was an easy fix to hang it on my grandmother.'

Jeremy still had hopes the prosecution case would be deemed as flawed. 'This is not a strong case. She was hanged for the murder of her husband on what can only be described as highly circumstantial evidence.'

In his submission to the judge, he pointed out that details about the secret questioning of Lucy Ostler were not made available to Lottie's defence teams: 'The vital weed killer statement of 19 January was the direct product of a whole day of unrecorded discussion with police – that's eight hours...

'In the course of that eight-hour period, Lucy Ostler's statement changed completely. So, in conclusion, had this material been available to the jury, the jury's verdict might have been different and in those circumstances my submission is that there is a real risk that there has been a miscarriage of justice here.'

However, Sasha was far less convinced. Although she began by feeling uneasy about the case against Lottie, the input of the professional witnesses – interviewed by her and Jeremy – had helped cement her opinion. In her submission, she set out the points that persuaded her about the legitimacy of the case: 'Firstly, the deceased died as a result of a deliberate ingestion of arsenic. Secondly, the tin that was so controversial did indeed contain quite large traces of arsenic. And the third point that David Osselton made, which was highly significant, is that the deceased's fingernails indicated that there had been previous episodes of arsenic poisoning. And most importantly, the jury saw Mrs Ostler, they were able to assess her credibility and, contrary to what Mr Dein has suggested, this was not cursory cross-examination, this was very forceful.'

Considering the case in modern times, Judge David Radford was assessing the evidence and its fairness, not the sentence.

Although a police report said Mrs Ostler appeared to be holding something back, Judge Radford noted that police suspicion of her subsided as time went by, partly because her information could be corroborated. There was, he said, no evidence of any lack of integrity by the police. In fact, said the judge, it was a 'very strong case'.

'It was, as it always is, a matter for the jury to determine where the truth lay, and whether they were satisfied of the accused's guilt before they returned their verdict. They were so satisfied and in my judgement there is nothing now which properly, legally, could recommend to me to reinvestigate this conviction.'

For David and William, it wasn't the verdict they wanted. It seemed they had come to the end of a roller-coaster journey and were leaving the reinvestigation empty-handed and broken-hearted.

Said David: 'It's more emotional than I thought it was going to be ... putting into context how times have changed in every respect, whether it be for five children who were left parentless, whether it was circumstantial evidence that's put together for a conviction and then the hanging and a burial in unconsecrated ground within the grounds of a prison.'

William had been compelled to stand at the graveside of his parents and reflect on how to say farewell to a significant someone he never knew. 'You just hold it in your heart and live with it,' he concluded.

Both remained convinced that Lottie was innocent and that there had been a miscarriage of justice. For them, there was no motive and they felt that Lottie, illiterate and uneducated, would not have been able to work out appropriate dosages for the sustained poisoning campaign that had been alleged. Mrs Ostler was the suspect they had in their sights. After getting advice from Jeremy and Sasha, they vowed to continue efforts to clear Lottie's name.

'I will never believe mother had done it,' declared William. 'As far as I'm concerned the case will never close.'

ACKNOWLEDGEMENTS

My thanks go to the programme makers who have brought these forgotten stories back to life and to the courageous descendants of those neglected women featured in this book, who helped them do so. Behind these accounts lies a rich social history too quickly forgotten. Much light was cast on the case of Sarah Chesham by Helen Barrell's books *Fatal Evidence* and *Poison Panic*. Rene Weis's book *Criminal Justice: The True Story of Edith Thompson* was a great help in giving context. Thanks to Emma Tucker, who helped give identity to Lily Waterhouse, one of history's invisible women, through her genealogical skills. *Dead Woman Walking: Executed Women in England and Wales 1900–1955* by Dr Anette Ballinger was a rich resource for ideas. In more general terms, *Daughters of Cain* by Renée Huggett and Paul Berry offered different insights to those we know today.

Online, there was assistance from a wealth of newspapers that covered these cases so sensationally, helping me to amply illustrate society's bias. The number of online sites visited are too numerous

ACKNOWLEDGEMENTS

to mention but capitalpunishmentuk.org was endlessly helpful in its scope.

Thanks to Albert and Nell at Penguin Random House for making this project fly, and to Nick Constable, an ideas man.